LIFECYCLE EVENTS AND THEIR CONSEQUENCES

LIFECYCLE EVENTS AND THEIR CONSEQUENCES

Job Loss, Family Change, and Declines in Health

Edited by Kenneth A. Couch, Mary C. Daly,

and Julie M. Zissimopoulos

STANFORD ECONOMICS AND FINANCE

AN IMPRINT OF STANFORD UNIVERSITY PRESS

STANFORD, CALIFORNIA

Stanford University Press
Stanford, California

Special discounts for bulk quantities of titles in the Stanford Economics and Finance Imprint are available to corporations, professional associations, and other organizations. For details and discount information, contact the special sales department of Stanford University Press. Tel: (650) 736-1782, Fax: (650) 736-1784

Printed in the United States of America on acid-free, archival-quality paper

Library of Congress Cataloging-in-Publication Data

Lifecycle events and their consequences : job loss, family change, and declines in health / edited by Kenneth A. Couch, Mary C. Daly, and Julie M. Zissimopoulos.
    pages cm
    Includes bibliographical references and index.
    ISBN 978-0-8047-8585-3 (cloth : alk. paper)
    1. Cost and standard of living—United States.
2. Wealth—United States.   3. Well-being—United
States.   4. Life change events—Economic aspects—
United States.   5. United States—Economic conditions.
I. Couch, Kenneth A. (Kenneth Alan), editor of compilation.   II. Daly, Mary C. (Mary Colleen), editor of compilation.   III. Zissimopoulos, Julie M. (Julie Margaretta), 1969- editor of compilation.
    HD6983.L54 2013
    339.4—dc23   2013009258

ISBN 978-0-8047-8643-0 (electronic)

Typeset by Newgen in 10/14 Sabon

CONTENTS

For additional data, please see the Web Appendix tables and figures for Chapters 3, 5, 7, 8, and 10 on our website: http://www.sup.org/ lifecycleevents.

Richard V. Burkhauser is the Sarah Gibson Blanding Professor of Public Policy in the Department of Policy Analysis and Management, Cornell University, and a professorial research fellow at the University of Melbourne's Institute of Applied Economic and Social Research. He is a member of the National Bureau of Economic Research, a research professor of the German Institute for Economic Research (DIW-Berlin), and an adjunct scholar for the American Enterprise Institute for Public Policy Research. His professional career has focused on how public policies affect the economic behavior and well-being of vulnerable populations, e.g., older persons, people with disabilities, and low-skilled workers. He received his PhD in economics from the University of Chicago.

Kenneth A. Couch is a professor in the Department of Economics at the University of Connecticut. His research interests include the long-term impacts of life-course events such as job displacement and changes in family structure. He is an associate editor of the *Journal of Policy Analysis and Management,* and his recent work has been published in *Demography* and in the *American Economic Review.* He received his PhD in economics from the University of Wisconsin in 1992.

Mary C. Daly is associate director of research and group vice president at the Federal Reserve Bank of San Francisco. Ms. Daly's research spans public finance, labor economics, and public policy. She has published widely on issues related to employment, wages, income inequality, and disability policy. In her role at the bank, Mary supports the monetary policy function and serves as a system resource on issues related to employee retirement and health benefits. Ms. Daly previously served on the technical panel of the Social Security Advisory Board, and is currently a fellow in the National Academy of Social Insurance and a visiting scholar at the Congressional Budget Office. Ms. Daly joined the bank as an economist in 1996 after completing a National Institute on Aging postdoctoral fellowship at Northwestern University. She earned a PhD in economics from Syracuse University and a BS from the University of Missouri.

Thomas DeLeire is professor of public affairs and economics and director of the La Follette School of Public Affairs at the University of Wisconsin–Madison. He is also a research associate of the National Bureau of Economic Research. His research focuses on labor and health economics.

Henry S. Farber is the Hughes-Rogers Professor of Economics and an associate of the Industrial Relations Section at Princeton University. Professor Farber graduated from Rensselaer Polytechnic Institute (BS, 1972), the New York State School of Industrial and Labor Relations, Cornell University (MS, 1974), and Princeton University (PhD, 1977). In addition to his faculty position at Princeton, Farber is a research associate of the National Bureau of Economic Research (NBER) and a research fellow of the Institute for the Study of Labor (IZA). He is also a fellow of the Econometric Society, the Society of Labor Economists, and the Labor and Employment Relations Association. Before joining the Princeton faculty in 1991, Farber was a professor of economics at the Massachusetts Institute of Technology (1977–91). Farber's current research interests include unemployment, liquidity constraints and labor supply, labor unions, worker mobility, wage dynamics, and analysis of the litigation process.

Colin S. Gardiner was formerly a researcher at the Federal Reserve Bank of San Francisco but now works as a product developer for Pearl.com, a startup focused on making professional services available to everyone. His research interests include labor and social welfare policy.

Robert Haveman is John Bascom Emeritus Professor in the Department of Economics and the La Follette School of Public Affairs at the University of Wisconsin–Madison. He is also an adjunct professor at the Research School of Economics at Australian National University. His research interests focus on the economic well-being of the low-income population and the evaluation of public policy measures, especially in low-income housing and higher education. He also studies the patterns of well-being among the older population, including the impact of shocks to health on wealth and assets. Professor Haveman received a PhD in economics from Vanderbilt University.

Karen Holden is professor emeritus of public affairs and consumer science, University of Wisconsin–Madison. Prior to her retirement, she was also a research associate at the Institute for Research on Poverty and a steering committee member at the Center for the Health and Demography of Aging and the Center for Demography and Ecology. She was co-PI (with Michael Collins) of the Social Security Administration's grant (2009–11) to the Center for Financial Security, one of three national centers in SSA's Financial Literacy Research Consortium. The major theme of her work has been on how Social Security and employer-provided pensions influence retirement timing and well-being after retirement and widowhood. Her current research includes an examination of the adequacy of retirement savings, the influence of early life cognition and school courses and grades on later life financial knowledge, differentials between men and women in voluntary retirement savings contributions, the influence of late life events on financial well-being, and children's understanding of financial concepts. She was an advisor to Sesame Workshop on a program (and DVD) teaching children about saving. While continuing with some research and teaching in retirement, increasingly her hours are spent playing music, including in an all-women Cajun band (see www.prairiebayoucajun.com). She received her BA in economics from Barnard College and her doctorate in economics from the University of Pennsylvania.

Andrew J. Houtenville is an associate professor of economics at the University of New Hampshire (UNH). He is also the research director of the UNH Institute on Disability and the director of the Rehabilitation Research and Training Center on Employment Policy and Measurement. He has written extensively about employment and program participation of working-age people with disabilities, with a focus on long-term time trends. He has also written extensively on the measurement of disabilities in the context of population-based surveys. He received his PhD in economics from UNH in 1997.

Michael D. Hurd is principal senior researcher and director of the RAND Center for the Study of Aging. His research interests include a wide range of topics in the economics of aging including retirement and the structure of private pensions and Social Security, the determinants of consumption and saving, the use of health care services, methods of assessing uncertainty in a population, bracketing and anchoring effects in the elicitation of economic information, and the relationship between socioeconomic status and mortality. He received his PhD in economics from the University of California, Berkeley.

Ariel Kalil is a professor in the Harris School of Public Policy Studies at the University of Chicago, where she directs the Center for Human Potential and Public Policy. She is a developmental psychologist who studies how economic conditions affect family well-being and behavior. Her work in this area includes studies of how job insecurity and job loss affect the health and well-being of older workers.

Juyeon Kim is a postdoctoral fellow of the Center on Aging at the University of Chicago and the National Opinion Research Center (NORC). She is a researcher for the first and second waves of the National Social Life, Health, and Aging Project (NSHAP). She is interested in the effects of social contexts, such as marital relationships, households, and social networks, on health outcomes. Her recent work examines the effect of the economic downturn on living arrangements, and other work focuses on how size and the complexity of role relationships of social networks influence older adults' health including depressive symptoms and hypertension.

Joyce Manchester heads up the Long-Term Analysis Unit at the Congressional Budget Office. Her research focuses on responses to public policy among older workers and workers with disabilities. She holds a PhD from Harvard University.

Bruce D. Meyer is the McCormick Foundation Professor at the Harris School of Public Policy Studies at the University of Chicago. He was a faculty member in the economics department at Northwestern University from 1987 through 2004. His work has appeared in the *American Economic Review, Quarterly Journal of Economics, Econometrica, Journal of Labor Economics, Journal of Public Economics,* and other refereed journals. His book titles include *Making Work Pay: The Earned Income Tax Credit and Its Impact on America's Families* and *Strategies for Improving Economic Mobility of Workers: Bridging Research and Practice* (co-editor in both cases).

Amalia R. Miller is an associate professor of economics at the University of Virginia and an adjunct economist at the RAND Corporation. Her research interests are primarily in labor and health economics. She has studied the effects of fertility delay and contraceptive access on women's professional and educational outcomes and is researching the role of workplace peer effects on fertility decisions. Her current work in health economics explores the determinants of health information technology adoption and its impacts on health care costs and outcomes. She received a Ph D in economics from Stanford University.

Wallace K. C. Mok is an assistant professor of economics at the Chinese University of Hong Kong. He received his PhD from Northwestern University in 2009. He works on disability, compensation, and measurement error in surveys and has published in the *Journal of Human Resources.*

Jeremy G. Moulton is an assistant professor of public policy at the University of North Carolina, Chapel Hill. His research interests include the economics of aging and intergenerational transmission of wealth and education. He received a PhD in economics from the University of California, Davis.

John W. R. Phillips is an economist at the National Institute on Aging (NIA) Division of Behavioral and Social Research, where he serves as health scientist administrator for the Economics of Aging section as well as project scientist for the Health and Retirement Study. Over the course of his career, he has published research on retirement, saving, and intergenerational resource allocation. His prior supervisory posts include director of the Social Security Administration (SSA) Office of Policy Research and chief of the Population and Social Process Branch at the NIA Division of Behavioral and Social Research. Earlier in his career he served as an economist and federal program officer at SSA conducting research on retirement and directing the Retirement Research Consortium program for SSA. He completed a two-year NIA postdoctoral research fellowship at the University of Pennsylvania, where he published work on early retirement, savings shortfalls, and intergenerational transfers. He received his PhD in economics from Syracuse University in 1997.

Gayle L. Reznik is an economist in the Office of Retirement Policy at the Social Security Administration. She earned her PhD in economics from Stony Brook University. Her current research interests include aging and retirement, Social Security, and life-course events. She has published in *Journal of Family and Economic Issues, The Gerontologist,* and *Social Security Bulletin.*

Jae Song is a senior advisor/economist at the Office of Quality Performance, Social Security Administration. His primary research interests are in the labor force activity of individuals with disabilities and their labor force exit behavior, work disincentive effects of Social Security programs, and earnings dynamics. He received a PhD in Economics from the State University of New York at Albany.

Ann H. Stevens received her PhD from the University of Michigan in 1995. Her research interests include the incidence and effects of job loss, understanding connections between economic shocks and health, and poverty dynamics. Stevens served on the faculty at Rutgers and Yale Universities prior to joining UC Davis in 2003. She has served as an investigator on several grants from the National Science Foundation, including a study currently underway to better understand the relationship between cyclical movements in unemployment and mortality. Stevens is also a faculty research associate with the National Bureau of Economic Research.

Christopher R. Tamborini is a senior research analyst in the Office of Retirement Policy at the U.S. Social Security Administration. He holds a PhD in sociology from the University of Texas at Austin. His current research interests include life course, family and marriage, aging and retirement, Social Security, and research methods. Recent publications include articles in *Journal of Marriage and Family, Social Forces, Sociological Methods & Research, Research on Aging, The Gerontologist,* and *Population Research and Policy Review.*

Jennifer R. Tennant is an assistant professor in the Department of Economics at Ithaca College. Previous to this appointment, she was a postdoctoral associate at Cornell University, a research assistant at the National Bureau of Economic Research, and an assistant vice president at Moody's Investors Service. Her areas of concentration are disability and mental health policy, labor force participation of vulnerable populations, and taxation issues. Current research topics include detailing how different definitions of disability are associated with different social success estimates for these populations, the effect of a change in government policy on the disability insurance participation of recent veterans, and the effect of the Great Recession on state and local finances. She received her PhD in economics from the Graduate Center, City University of New York, in 2006.

Till von Wachter is an associate professor of economics at the University of California, Los Angeles. He is a faculty research associate of the National Bureau of Economic Research, the California Center for Population Research, the Center for Economic Policy Research, and the Institute for the Study of Labor (IZA). He was also a visiting scholar at the Russell Sage Foundation in 2010 and 2011. He earned his master's degree in economics from the Economic University of Bonn, Germany, and his doctorate from the University of California, Berkeley. Von Wachter's current fields of interest include the long-term effects of job displacement on career and family outcomes, the labor market determinants of retirement and disability, and the effect of public programs such as disability insurance and unemployment insurance. Von Wachter is topic leader of the EPRN Unemployment Jobs Deficit/Growth research cluster, and has advised the U.S. Congress, the OECD, the World Bank, and the IMF on job loss and unemployment insurance.

Linda J. Waite is Lucy Flower Professor of Sociology and director of the Center on Aging at the University of Chicago and the National Opinion Research Center (NORC). Waite is the principal investigator for the National Social Life, Health, and Aging Project (NSHAP), supported by a MERIT Award to Waite from the National Institute on Aging. She is coauthor, with Frances Goldscheider, of *New Families, No Families: The Transformation of the American Home* (University of California Press, 1991), winner of the Duncan Award from the American Sociological Association. She is also coauthor, with Maggie Gallagher, of *The Case for Marriage: Why Married People are Happier, Healthier, and Better Off Financially* (Doubleday, 2000), which won the 2000 Outstanding Book Award from the Coalition for Marriage, Family, and Couples Education. She is past president of the Population Association of America. Her current research focuses on social connections at older ages and aging.

Geoffrey L. Wallace is associate professor of public affairs and economics at the University of Wisconsin–Madison. His research is in the areas of labor economics, the economics of marriage and the family, and policy issues relating to poverty. Current projects examine the effects of changing economic conditions on living arrangements among young people, the effects of competition on educational outcomes, and issues of child support enforcement. His research on educational outcomes includes a study of the effects of Milwaukee's public school choice program on student achievement. Professor Wallace received his doctorate in economics from Northwestern University.

Robert J. Willis is a professor in the Department of Economics and a research professor in the Survey Research Center and the Population Studies Center of the Institute for Social Research at the University of Michigan. He has long-standing interests in the economics of the family including theoretical and empirical research on fertility, marriage, divorce and out-of-wedlock childbearing, education and earnings, intergenerational transfers, and the determinants of poverty among elderly widows. In the past decade, he has begun a new area of research on cognitive economics dealing with the relationship between cognitive ability and economic behavior. He received his PhD in economics from the University of Washington.

Barbara Wolfe is professor in the Departments of Economics, Population Health Sciences, and the La Follette School of Public Affairs at the University of Wisconsin–Madison. She also has an appointment at the Research School of Economics at Australian National University. Her research focuses on issues of importance for improving the situation of vulnerable persons including children in low-income families and persons with disabilities and in understanding the link between income and both health and cognitive abilities. She received a PhD from the University of Pennsylvania in economics.

Julie M. Zissimopoulos is a research associate professor in the Department of Clinical Pharmacy and Pharmaceutical Economics and Policy at the University of Southern California and the associate director of the Leonard D. Schaeffer Center for Health Policy and Economics. She specializes in the economics of aging. Topics of special interest are medical expenditures at older ages, savings and wealth, labor force behavior, and financial and nonfinancial support between generations of family members. She received her PhD in economics from the University of California, Los Angeles.

LIFECYCLE EVENTS AND THEIR CONSEQUENCES

CHAPTER ONE

Introduction

Kenneth A. Couch, Mary C. Daly,
and Julie M. Zissimopoulos

Negative events in peoples' lives can have profound effects on their life-cycle outcomes. Events such as job loss, changes in family structure, and declines in health can reduce individuals' economic and noneconomic well-being, leaving them permanently worse off than they were before the event, unable to regain their prior standing. The impact of these shocks may not be limited to the individuals affected but can spill over to families and even to future generations, when children in affected households have limited access to economic and emotional resources.

Understanding and documenting the impact of these commonly encountered negative events is the focus of this book. Although the literature on these topics is extensive, there have been few comprehensive examinations that bring together complementary interdisciplinary analyses on a range of negative lifecycle shocks. This book begins to fill the gap with a collection of chapters authored by leading researchers in economics, demography, and sociology, all focused on three common lifecycle events: involuntary job loss, changes in family structure, and declines in health or functioning.

A key contribution of the book is the construction of a research framework that facilitates comparisons across various types of shocks. It is built around a set of key questions that are important for evaluating the individual and social costs of any lifecycle event. The questions are:

We would like to express our gratitude to the Federal Reserve Bank of San Francisco for its support of the research in this volume. Also, we thank Natalie Zohuri for her assistance with the logistics of producing the text.

1. How likely are individuals to experience the event?
2. What are the short-term economic impacts?
3. What are the long-term economic impacts?
4. What are the noneconomic impacts?

For each of the lifecycle events studied, a chapter in the book examines one or more of these key questions. This structure gives readers the ability to compare these events in terms of the portion of the population affected as well as the short- and long-term impact of these events on economic and noneconomic well-being. By addressing these four basic questions, the chapters in this volume provide a foundation for those interested in pursuing multidisciplinary research on one or all of these topics.

A second contribution of the book is the studies themselves, which provide excellent introductions to researchers and policymakers interested in the consequences of lifecycle events. The collected chapters also showcase the range of analysis being done by top academics and highlight some of the emerging public data sources and statistical techniques available to researchers interested in these issues. For example, several of the papers draw on cross-sectional surveys that allow researchers to document the importance of each type of risk in the population at a point in time. Other chapters rely on data drawn from panel surveys that collect information on the same person over time, allowing researchers to analyze the long-term impact of lifecycle disruptions on well-being. Still others use panel surveys linked to administrative records from government programs that have only recently become available to researchers. The linkage of traditional survey information with administrative records collected by government agencies builds on the strengths of each source of information. The administrative records contain valuable information, such as the annual earnings of individuals, as well as private and public retirement benefits untainted by the measurement error that is common in self-reported data. The surveys contain information on demographics and other life details not available in the administrative records. Using these combined data sources, researchers can accurately track the impact that a variety of events have on people's lives over long periods.

Of course there are many subjects the book does not address that bear noting. A number of negative shocks are not examined by the authors.

As noted earlier, the book focuses on the three highly prevalent events associated with adverse impacts for which various public and private insurance and transfer schemes have been developed. Future research agendas might focus on how other negative events compare to the ones discussed here. Another issue not taken up in this book is the impact of these negative events on children. This subject has received considerable attention of late as researchers attempt to understand the long-term impact of reduced parental income on children. While the findings in this book are suggestive of potential negative effects on children as a result of reduced family income, a rigorous treatment is left for future research. Finally, there is emerging evidence that the negative events discussed here are often interrelated, either because there is a higher risk for all events among particular groups or because one event leads to another. A comprehensive treatment of these interrelationships is, again, beyond the scope of this book, but the authors point out evidence for such inter-relationships when relevant.

GUIDE TO THE CHAPTERS IN THIS VOLUME

Job Loss: Chapters 2–6

In Chapter 2, Henry Farber discusses the incidence of job loss in the United States and examines the short-term impact on earnings following reemployment. He finds that the incidence of displacement rises and falls with the economy and that it was especially high during the recent severe recession. In contrast, the penalty for displacement varies less with economic conditions because displaced workers generally experience sharp earnings decreases following job loss. These results point to a substantial short-term cost associated with job loss in the United States.

Chapter 3, by Till von Wachter, Jae Song, and Joyce Manchester, considers whether short-term losses experienced by displaced workers persist over time. They find that workers released in mass layoffs experience significant reductions in work activity in later life. Such reductions will result in sizeable decreases in available resources both in working age and in preparedness for retirement. The authors conclude that "displacement appears to be an extraordinary event shaping workers' long-term cumulated earnings" (p. 52).

The impact of job loss on the period of retirement is considered in more detail in Chapter 4 by Ann Stevens and Jeremy Moulton. They compare retirement wealth for individuals who experience a job loss with those who do not and find sizeable differences, especially when the job loss occurs at young ages. They find little evidence that displaced workers can make up these differences by shifting retirement to a later date. The inability to recover appears related to both the difficulty in becoming reemployed and, if a new job is found, working sufficiently long before retirement to offset the initial declines in assets.

Lasting reductions in earnings and wealth due to job loss may have consequences on well-being beyond financial concerns. Chapter 5 by Ariel Kalil and Thomas DeLeire examines the impact of job loss on two different measures of self-reported psychological well-being, one meant to capture life satisfaction and another that gauges sense of purpose in life. They find that job loss, independent of a variety of background factors, reduces satisfaction by roughly 25 to 50 percent and that self-assessment of purpose in life decreases by roughly 15 percent. This work suggests that job loss takes a toll on the nonfinancial as well as the financial well-being of individuals.

In Chapter 6 Michael Hurd discusses these studies on job loss and suggests interesting extensions to them.

Family Change: Chapters 7–11

In Chapter 7, Amalia Miller examines the impact of changing demographic trends in the timing of marriage and motherhood over the past several decades on the earnings and assets of women and their spouses. Delaying a first birth appears to have a large and durable impact on women's earnings. Moreover, delay of marriage and childbirth alters household income. While these effects have only a modest impact on asset accumulation, they cumulate over time; thus, delay can have a lasting impact on the economic well-being of women and their families over the lifecycle.

The authors of Chapter 8, Kenneth Couch, Christopher Tamborini, Gayle Reznik, and John Phillips, examine the impact of divorce and remarriage on labor supply and Social Security retirement benefits among women. They find that women who divorce and never remarry significantly increase their labor supply, and thus earnings, and retire later than women who are continuously married or remarry after divorce. Taking spouses into account reveals that total Social Security retirement benefits flowing to the households of women who experienced a divorce and never remarried are much lower compared to those who either remarried or were continuously married.

Julie Zissimopoulos examines the impact on net worth and savings of changes in family structure at older ages in Chapter 9. Married couples have more wealth than unmarried individuals. While it is tempting to conclude that family structure is the primary determinant of wealth levels near retirement, Zissimopoulos finds that higher lifetime earnings, lower mortality risk, and other factors also explain why married couples have higher wealth at older ages compared to unmarried individuals. She finds that changes in family structure at older ages do have an impact on wealth: divorce both splits and consumes wealth while remarriage rebuilds assets and divorce at all ages has negative and long-lasting consequences on wealth accumulation.

In Chapter 10, Juyeon Kim and Linda Waite examine the influence of changes in family size and complexity of living relationships on a family's economic well-being during the Great Recession. The authors find that the average size of households did not change markedly following the Great Recession. However, the stable average conceals considerable churning: about one-third of households added or lost members. The authors find that decreases in household size and complexity, on average, are associated with higher standards of living in the household for white families, no change for African American families, and a lower standard of living for Hispanic families. While families play an important role in providing income support in difficult economic times, changes in living arrangements that increase family size typically result in decreases in economic welfare.

Chapter 11 by Robert Willis reviews the chapters that consider the consequences of changes in household structure, placing each in the broader context of the field of family economics.

Declines in Health: Chapters 12–16

Richard Burkhauser, Andrew Houtenville, and Jennifer Tennant discuss, in Chapter 12, the conceptual and practical challenges of measuring the prevalence of debilitating declines in health in the population. The authors show that decisions about measurement can have a significant impact on estimates of the size and composition of the population affected. Using two nationally representative data sources, Burkhauser et al. show that no single question or measure captures everyone currently targeted by public policies for those with disabilities. Therefore, the authors conclude that a combination of questions historically and currently being used in U.S. surveys is optimal and represents best practice for researchers interested in studying how declines in health affect employment, income, and public benefit receipt.

The authors of Chapter 13, Bruce Meyer and Wallace Mok, assess the incidence of disability among working-age men and the impact it has on income and benefit receipt. The authors estimate that about 30 percent of men experience some form of disability and that the economic consequences are similar to those experienced by displaced workers—substantially lower earnings and income. For those who report chronic, severe disabilities, the costs are especially large and are not offset by increased income from other sources. Thus, disability comes with economic costs for the individual that are not offset by either government or family support.

In Chapter 14, Geoffrey Wallace, Robert Haveman, Karen Holden, and Barbara Wolfe consider how the onset of a physical or mental problem in functioning affects economic well-being during retirement. They examine how reductions in physical and mental functioning relate to annuitized net wealth. The authors find that difficulties with both mental and physical functioning are associated with declines in wealth and that the impact is larger for single adults. This pattern is driven by individuals spending down resources to pay for health care and assistive services.

Mary Daly and Colin Gardiner examine the relationship between disability, its onset, and subjective well-being in Chapter 15. The authors find that having a work-limiting disability is associated with lower levels of self-reported life satisfaction. Consistent with previous studies, the authors find a negative relationship between disability status and subjective well-being. Although the effect of disability is somewhat mitigated by employment, income and wealth, it emerges as a salient determinant of subjective well-being throughout the analysis.

Chapter 16 by Robert Haveman reviews the chapters in the section and highlights areas of research where further analysis is needed.

IDEAS FOR FUTURE RESEARCH

The chapters in this volume show that negative lifecycle events can have large and lasting effects on both the economic circumstances and health of individuals and their families. Future research can take advantage of expanding data resources that allow researchers to trace individuals throughout their lifetimes and follow their children as they age into adulthood. Similar data for other countries also will be useful for improving our understanding of how public programs and private institutions amplify or attenuate losses associated with negative lifecycle shocks. Given the size of the consequences documented in this volume, continued research in this area is an important goal.

PART I
JOB LOSS

CHAPTER TWO

Job Loss

Historical Perspective from the Displaced
Workers Survey, 1984–2010

Henry S. Farber

INTRODUCTION

The Great Recession from December 2007 to June 2009 is associated
with a dramatic weakening of the labor market, which is now only
slowly recovering. The unemployment rate remains stubbornly high, and
durations of unemployment are unprecedentedly long. In this chapter I
use the Displaced Workers Survey (DWS), administered every two years
from 1984–2010, as a supplement to the Current Population Survey
(CPS), to examine the experiences of job losers in the Great Recession
and compare them to those of job losers in previous years, both in and
out of recessions. The January 2010 DWS is of particular interest because it covers job loss during the Great Recession (2007–09).[1]

An important concern in the aftermath of the recession is the high
unemployment rate, which remained at 9.6 percent in the fourth quarter
of 2010, more than one full year after the "official" end of the recession
in June 2009.[2] The first panel of Figure 2.1 contains a plot of the quarterly, seasonally adjusted civilian unemployment rate from 1978 through
the second quarter of 2011.[3] Labor market conditions over the period
covered by the DWS (1981–2009) have varied substantially. The early
1980s saw a sharp increase in the unemployment rate to more than 10
percent during the July 1981 to November 1982 recession. This increase
was followed by a long decline during the remainder of the 1980s. The
unemployment rate then increased to almost 8 percent in 1992 before
beginning another long decline to about 4 percent in 2000. After the
comparatively mild recession in 2001 (when the unemployment rate was

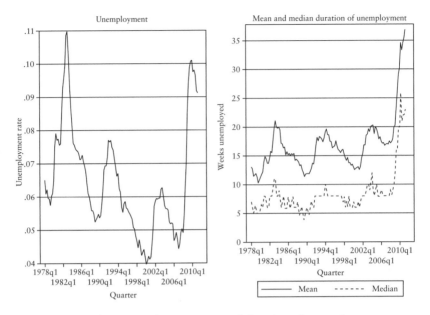

Figure 2.1 Civilian unemployment rate and duration of unemployment, seasonally adjusted

6 percent), the unemployment rate again declined to about 4.5 percent in 2007 before increasing sharply to about 10 percent by early 2010. Since that time the unemployment rate has fallen slowly.

A related concern is the unprecedentedly long durations of unemployment. This is illustrated in the second panel of Figure 2.1, which shows both the mean and median seasonally adjusted duration of unemployment for spells in progress, quarterly from 1978 to the second quarter of 2011. This figure clearly shows the countercyclical nature of unemployment duration. The mean duration of unemployment reached about 20 weeks in the three earlier recessions but rose to 35 weeks in the Great Recession. The median showed a similar pattern, reaching about 10 weeks in earlier recessions but increasing to 25 weeks in the most recent recession. The figure further indicates a continuing increase in mean unemployment duration into 2011 (mean duration 37 weeks in the second quarter of 2011) as the recovery continued to falter.

Clearly, the dynamics of unemployment in the Great Recession are fundamentally different from unemployment dynamics in earlier recessions. I turn now to analysis of the experience of displaced workers to shed more light on how this recession has differed from earlier recessions with regard both to the incidence and costs of job loss. After presenting a brief description of the Displaced Workers Survey, I begin my analysis with the presentation of some facts on the rate of job loss. I then examine two sets of outcomes for displaced workers. The first set concerns post job-loss employment and unemployment experience, including rates of employment, unemployment and nonparticipation. The second set of outcomes concerns hours and earnings among reemployed job losers. I examine the full-time or part-time status of reemployed job losers at the DWS survey date as well as the change in weekly earnings for displaced workers between the predisplacement job and the job held at the DWS survey date. Because the earnings of displaced workers likely would have changed had the workers not been displaced, I also use a control group of workers from the outgoing rotation groups of the CPS to compute the change in earnings over the same period covered by each DWS for workers who were not displaced. This allows me to break the earnings loss into two components: 1) the difference between the earnings received by job losers on their postdisplacement jobs and the earnings they received prior to displacement and 2) foregone earnings growth measured by the earnings growth received by the control group of nondisplaced workers. I then use these changes to compute difference-in-difference (DID) estimates of the effect of displacement on the earnings of reemployed workers.

The Displaced Workers Survey

I analyze data on 1,058,244 individuals between the ages of twenty and sixty-four from the DWS conducted as part of the January or February CPS in even years from 1984 through 2010. The survey is meant to capture worker terminations as the result of business decisions of the employer (e.g., a plant closing, a layoff, the abolition of a job) unrelated to the performance or choices of the particular employee. As such, it is not meant to capture voluntary job changes (quits) or termination "for cause." While the precise question asked varied somewhat over time, in January 2010 respondents were asked:

> During the last 3 calendar years, that is, January 2007 through December 2009, did (name/you) lose a job or leave one because: (your/his/her) plant

or company closed or moved, (your/his/her) position or shift was abolished, insufficient work or another similar reason?

I count as job losers workers who reported a job loss in the three calendar years prior to the survey.[4]

To investigate the consequences of job loss, I use a set of follow-up questions in the DWS asked of workers who report having lost a job. Unfortunately, since 1994, the follow-up questions were asked only of job losers whose reported reason for the job loss was slack work, plant closing, or position/shift abolished. I term these the "big three" reasons. Workers who lost jobs due to the ending of a temporary job, the ending of a self-employment situation, or "other" reasons were not asked the follow-up questions. To maintain comparability across years, my analysis of post-job-loss experience, regardless of year, uses only workers who lost jobs for the "big three" reasons. In addition, to have a consistent sample over time, I do not use information on the post-job-loss experience of job losers in the 1984–92 DWS whose reported job loss was more than three years prior to the interview date.

THE RATE OF JOB LOSS

Information on rates of job loss is presented most accessibly in graphical form, and the discussion here is organized around a series of figures.[5]

Figure 2.2 contains plots of adjusted three-year job-loss rates computed from each of the ten surveys from 1984 to 2010 along with the civilian unemployment rate for the year preceding each survey. The cyclical behavior of job loss is apparent, with job-loss rates clearly positively correlated with the unemployment rate ($\rho = 0.80$).[6] Both unemployment and job-loss rates were very high in the two most serious recessionary periods (1981–83 and 2007–09, the 1984 and 2010 survey years, respectively). While the unemployment rates were comparable in 1983 and 2009 (9.6 percent versus 9.3 percent), the job-loss rate was much higher in the 2007–09 period than in the 1981–83 period (16.0 percent versus 12.8 percent). This suggests that the Great Recession was associated with a much higher job-loss rate than the norm, which makes it particularly interesting to study the consequences of job loss in the most recent period.

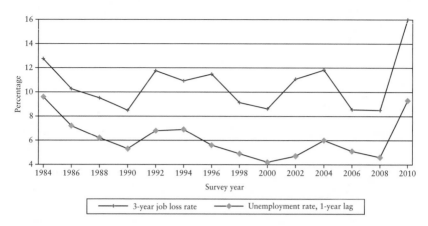

Figure 2.2   Unemployment and job loss rates, by survey year
sources: Displaced Workers Survey and Current Population Survey.

The first panel of Figure 2.3 contains three-year rates of job loss by year for each of four education categories. Not surprisingly, job-loss rates are dramatically higher for less-educated workers than for more-educated workers. For example, the job-loss rate for workers with twelve years of education was 9.4 percent in 1997–99 (the lowest in the sample period) compared with 14.3 percent in 1981–83 and 19.4 percent in 2007–09. In contrast, the job-loss rate for workers with at least sixteen years of education was 5.4 percent in 1987–89 compared with 6.9 percent in 1981–83 and 11.0 percent in 2007–2009. Clearly, there is a cyclical pattern in job-loss rates for all educational groups, but the cyclical fluctuations are much larger for less-educated workers.

Cyclical fluctuations in job-loss rates have grown over time for more-educated workers. Early on, there was little cyclical movement of job-loss rates for workers with at least sixteen years of education. Job-loss rates for these workers fell only slightly in the recovery from the recession of the early 1980s. However, the rate of job loss increased substantially in the 1989–91 period, did not fall much during the subsequent recovery, and increased again from 1997–2003 before falling through 2007. In the most recent period (2007–09), the job-loss rate of college graduates increased sharply (from 6 percent in 2005–07 to 11 percent in 2007–09). While the 2007–09 rate of job loss for college graduates is substantially below the rate for workers with less education, it is at a historically high

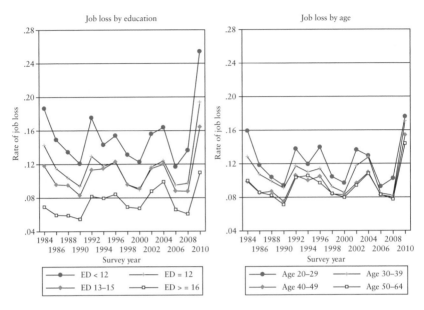

Figure 2.3   Three-year job loss rates by education and age, 1981–2009

level. The conclusion is that more-educated workers are less vulnerable to job loss, but even their vulnerability has increased over time.

The second panel of Figure 2.3 contains three-year job-loss rates by year for four age groups covering the range from ages twenty to sixty-four. Job-loss rates are highest for the youngest workers (twenty- to twenty-nine-year-olds) and generally show the standard cyclical pattern. The job-loss rates of the oldest two groups, ages forty to forty-nine and fifty to sixty-four, are very similar. There has been some convergence over time in rates of job loss by age, with the rates for older workers increasing relative to those for younger workers.

CONSEQUENCES OF JOB LOSS: EMPLOYMENT
AND UNEMPLOYMENT

Postdisplacement (Survey Date) Labor Force Status

In this section, I examine how the distribution of survey-date labor force status of workers has varied over time and how survey-date employment rates have varied over time by education and age. Figure 2.4 contains plots of the fraction employed, unemployed, and not in the labor force

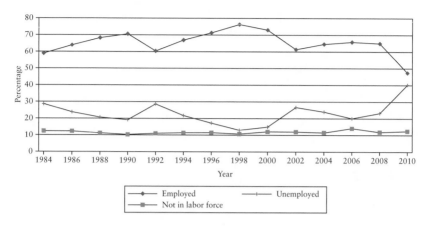

Figure 2.4   Survey date labor force status of job losers
SOURCE: Displaced Workers Survey.

at the DWS survey dates for job losers in each of the DWS's. It is clear from this figure that the postdisplacement employment rate is procyclical, with relatively low employment rates in surveys covering the slack labor markets of 1984, 1992, 2002, and 2010. The most striking feature of this plot is that the postdisplacement employment rate is substantially lower, at less than 50 percent, in the 2010 survey (covering job loss in the 2007–09 period of the Great Recession) than in any earlier period.

Not surprisingly, the survey-date unemployment rate among job losers moves countercyclically, with peak unemployment rates at the 1984, 1992, 2002, and 2010 survey dates. The most striking feature of the unemployment plot is that the postdisplacement unemployment rate is substantially higher, at about 40 percent, in the 2010 survey than in any earlier period. The survey-date fraction of job losers not in the labor force is remarkably constant across all years, at about 10 percent. There is no evidence that job losers are disproportionately discouraged in recessions, including the most recent recession, leading them to withdraw from the labor force. It is clear from Figure 2.4 that the reemployment experience of job losers is substantially worse for those who lost jobs in the Great Recession than at any other period in the last thirty years.

Postdisplacement Employment Status by Education and Age. An important dimension along which there are differences in postdisplace-

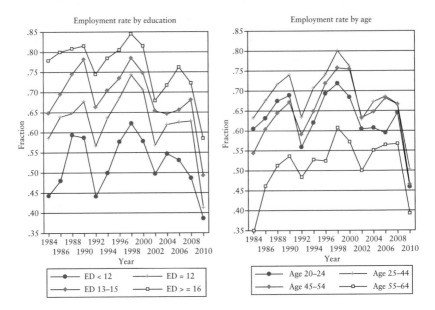

Figure 2.5   Survey date employment status of job losers, by education and age

ment labor force status is education. The first panel of Figure 2.5 contains plots of survey-date employment probabilities for displaced workers by year broken down by education. Not surprisingly, the likelihood of postdisplacement employment rises with education, although the differences by education group have moderated somewhat over time. The usual cyclical pattern of the employment fraction exists at all education levels, and the Great Recession has been hard on workers in all education groups. Only 41 percent of job losers with a high school education were employed in January 2010. This compares with a 59 percent post-job-loss employment rate for high school graduates in 1984, the survey year covering the 1982 recession. The post-job-loss employment rate for college graduates was 59 percent in January 2010 compared with a 78 percent reemployment rate for college graduates in 1984.

There are somewhat weaker differences in postdisplacement employment status by age. The second panel of Figure 2.5 contains plots of survey-date employment probabilities for displaced workers by year broken down by age. As with education, the usual cyclical pattern of the employment fraction exists at all age levels. The most striking differences in post-job-loss employment rates by age are that the oldest workers (ages fifty-five to sixty-four) are substantially less likely to be employed than are younger workers and that the youngest workers (ages twenty to twenty-four) are less likely to be employed than prime-age workers (ages twenty-five to fifty-four).

All age groups have suffered in the Great Recession. Even job losers ages forty-five to fifty-four have an employment rate of about 45 percent, while workers ages fifty-five to sixty-four have an employment rate of 40 percent. Although the statistics are not shown here, it appears that even the oldest job losers in the Great Recession do not have an increased rate of withdrawal from the labor force. In contrast, there has been some increase in the fraction not in the labor force for the youngest job losers, probably reflecting reenrollment in school.

CONSEQUENCES OF JOB LOSS: HOURS AND EARNINGS

Postdisplacement Full-Time/Part-Time Status

Many reemployed job losers are employed part-time subsequent to job loss. Some of these workers had lost part-time jobs but many had lost full-time jobs. It is well known that part-time workers, in addition to having lower weekly earnings, have substantially lower hourly wage rates and less access to fringe benefits like health insurance and pensions than do full-time workers (Farber and Levy 2000). The DWS collects information on part-time status (less than 35 hours per week) on the lost job, and it is a straightforward operation to compute part-time status on postdisplacement jobs from the standard CPS hours information. The analysis in this section focuses only on individuals employed at the survey date, and all part-time rates are computed based on this group of workers.

Figure 2.6 contains a plot of the fraction of employed job losers who are employed part-time at each survey date conditional on part-time status on the lost job.[7] Not surprisingly, workers who lost part-time jobs are substantially more likely to have part-time jobs at the survey date. Many of these workers are part-time due to labor supply choices, and it is reasonable to expect that these workers would continue to choose to work part-time. It is noteworthy, then, that almost 50 percent of part-time job losers were working full-time at the survey date, although this

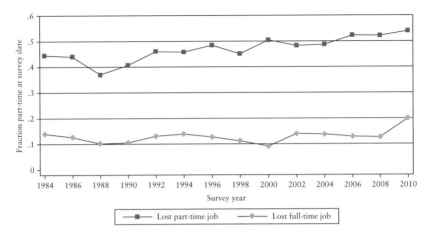

Figure 2.6   Fraction part-time at survey date, by part-time status on lost job

fraction has decreased substantially since the late 1980s. Among reemployed part-time job losers in the 2007–09 period, about 46 percent were working full-time in January 2010.

In terms of the cost of job loss, a more interesting group to study consists of those workers who lost full-time jobs. Between 10 percent and 15 percent of these job losers were working part-time at the survey dates from 1984–2008. The part-time rate among full-time job losers increased substantially, to 20 percent in 2010. Thus, even among the 50 percent of job losers who were reemployed, a substantial fraction of full-time job losers did not find full-time employment. More generally, there is a cyclical component to the ability of full-time job losers to find full-time employment. The postdisplacement part-time rate among full-time job losers is higher in each of the slack labor market periods, but the part-time rate was highest in the Great Recession.

The Loss in Earnings Due to Displacement

The analysis of the loss in earnings of reemployed displaced workers proceeds in two stages. First, I investigate the change in earnings between the lost job and the job held at the DWS survey date. Had the displaced worker not lost his or her job, however, earnings likely would have grown over the interval between the date of job loss and the DWS survey date. Thus, second, I investigate the earnings loss suffered by displaced workers, including both the decline in their earnings and the increase in earnings enjoyed by nondisplaced workers that is foregone by displaced workers. For this earnings loss to be measured, a control group of nondisplaced workers is required; later in this section I provide such a control group using data from the CPS outgoing rotation groups.

Difference Estimates of the Change in Earnings as a Result of Job Loss. I begin the analysis of earnings changes by examining the difference in real weekly earnings for job losers between the postdisplacement job and the job from which the worker was displaced.[8] The solid line in the first panel of Figure 2.7 shows the average proportional decline, by survey year, in real weekly earnings between the lost job and the survey-date job for all workers who lost a job, were reemployed at the survey date, and were not self-employed on either the lost job or the new job. There is a cyclical component to the earnings decline, with larger declines in slack labor market periods. The average earnings decline in the last recession was the largest since 1984, at 17.5 percent. This compares with a decline of 14.1 percent in 1984 and 15.9 percent in 1992.

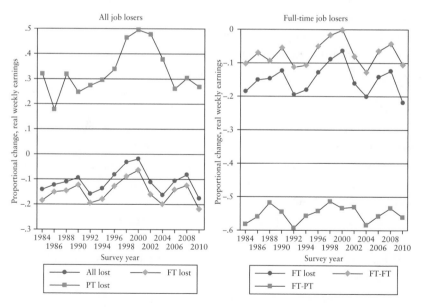

Figure 2.7   Proportional change in real weekly earnings for job losers

Because my measure of earnings is weekly, part of the measured earnings change reflects voluntary or involuntary changes in hours worked (movement to or from full-time work). The lower dashed line in the first panel of Figure 2.7 is the average earnings change of full-time job losers. This parallels the earnings change of all job losers (correlation 0.986) because most reported loss is of full-time jobs (almost 90 percent). The reason full-time job losers have larger average earnings declines is that some full-time workers are reemployed on part-time jobs (Figure 2.6). The upper dashed line in the first panel of Figure 2.7 is the average earnings change of part-time job losers. This is positive in every period because many losers of part-time jobs are employed subsequently on full-time jobs (48 percent overall, Figure 2.6). In summary, job losers suffer substantial earnings declines on average, and the average decline is largest in the most recent period.

Given that a large majority of job losers lost full-time jobs, I focus on the experience of these workers. The solid line in the second panel of Figure 2.7, which reproduces the lower dashed line in the first panel, is the average earnings change of full-time job losers. The upper dashed line in the second panel of Figure 2.7 is the average earnings change of job losers who make a full-time to full-time transition. This closely parallels the earnings change of all full-time job losers (correlation 0.956) because most reemployed full-time job losers are reemployed on full-time jobs (87 percent). The lower dashed line in the second panel of Figure 2.7 is the average earnings change of job losers who have made a full-time to part-time (FT-PT) transition. This is substantial and negative because of the decline in weekly hours in moving from full-time to part-time.

All of these series show a cyclical pattern, with larger earnings declines in weaker labor markets. That this decline is largest in the most recent recessionary period is due entirely to the higher incidence of part-time employment on the new job among both full-time and part-time job losers. The earnings decline holding FT-PT status fixed is not particularly large in the current period relative to other slack labor market periods.[9]

I carried out a multivariate regression analysis (not presented here) of the log earnings change of reemployed displaced workers, controlling for year, education, age, race, sex, and tenure on the lost job. That analysis shows no significant relationship with race or sex.[10] Workers with less than a high school education suffered larger earnings losses than workers with at least a high school education. There is a strong relationship between age and the change in real earnings, with older workers suffering larger earnings declines. In addition, there is a very strong relationship between the change in earnings and tenure on the lost job. The average earnings loss is much larger when the worker had accumulated substantial tenure on the lost job. This is consistent with the destruction of job- or industry-specific human capital when a long-term job ends.[11]

Difference-in-Difference Estimates of the Effect of Job Loss on Earnings. To account for the extent to which earnings might have grown had the workers not been displaced, I generate a comparison group of workers using a random sample from the merged outgoing rotation group (MOGRG) files of the CPS for the three calendar years prior to each DWS (period 0) together with all workers from the outgoing rotation groups of the CPSs containing the DWS's (period t). The data from the MOGRG files provide the period 0 earnings, and the data from the outgoing rotation groups DWS's provide the period t earnings.

This analysis is restricted to full-time workers. In particular, the job losers considered are only those who are reemployed and make full-time to full-time transitions. Therefore, it will understate the true earnings loss of displacement for two reasons. First, it considers only those who are reemployed (50 percent of job losers in the most recent period). Second, it ignores the fact that many full-time job losers are reemployed in part-time jobs (about 20 percent in the most recent period), offset to some extent by those part-time job losers who are reemployed in full-time jobs.

Define the change in log real earnings for displaced workers as

$$(1) \qquad \Delta_d = (\ln W_{dt} - \ln W_{d0}),$$

and define the difference in log real earnings for workers in the comparison group as

$$(2) \qquad \Delta_c = (\ln W_{ct} - \ln W_{c0}),$$

where d refers to displaced workers (the "treatment" group), c refers to nondisplaced workers (the control group), t refers to the current (postdisplacement) period, and 0 refers to the initial (predisplacement) period. The difference-in-difference estimate of the loss in log real weekly earnings due to job loss is computed as

(3) $\Delta\Delta = \Delta_d - \Delta_c.$

Assuming average earnings would have grown rather than declined in the absence of displacement, Δc will be positive so that the difference-in-difference estimate of the average earnings decline ($\Delta\Delta$) will be larger in absolute value than the simple difference estimate (Δ_d). I generated initial earnings for the comparison group ($\ln W_{g0}$) from a random subsample of the merged outgoing rotation group CPS file (MOGRG) each year from 1981–2009.[12] The resulting comparison sample of initial earnings for full-time workers contains 154,272 observations.

The CPS's containing the DWS's have two outgoing rotation groups (OGRGs) with earnings data for all workers. These provide the observations on current earnings for the comparison group of nondisplaced workers ($\ln W_{gt}$). This sample contains observations on full-time earnings for 150,935 workers at the DWS survey date.

Ideally, these comparison groups would contain only workers who had not lost a job during the relevant period. While I can identify the displaced workers in period t (because the data come from the CPSs with DWS's), I cannot identify the workers who will be displaced in the MOGRG samples. To the extent that earnings growth for displaced workers is different from that for nondisplaced workers, earnings growth computed from the control group as defined here would lead to biased estimates of earnings growth for a group of nondisplaced workers. To address this problem, I adjusted the estimates based on the outgoing rotation groups to provide unbiased estimates of the earnings change for a control group of nondisplaced workers. This adjustment is described in the appendix at the end of the chapter.

The source of data for the treatment group earnings is the DWS's, where $\ln W_{dt}$ is survey-date earnings for displaced workers, and $\ln W_{d0}$ is earnings on the lost job. The predisplacement sample consists of all displaced workers who were not self-employed but were employed full-time on the lost job and who were employed with earnings available at the survey date (n=26,788). The postdisplacement sample consists of all displaced workers who were not self-employed but were employed full-time at the survey date and who had earnings data on the lost job (n=24,057).

The difference-in-difference estimates are derived using the data from separate ordinary least squares (OLS) regressions for each DWS survey year of log real earnings (deflated by the CPI) on a set of worker characteristics and an indicator for time period (before or after displacement), an indicator for whether the observation is part of the "contaminated" control sample or part of the displacement sample, and the interaction of the time period and sample indicators.[13] This OLS regression is of the form year of the form,

$$(4) \qquad \ln W_{is} = X_{is}\,\beta + \gamma_1 T_s + \gamma_2 D_i + \gamma_3\,T_s\,D_i + \varepsilon_{is},$$

where $\ln W_{is}$ measures log real full-time earnings for individual i in period s (either 0 or t), X is a vector of individual characteristics, β is a vector of coefficients, T_s is a dummy variable indicating the postdisplacement period, D_i is a dummy variable indicating the displacement sample, and ε is an error term.[14] The estimates of the parameters γ_j are used along with information from the DWS on period-specific job-loss rates to compute estimates of the earnings effects as described in the appendix.

Figure 2.8 contains the overall regression-adjusted difference-in-difference estimates of the proportional earnings loss from job loss for

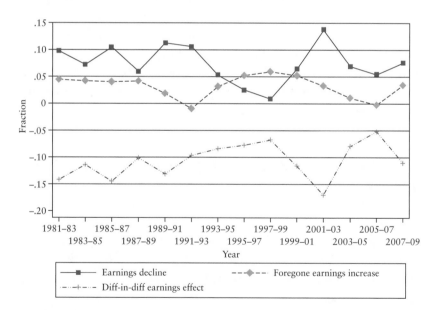

Figure 2.8 Proportional earnings loss, difference-in-difference analysis, FT-FT transitions

each year.[15] So that the figure can be read clearly, the earnings loss for displaced workers is presented as a positive number (the negative of the earnings change for displaced workers: $-\Delta_d$). The foregone earnings increase is Δ_c, and the difference-in-difference earnings effect is $\Delta\Delta$. Note that these estimates account for the effect of normal growth along the age-earnings profile. This is because the age variables in the regression are measured at the DWS survey date (period t) for both the period 0 and period t observations.[16]

The results show that in the 1980s displaced workers earned about 9 percent less on average after displacement than before, while the control group's earnings rose by about 4.5 percent over the same period. The difference-in-difference estimate of the earnings loss is the difference between these numbers, which is a loss of about 13 percent during the 1980s.[17] The 1990s show a different pattern. The earnings decline of displaced workers in the 1990s dropped sharply during the decade, from 11.3 percent in the 1989–91 period to a statistically insignificant 0.9 percent in 1997–99. During the same period, the earnings growth of the control group increased from 1.9 percent in 1989–91 to 5.9 percent in 1997–99, reflecting the general increase in real wages in the late 1990s. The difference-in-difference estimate of the earnings loss associated with job loss decreased during the 1990s (from a high of 13.1 percent in 1989–91 to a low of 6.8 percent in 1997–99), reflecting the fact that the earnings decline of displaced workers fell by more than earnings grew among the comparison group.

The picture changed in the last ten years. The foregone earnings increase fell somewhat, from 5.9 percent in 1997–99 to zero in 2005–07, while the earnings decline suffered by displaced workers increased substantially, from 0.9 percent in the 1997–99 period to 13.7 percent in 2001–03, before declining to 5.4 percent in 2005–07. In the period covering the Great Recession (2007–09), the earnings decline of job losers making a FT-FT transition was 7.6 percent, with a foregone earnings increase of 3.5 percent. This implies a total earnings loss from job displacement for these workers of 11 percent, which is not unusually large by historical standards.

It is clear from Figure 2.8 that earnings growth foregone by job losers has been an important part of the cost of job loss in some periods.

Interestingly, the period of the Great Recession has not been marked by unusually large real earnings losses for reemployed job losers making a FT-FT transition. The earnings loss in this period is split into about one-third foregone earnings growth and two-thirds earnings decline.

CONCLUDING REMARKS

Job loss and worker dislocation are facts of life in the U.S. economy, and they are part of an efficient labor allocation process. However, the costs of job loss have been particularly severe in the Great Recession. During this period (job loss in 2007–09) I found the following:

- About 16 percent of people ages twenty to sixty-four reported having lost a job.
- Less than 50 percent of job losers were employed in January 2010 (a much lower fraction than in earlier periods).
- About 20 percent of reemployed full-time job losers were holding part-time jobs (a much higher fraction than in earlier periods).
- Job losers who found a new job earned, on average, 17.5 percent less on their new job than on the lost job.
- Losers of full-time jobs who found a new job earned 21.8 percent less, on average, on their new job than on the lost job, due in large measure to the substantial fraction (20 percent) of full-time job losers who were employed in part-time jobs subsequent to job loss.
- Losers of full-time jobs who found a new full-time job earned 10.5 percent less, on average, on their new job than on the lost job. This is comparable to earnings losses in earlier periods with a slack labor market (1984, 1992, 1994, and 2004).
- Counting foregone earnings increases enjoyed by non-job-losers, full-time job losers who found new full-time jobs suffered a total earnings loss of about 11 percent less on average on their new jobs than they would have earned had they not been displaced. This is not unusual compared with earlier periods.

The measures on which this chapter is focused likely understate the true economic cost of job loss substantially. First, time spent unemployed by those workers who were reemployed is not considered. Second, more hinges on employment, particularly full-time employment, in the United States than in other developed countries. Health insurance and pensions are closely linked to employment, and many workers do not have alternative access to these important benefits. This makes job loss an expensive and damaging event on average.

To conclude, while job loss is a fact of life in the United States, the consequences of job loss in the Great Recession have been unusually severe. Most important, those who lost their jobs in the Great Recession have been much less successful at finding new jobs (particularly full-time jobs) than job losers were in the aftermath of earlier recessions. It is not yet clear what will be the long-run consequences of prolonged inability to find work for job losers on their future labor market outcomes.

APPENDIX: DETAILS OF THE DIFFERENCE-IN-DIFFERENCE PROCEDURE

The observed log wage change of workers in the outgoing rotation groups (which include both displaced and nondisplaced workers) is a probability-of-job-loss weighted average of the change in log earnings for displaced and non-displaced workers. Define the change in log earnings for the outgoing rotation groups as

(5) $$\Delta_g = (1-\theta)\Delta_c + \theta\Delta_d,$$

where Δ_g is the log earnings change in the outgoing rotation group sample $\ln W_{gt} - \ln W_{g0}$ and θ is the fraction of workers in the outgoing rotation group sample who lost a job (the displacement rate).

The observable quantities are Δ_g and Δ_d, but calculation of the difference-in-difference estimate of the log earnings change due to job loss requires both Δ_d and Δ_c—equations (1) and (2).[18] I can compute Δ_c with the available data on Δ_g, Δ_d and θ. Using equation (5), the change in log earnings for the comparison group is

(6) $$\Delta_c = \frac{\Delta_g - \theta\Delta_d}{(1-\theta)}$$

and the difference-in-difference estimate of the effect of job loss on earnings is

(7) $$\Delta\Delta = \frac{\Delta_d - \Delta_g}{(1-\theta)}.$$

Intuitively, the samples from the outgoing rotation groups are "contaminated" with displaced workers so that the difference-in-difference estimate computed using this contaminated control group needs to be scaled up by the factor $\frac{1}{1-\theta}$ to compensate.

The parameters γ_j, estimated by separate OLS regressions for each DWS survey year from equation (4), are used, along with information from the DWS on period-specific job loss rates (θ), to compute estimates of the log earnings effects as follows:

(8) $$\Delta_d = \gamma_1 + \gamma_3,$$

(9) $$\Delta_c = \gamma_1 - \frac{\theta\gamma_s}{(1-\theta)}, \text{ and}$$

(10) $$\Delta\Delta = \frac{\gamma_s}{(1-\theta)}.$$

NOTES

1. Examples of earlier work using the DWS include Farber (1993, 1997, 1998, 2005); Podgursky and Swaim (1987); Kletzer (1989); Topel (1990); Gardner (1995); Neal (1995); Esposito and Fisher (1997); and Hipple (1999). See Fallick (1996) and Farber (2004) for reviews of the earlier literature.

2. This is the National Bureau of Economic Research (NBER) dating of the recession. See http://www.nber.org/cycles.html and NBER (2010) for more information on the NBER business cycle dating procedure. The labor market historically lags behind the NBER dates, which are based largely on GDP growth. For example, the unemployment rate in the recent period reported by the U.S. Bureau of Labor Statistics peaked in October 2009, while the NBER dated the end of the recession in June 2009.

3. These unemployment rates are based on my own calculations using the individual-level Current Population Survey (CPS) data available for this period. I weight by the CPS final sampling weights. To seasonally adjust a series Y_t with overall mean $\overline{Y}$, I regress Y_t on a complete set of seasonal dummy variables and calculate the residuals, e_t. I then compute the seasonally adjusted series as

$$Y_t^{sa} = \overline{Y} + e_t.$$

4. Important issues of measurement and interpretation arise when comparing job-loss rates calculated using the Displaced Workers Survey (DWS) over time, including changes in wording of the key questions and a change in 1994 in the recall period from five years to three years. See Farber 1997 and 2004 for detailed discussions of these issues and the procedures I use to reweight the data to yield adjusted job-loss rates that are comparable over time.

5. All counts are weighted using the CPS sampling weights.

6. Another possibility would be to use the average unemployment rate for the three years preceding each survey. However, reported rates of job loss are always higher in the year immediately preceding the survey relative to the rates of job loss two and three years preceding the survey. This may be the result of recall bias noted by Topel (1990). Empirically, the correlation of the rate of job loss with the unemployment rate in the year preceding the survey ($\rho = 0.80$) is much higher than the correlation of the rate of job loss with the average unemployment rate in the three years preceding the survey ($\rho = 0.42$).

7. Note that there is a problem of temporal comparability of the data on part-time employment at the survey date. The new survey instrument, first used in the 1994 CPS, asks a different battery of questions about hours of work on the current job, and this may have the effect of raising the fraction of workers reporting that they are currently working part-time (Polivka and Miller 1998). The survey question regarding whether the lost job was part-time is unchanged in the 1994 and later DWSs.

8. Earnings are deflated by the 1982–84=100 consumer price index (CPI). The CPI in the reported year of displacement is used to deflate earnings on the old job. The CPI for the DWS survey month is used to deflate current earnings.

9. The differences between the earnings decline holding FT-PT status fixed between 2010 and earlier slack labor market periods (1984, 1992, 1994, and 2004) are not statistically significant.

10. See Farber 2004 for presentation of regression results on the earnings change through the 2002 DWS.

11. Kletzer (1989), Neal (1995), and Parent (2000) address the issue of job loss and specific capital, both at the firm and industry level.

12. The size of the random sample was set so that 1) the size of the sample with initial earnings on the control group was expected to be the same size as that with current earnings on the control group (two rotation groups), and 2) the distribution of years since the associated DWS survey date roughly mimicked the distribution of years since displacement in the sample of displaced workers. In other words, a separate control sample was drawn for each DWS from the three MOGRGs for the years immediately prior to the DWS that reflected the distribution of time since job loss. Each MOGRG file has 24 rotation groups (2 per month for 12 months). Denote the share of reported job loss one, two, and three years prior to the survey date t as p_{1t}, p_{2t}, and p_{3t}, respectively. In order to get the appropriate sample size in survey year t, I took a random sample with probability $(p_{1t})(2)/24$. Similarly, for the second and third years prior to the DWS I took random samples with probability (p_{2t}) $(2)/24$ and $(p_{3t})(2)/24$, respectively.

13. Note that I do not calculate first-differenced estimates for the displaced workers, as I did previously, despite the fact that the observations are paired. This is because observations for the control group are from a set of cross-sections and are not paired. I do not account for the correlation over time in the two observations for each displaced worker.

14. The X vector includes constant, dummy variables for sex, race, nine age categories, and four educational categories.

15. Note that the differences (or DIDs) in log earnings are approximations to the appropriate proportional differences (or DIDs) in earnings. I transform the differences in log earnings to proportional differences using the usual relationship that, with a log difference of δ, the proportional difference is $e^{\delta-1}$. The difference-in-difference estimate plotted in the figure is then calculated as the difference of the transformed differences

$$(\Delta\Delta = e^{\Delta d} - e^{\Delta c}).$$

16. This is one reason why it was important that the sample fractions in the initial-earnings control group mimic the fractions in the treatment group with respect to the time until the DWS survey date.

17. Because in the figure I present the earnings loss rather than the earnings change for displaced workers, the difference-in-difference estimate is the negative of the sum of the earnings decline for displaced workers and the foregone earnings increase.

18. Note that I do not use the information on who is displaced that is available in the DWS outgoing rotation groups. My estimate of Δ_g includes both displaced and nondisplaced workers at both time 0 and time t.

REFERENCES

Fallick, Bruce C. "A Review of the Recent Empirical Literature on Displaced Workers," *Industrial and Labor Relations Review* 50 (October 1996): 5–16.

Farber, Henry S. "The Incidence and Costs of Job Loss: 1982–91," *Brookings Papers on Economic Activity: Microeconomics* (1993): 73–119.

Farber, Henry S. "The Changing Face of Job Loss in the United States, 1981–1995," *Brookings Papers on Economic Activity: Microeconomics* (1997): 55–128.

Farber, Henry S. "Has the Rate of Job Loss Increased in the Nineties?" *Proceedings of the Fiftieth Annual Winter Meeting of the Industrial Relations Research Association* Vol. 1, 1998: 88–97.

Farber, Henry S. "Job Loss in the United States, 1981–2001," *Research in Labor Economics* 23 (2004): 69–117.

Farber, Henry S. "What Do We Know About Job Loss in the United States? Evidence from the Displaced Workers Survey, 1981–2004," *Economic Perspectives*, Federal Reserve Bank of Chicago (Second Quarter, 2005): 13–28.

Farber, Henry S., and Helen Levy. "Recent Trends in Employer-Sponsored Health Insurance Coverage: Are Bad Jobs Getting Worse?" *Journal of Health Economics* (January 2000): 93–119.

Gardner, Jennifer M. "Worker Displacement: A Decade of Change," *Monthly Labor Review* 118 (April 1995): 45–57.

Hipple, Steven. "Worker Displacement in the mid-1990's," *Monthly Labor Review* 122 (July 1999): 15–32.

Kletzer, Lori G. "Returns to Seniority after Permanent Job Loss," *American Economic Review* 79 (June 1989): 536–43.

National Bureau of Economic Research. "The NBER's Business Cycle Dating Committee," September 20, 2010. Available at http://www.nber.org/cycles/recessions.html.

Neal, Derek. "Industry-Specific Capital: Evidence from Displaced Workers," *Journal of Labor Economics* 13 (October 1995): 653–77.

Parent, Daniel. "Industry-Specific Capital and the Wage Profile: Evidence from the National Longitudinal Survey of Youth and the Panel Study of Income Dynamics," *Journal of Labor Economics* 18 (April 2000): 306–23.

Podgursky, Michael, and Paul Swaim. "Job Displacement Earnings Loss: Evidence from the Displaced Worker Survey," *Industrial and Labor Relations Review* 41 (October 1987): 17–29.

Polivka, Anne E., and Stephen M. Miller. "The CPS After the Redesign: Refocusing the Lens," in *Labor Statistics Measurement Issues*, John Haltiwanger, Marilyn Manser, and Robert Topel, eds., University of Chicago Press, 1998, 249–89.

Topel, Robert. "Specific Capital and Unemployment: Measuring the Costs and Consequences of Job Loss," *Carnegie Rochester Conference Series on Public Policy* 33 (1990): 181–214.

CHAPTER THREE

The Effect of Job Displacement on Cumulated Years Worked

Till von Wachter, Jae Song, and Joyce Manchester

INTRODUCTION

An increasing number of studies document that job loss during recessions can have lasting consequences for workers and their families. Loss of a stable job can lead to substantial reductions in earnings (e.g., Ruhm 1991; Jacobson, LaLonde, and Sullivan 1993; Schoeni and Dardia 2003; Couch and Placzek 2010), which for workers displaced from good employers can last up to fifteen to twenty years (von Wachter, Song, and Manchester 2011). Job displacement can also lead to persistent increases in mobility across jobs, industries, and states (Stevens 1997; von Wachter, Song, and Manchester 2011). A job displacement can also lead to increases in mortality (Sullivan and von Wachter 2009), with substantial consequences for life expectancy.

The difficulty faced by workers in finding employment in the short term is the focus of Henry Farber in "Historical Perspective from the Displaced Workers Survey: 1984–2010," in this volume. Farber documents how, especially in larger recessions, job losses can lead to substantial short-run reductions in employment. In this chapter, we study the effect of job displacement on *total* employment over a horizon of up to twenty years after job loss. To do so, we use longitudinal administrative data covering thirty years of information on employment and firm

---

The findings and views expressed here are those of the authors and should not be interpreted as those of the Social Security Administration or the Congressional Budget Office.

characteristics covering the entire U.S. labor market. The available data allow us to isolate male workers who were displaced when their employer suffered a sudden large reduction in employment during the recession of the early 1980s. We then compare the total number of years with positive earnings until 2003 for displaced workers with similar workers who did not separate from their employer during the early 1980s.

The focus on cumulated years of employment is relevant for several reasons. The public debate on the effect of economic contractions focuses largely on measures of nonemployment. This is partly because many of the programs potentially providing assistance to workers during recessions are geared toward the nonemployed. Those programs include unemployment insurance, job search assistance, or subsidies for retraining. Other programs not explicitly geared toward job losers are nevertheless influenced by the incidence of nonemployment, such as Social Security Disability Insurance (SSDI). Workers experiencing a longer spell of nonemployment may be more likely to become eligible for SSDI, and also face lower opportunity costs of applying for SSDI.

Gaps in workers' employment histories also matter for workers' well-being in the long run. To the extent that workers cannot recoup their losses by working longer or gaining higher earnings, their permanent income and lifetime consumption choices may be affected (Friedman 1957). For example, employment gaps may lower both the base from which Social Security benefits are calculated and workers' ability to accumulate assets, including pension assets. Multiple or prolonged spells of nonemployment after job displacement can thus have consequences beyond one's working life. Because long spells of nonemployment tend to be concentrated among a subset of job losers, the effect of job loss may lead not only to lower levels, but also to greater inequality in retirement benefits and income.

Few data sources are adequate for the study of measures of total employment over long stretches of time for large samples of workers. As a result, we have information on the immediate effect of job loss on employment (see Farber 1999 and Chapter 2 of this volume; Chan and Stevens 2001) but few measures of the *long-term* reduction in employment following job displacement in recessions. Yet, given the widespread increase in layoffs and nonemployment in major recessions, the persistent effects of job loss found for earnings and other outcomes, and the important role of nonemployment in many public programs, documenting and understanding the effects of job displacement on cumulated employment is important.

In this chapter, we first use our data to provide new evidence on the potential degree of job and employment instability male workers may face over their working lives. As found by others, we show that transitions between jobs are frequent throughout workers' careers, but decline substantially with age. We find job transitions rise in booms, which is often interpreted as suggestive evidence that many of those transitions are voluntary. In recessions, however, transitions to nonemployment rise and (presumably voluntary) job-to-job transitions decline. As a result, the risk of an involuntary job separation is likely to rise significantly in recessions. For the early 1980s, we show that this increase coincides with a substantial incidence of job displacement during mass layoffs.

We then show that those job displacements can have substantial effects on cumulated years of employment of previously stable male workers employed at midsized firms. Workers who lost their jobs during a mass layoff in the early 1980s suffered a loss of about 1.5 to 3 years in total years worked, depending on the age at displacement and the horizon over which we follow workers after job loss. Relative to the potential maximum years worked, the loss ranges from 6 percent to 14 percent. None of the other potential determinants of total years worked in our sample—including average initial earnings or initial wage growth, industry, or firm size—leads to effects that are nearly as large. We find that those employment losses are concentrated among the lower tail of the distribution, especially for younger displaced workers. Among those workers, a large fraction suffers at least one spell of a single year of nonemployment.

Our results suggest that job displacements in recessions lead to a substantial rise in the incidence of longer spells of nonemployment lasting at least one year and hence to a substantial reduction in total years worked over a twenty-year horizon after job loss. We cannot measure nonemployment spells that do not span an entire calendar year. Because a large share of unemployment spells are shorter than a year, and even longer nonemployment spells may straddle two calendar years, our estimates are likely to underestimate the total effect of job displacement on time worked. Conversely, our estimates may overstate the effect of job displacement because any nonemployment spell that occurs during a mass layoff is interpreted as a displacement. Hence, in principle we may measure nonemployment occurring for reasons other than job loss, such as care for relatives, adverse health, self-employment, or time spent in further education. Given that our results are robust to controlling for age at displacement and are not affected by a range of control variables, we suspect that the nonemployment trends in our control group are sufficient to control for the time pattern of those other events. As further explained below, this robustness as well as our research design focusing on stable male employees displaced during mass layoffs also leads us to believe that it is unlikely that our estimates arise because job losers have higher inherent propensity to suffer nonemployment. Nevertheless, the inherent potential limitations of the research design based on nonrandomized analysis of administrative data have to be borne in mind when interpreting our results.

Clearly, even if our estimates of work years lost are the true causal effect of a job displacement, they may capture both a rise in involuntary unemployment and an increase in potentially beneficial nonmarket activities in response to job loss, such as obtaining additional education or training. Hence, without additional information our estimates do not translate directly into an estimate of changes in worker welfare. Yet the estimates unambiguously imply a reduction in covered market employment. Moreover, at least on average, reductions in employment of at least a year correlate strongly with above-average permanent reduction in earnings. Thus it is unlikely that on average workers use the long nonemployment spells we find here for investments in skills with high market value.

In the next section, we describe our data sources and the construction of our sample of displaced workers. In the following sections we describe the incidence of job mobility and nonemployment transitions; analyze the effect of job displacement on cumulated years worked; and adjust the differences between displaced and nondisplaced workers using predetermined characteristics.

DATA AND SAMPLE

Longitudinal Worker Data

As in von Wachter, Song, and Manchester (2011), the sample of workers used for our analysis is based on three data sets: the 2004 Continuous

Work History Sample (CWHS) active file, a 1 percent extract from the Master Earnings File (MEF), and a 1 percent extract from the Longitudinal Employee-Employer Data (LEED). First, we merge the 1 percent baseline sample of individuals covered by Social Security from the CWHS with information from the MEF on workers' total uncapped annual earnings for each job in each year from 1978 through 2004. Besides annual earnings and an identification number for each employer (EIN), the MEF also contains information on the industry for each job. Second, we complement the data on uncapped earnings with information on annual earnings for each job from 1974 to 1977 from the LEED. The Data Appendix of von Wachter, Song, and Manchester (2011) has more-detailed information.

Our sample was explicitly chosen to be comparable to the seminal work of Jacobson, LaLonde, and Sullivan 1993 (henceforth, JLS), who studied the effect of job loss during the early 1980s in Pennsylvania on workers in stable employment from 1974 to 1979. For our sample to be comparable to JLS, two modifications are necessary. First, we follow a simple imputation procedure described in Kopczuk, Saez, and Song (2007) to make the capped earnings levels from the LEED comparable to the uncapped earnings in the MEF. Second, we exclude job separations from public administration, several social services (such as health and legal services), and agriculture to maintain consistency of our sample over time. To avoid censoring of our earnings observations, those sectors remain as sources of postseparation employment. Excluding those sectors also helps to avoid changes in EINs occurring for administrative reasons.

From that sample, we extract two groups of male workers with high employer attachment: workers in stable employment from 1977 to 1979 and from 1974 to 1979. We focus on the latter group with six or more years of job tenure here, but all results are robust to considering workers with three or more years of job tenure. We also follow JLS in requiring that workers be born in or after 1930. Hence the average age at the time of job separation is roughly forty years, and the majority of the sample is in their prime working years during the follow-up period. To avoid an increasing fraction of workers dropping out of the labor force over time, we restrict workers in our initial analysis to no older than fifty-five.

Because we are also interested in the employment response of mature and older displaced workers, we consider a sample that includes employment up to age seventy. In the future, we will be able to directly examine the receipt of public pension and disability insurance using administrative data on benefit receipt from the Master Beneficiary Record (MBR).

A crucial step in our analysis is the dating of job separations. The most straightforward definition is simply a change in EIN from the EIN of the employer of the stable job held in the late 1970s. Alternative definitions yielded very similar results (von Wachter, Song, and Manchester 2007). Following JLS, we define a worker as displaced from his previous job when the firm experiences a mass-layoff event.

Longitudinal Firm Data

As in von Wachter, Song, and Manchester (2011), we use firm-level employment data covering any employer operating in the United States from 1978 to 2004 that reports earnings covered by Social Security.[1] For workers with multiple employers in one year, we include only the employer at which the worker received the highest earnings to avoid double-counting workers who switch employers within a year or workers who hold multiple jobs.[2]

We define mass layoffs as instances where the employment of a firm drops by at least 30 percent and restrict ourselves to firms with at least fifty employees in 1979. Because our employment measures are based on annual earnings, if workers receive earnings for part of the year at the old employer, even a sudden drop in firm size may not appear immediately as a drop in employment. Thus, we consider changes in firm size over two years. To make sure we capture a permanent decline and not temporary fluctuations in a firm's workforce, we also require employment at the firm to have a minimum amount of stability before and after a sudden drop in employment.

The resulting incidence of mass layoffs at the firm level and job destruction at the worker level suggests a large spike of layoffs in the early 1980s. Below, we show the transition rate to nonemployment was especially high in the early 1980s, consistent with a high rate of layoffs. We then analyze the effect of separating from a stable job during a mass layoff on cumulated years worked.

TRENDS IN JOB SEPARATIONS AND AVERAGE
CHARACTERISTICS OF SEPARATORS

We begin with a description of job separation rates and the average characteristics of workers separating from long-term jobs. The total annual separation rate and the rate of transition between two EINs reveal three observations (see Figures 3.1 and 3.2). First, the average job separation rate is high, fluctuating around 35 percent. That rate is actually somewhat lower than the annual rate of job separation implied by other estimates using administrative data (Anderson and Meyer 1994). Second, the job-separation rate is highly procyclical, suggesting that the bulk of job separations are driven by voluntary job mobility (Shimer 2005; Elsby, Michaels, and Solon 2009). Third, an important part of the level and movements of overall job separations is driven by job-to-job transitions (Figure 3.2). This confirms that a large share of job transitions are likely to be voluntary. The two figures also show job separations by three age groups. As is typically found, job-separation rates are highest and most procyclical for younger workers (Topel and Ward 1992). However, the rates remain substantial for workers between ages thirty and fifty, and even for workers above age fifty.

We next examine transitions from jobs into nonemployment, where nonemployment is defined as a calendar year without any earnings. Given that most nonemployment spells are short, our measure understates the job-to-nonemployment transition rate. The transition into nonemployment is a measure of involuntary job loss, albeit an imperfect one, because many involuntarily displaced workers find a job immediately or after a short spell of nonemployment. Clearly, some transitions into nonemployment are voluntary, although this is likely to be more important for older workers and women than for male workers in prime working age. Consistent with this interpretation, transitions to nonemployment jumped dramatically in 1982, a strong recession (Figure 3.3). Similarly, they rose prior to the 1991 recession and increased considerably between 2000 and 2002. As observed elsewhere using related measures (e.g., Davis 2008), during the 1980s and 1990s overall, the trend in the transition rate to nonemployment declined.

The remaining lines in the figure show the transition rate to nonemployment by three broad age groups. All age groups experienced a large

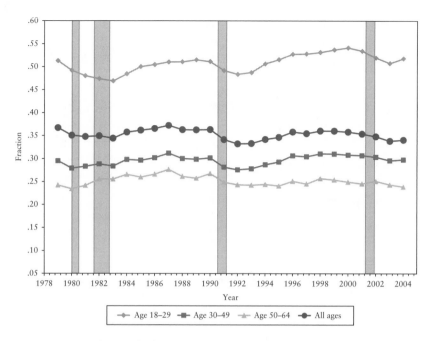

Figure 3.1 Incidence of job separations from one year to the next among men by calendar year; all ages and separately by age groups

SOURCE: Authors' calculations using a 1 percent sample of Social Security Administration data.

NOTES: Includes only workers born after 1930. The figure shows the fraction of male employees earning positive earnings in the previous year (t–1) who have left their main employer in the following year (t). Vertical bars represent National Bureau of Economic Research business cycle dates.

increase in transitions to nonemployment in 1982 and a clear countercyclical pattern afterward. All three groups also show a secular decline, although it appears most pronounced for those ages fifty to sixty-four. Not surprisingly, that group has by far the highest transition rate to nonemployment. Explaining the secular decline in nonemployment transition goes beyond the scope of this chapter but, as the figure suggests, it is likely associated with the slowing trend toward early retirement among older workers and the younger average age of workers as the baby-boom cohort entered prime working age.

The main message of Figures 3.1–3.3 is that workers face a potentially high degree of job and employment instability over their working

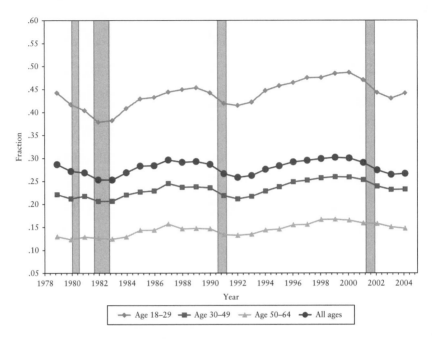

Figure 3.2   Incidence of job-to-job transitions from one year to the next among men by calendar year; all ages and separately by age groups

SOURCE: Authors' calculations using a 1 percent sample of Social Security Administration data.

NOTES: Includes only workers born after 1930. The figure shows the fraction of male employees earning positive earnings in the previous year (t–1) who have left their main employer in the following year (t) but continue to have positive earnings. Vertical bars represent National Bureau of Economic Research business cycle dates.

lives, which declines with age. Many of those transitions may be voluntary, but the risk of involuntary transitions and transitions into nonemployment increases in recessions. Changes in the overall rate of job separation mask changes in the composition of the group of separators. Although the rate of overall job separations declines in recessions (Figure 3.1), the fraction of involuntary separators among all separators is likely to rise sharply in economic downturns (Figure 3.3). Given that annual job-to-nonemployment transitions are likely to severely understate involuntary job loss (both because the vast majority of nonemployment spells are short and because many job losers may find a job immediately), it is fair to assume that an important fraction of job separations in the 1982 recession were involuntary.

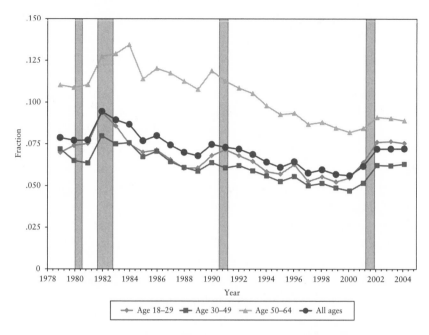

Figure 3.3   Incidence of job separations leading to nonemployment among men by calendar year; all ages and separately by age groups

SOURCE: Authors' calculations based on a 1 percent sample of Social Security Administration data.

NOTES: Includes only workers born after 1930. The figure shows the fraction of male employees earning positive earnings in the previous year (t–1) who have zero earnings on their W2 in the current year (t). Vertical bars represent National Bureau of Economic Research business cycle dates.

Workers with high job attachment who suffer job separation are especially likely to experience involuntary job loss. In results not shown here, the annual rate of job separation for our sample of high-attachment workers at stable jobs from 1974 to 1979 declines sharply with tenure. The rate of job separation is lowest for workers with six years of tenure, among whom voluntary movers in the early 1980s recessions are unlikely, especially during mass layoffs. The rate is somewhat higher for workers with three years of job tenure (in stable jobs from 1977 to 1979). Thus, when considering this broader group, we rely more strongly on the control group of nonseparators to net out the contribution of voluntary job mobility.

On average, stable workers who left their jobs during the early 1980s are likely to have left their employer involuntarily. However, clearly voluntary moves are included in the definition of job separations and non-employment transitions in Figures 3.1 to 3.3. To study the effect of job loss on employment, we want to have as much information as possible on the reason for job separation. In our main analysis, to isolate workers who left their job involuntarily due to external forces, we call a worker displaced if he leaves his stable job in a period in which the firm experiences a sudden large drop in employment. The majority of workers leaving the firm during such a mass layoff should leave their jobs involuntarily, especially during a strong recession. Again, some workers may have left the firm voluntarily as well. If voluntary movers tend to have shorter employment spells, this would lead us to understate the effect of layoffs. Another important concern is that employers may selectively lay off their least productive workers. Such selectivity may be less of a concern during large layoffs because employers may be unable to be as selective regarding which workers to lay off. This was true especially during the 1980s, when most firms—whether unionized or not—were bound by seniority rules (Abraham and Medoff 1984). We address the concern of selective displacement directly in our regression analysis.

Basic characteristics of our sample by mobility status during the years 1980–86 appear in Web Appendix Table A3.1. We show sample statistics for workers not separating during that period, those leaving their long-term employer during a mass layoff, and non-mass-layoff separators. The entries in the table confirm important differences in characteristics of workers leaving their long-term employer in 1980–85 relative to other workers not experiencing a permanent separation during that period. Job separators are on average younger and have 15 percent to 20 percent lower annual earnings in 1979. Displacements are more likely in construction and manufacturing and less likely in transportation. Non-MLF separations are more likely in trade and finance, insurance, and real estate (FIRE). Interestingly, manufacturing and construction do not emerge as high-layoff industries. Given those significant preseparation differences, it is important to account for the potential of selective job displacement when comparing the employment experience of displaced workers with a control group, something we will address in our regression analysis.

AVERAGE DIFFERENCES IN CUMULATED YEARS WITH POSITIVE EARNINGS

We now turn to the analysis of the effect of job displacement and job separation during recessions on years worked over the longer term. Given the nature of our data, our measure of time worked is whether a worker has any positive earnings from dependent employment (i.e., he received a W-2, as self-employment income is excluded) during a calendar year. A key advantage of our data source is that we can measure the incidence of years of nonemployment over a period of more than twenty years after a job separation. Moreover, the earnings measure—although not perfect—is very precise, and we can base our statistics on large samples. This is an improvement over most other data sources commonly used to measure lifetime labor supply; longitudinal surveys are mostly too small and suffer from retrospective measurement error, and administrative records typically do not reach as far back in time.[3]

Clearly, our measure also has several disadvantages. First, the reason for nonemployment is unknown. This is not a problem for causal inference if we assume that the group of nondisplaced workers we use as the control group experiences the same incidence of events that led to nonemployment spells other than unemployment—such as long spells of sickness, caring for a relative, self-employment, or obtaining additional education.[4] However, as discussed at the outset, it could affect the interpretation of our estimates. Second, our measure does not capture any spell of nonemployment shorter than a year, suggesting that our results likely understate the effect of job displacement on time worked.

Basic characteristics of our sample and of our measure of years worked appear in Table 3.1 and Web Appendix Table A3.1. We consider about 90,000 men who had six years of job tenure in 1979 with employers having at least fifty employees in that year. From 1980 to 1986, roughly 17,000—about 20 percent—of these men separated from their jobs during a mass layoff; we call them displaced workers (including workers later recalled to their firms). The first rows of Table 3.1 show the total (cumulated) number of years worked from 1974 to 2003 separately for those displaced and those not separating from their employer during the same time period.[5] In Panel A, we consider only years until a worker turns fifty-five to focus on an age range in which we would expect most

TABLE 3.1

Total years with positive earnings from 1974 to 2003 for male workers in stable employment from 1974 to 1979 in firms with at least 50 employees in 1979; by displacement status in mass layoffs from 1980 to 1986; and by age before displacement

Age in 1979 before displ.	Displaced in 1980–1986	Average age in 1979 (1)	Maximum potential years worked (2)	Mean no. of years with positive earnings (3)	Fraction working all years (4)	Fraction never working post displ. (5)	Sample size (6)
PANEL A: WORKING UNTIL AGE 55 (62 FOR 50–60 YEAR-OLDS)							
All ages	No	42.2	20.0	19.6	86.5	0	40,441
	Yes	43.9	18.8	16.9	54.4	24.5	17,345
20–29	No	27.2	30.0	28.9	79.1	0	3,233
	Yes	27.1	30.0	27.0	51.1	2.0	1,650
30–39	No	34.8	26.1	25.3	79.3	0	13,736
	Yes	34.6	26.3	23.5	49.2	3.5	4,847
40–49	No	44.4	16.6	16.4	91.6	0	13,263
	Yes	44.5	16.5	14.9	54.9	12.8	4,553
50–60	No	53.9	13.1	13.0	91.7	0	10,209
	Yes	55.2	11.8	10.6	59.0	55.0	6,295
PANEL B: WORKING UNTIL AGE 70							
All ages	No	42.2	27.8	24.4	39.2	0	40,441
	Yes	43.9	26.5	20.4	22.2	16.5	17,345
20–29	No	27.2	30.0	28.9	79.1	0	3,233
	Yes	27.1	30.0	27.0	51.1	2.0	1,650
30–39	No	34.8	30.0	28.3	64.2	0	13,736
	Yes	34.6	30.0	26.0	41.9	3.4	4,847
40–49	No	44.4	29.4	24.5	23.7	0	13,263
	Yes	44.5	29.4	21.8	13.8	7.9	4,553
50–60	No	53.9	22.1	17.5	13.2	0	10,209
	Yes	55.2	20.8	13.5	5.4	36.7	6,295

SOURCE: Authors' calculations using a 1 percent sample of Social Security Administration data.
NOTE: Includes only workers born after 1930.

individuals would be attached to the labor market. Starting at age fifty-five, eligibility for SSDI and many private pension plans begins to rise.

The average number of cumulated years worked for nondisplaced and displaced workers was 19.6 and 16.9 years, respectively (column 3). The difference in total years worked is sizeable, at 2.7 years. To put the total years worked and the gap for displaced workers in perspective, the table also shows the *maximum* number of potential total years worked (column 2). Given the age restriction, the average maximum potential number of years in employment for our sample was about 18.8 for displaced and 20 for nondisplaced workers. The difference arises from a slight difference in age in 1979 (before layoff) between displaced and nondisplaced workers shown in Table 3.1, column 1. Adjusting the raw mean difference by the difference in the maximum, we are left with a gap for displaced workers in total years worked of 1.5, arising in the course of nineteen potential work years.

The table also shows the fraction of individuals with at least one year of nonemployment during their remaining potential years of employment (column 4). The fraction for nondisplaced workers is 13.5 percent, confirming that a non-negligible fraction of individuals spend at least a year out of employment over their working lives. Yet the fraction is notably larger for displaced workers, among whom about 45 percent have at least one spell of nonemployment lasting at least one year. This is not driven purely by those never working again after displacement. That proportion, shown in column 5, is about 24.5 percent of displaced workers—a sizeable fraction (as discussed below, mostly driven by older displaced workers), but significantly lower than the fraction with at least a gap in employment of one calendar year.[6]

In Panel B of Table 3.1, we replicate the results including employment spells up to age seventy. Given the expanded time horizon, the maximum potential total years worked over 1974 to 2003 rise to twenty-eight and twenty-seven years for nondisplaced and displaced workers, respectively. Nondisplaced workers on average work 24.4 years, whereas displaced workers work 20.4 years, leading to a gap of four years. Discounting by the predisplacement age difference, the gap shrinks to 2.7 years. As expected, a substantially smaller fraction work all potential years in both groups, and a smaller fraction of displaced workers never return to work.

We will return to those differences when discussing differences by age at displacement.

We can also assess differences in the distribution of total years worked among nondisplaced and displaced workers. Until age fifty-five the median displaced worker has fifteen years of total employment, whereas nondisplaced workers have eighteen years (results not shown). Discounting that gap for the difference in median maximum potential years (seventeen and nineteen, respectively) leads to a loss in total lifetime employment of about two years. The fact that the difference in the medians is larger than the difference in means suggests that most of the losses occur in the lower tail of the distribution. That conclusion is borne out by considering percentiles of the total employment distribution—the difference is two years at the 75th percentile and four years at the 25th percentile.

The difference in the distribution is larger when the potential time period over which workers can lose employment years is longer. When years until age seventy are included, the difference in the medians is five years, and the median potential maximum is thirty years for both groups. Even more strikingly, the difference is one year at the 75th percentile and six years at the 25th percentile. As we discuss next, it is unlikely that the difference is driven by an uneven age distribution among displaced and nondisplaced workers. Instead, it appears that the losses in years worked are unequal across populations of job losers.

The remaining rows of Table 3.1 show the same results by four groups of age at displacement. Several interesting patterns emerge. First, the two older age groups suffer larger employment losses than the two younger age groups, especially when the comparison includes years up to age seventy. In particular for those displaced at ages fifty to sixty, a substantial fraction never return to employment. Yet, it appears that differences in mean age among displaced and nondisplaced are concentrated among the oldest group, something that we will take into account directly below. Second, even among younger workers, about half of the population has at least one nonemployment spell lasting one year or more (column 4). Third, for both younger and mature displaced workers, the effect on years worked is to a large degree driven by losses in total years worked in the lower half of the distribution (results not shown). The difference is zero at the median for those displaced at ages twenty to thirty and one year for those displaced at ages thirty to forty. In fact, for those two age groups the fraction never returning to employment after a displacement is below 5 percent (column 5). In Table 3.2, we will revisit the differences across age groups controlling for differences in age and other characteristics explicitly.

The numbers in Table 3.1 reveal that those displaced from their main jobs during a recession experience substantial losses in total years worked. In conjunction, the fraction of workers with at least one nonemployment spell lasting one year or more is noticeably higher. Given that those estimates do not account for nonemployment spells shorter than one year, they may severely undercount the impact of a displacement on long-term labor supply. The losses are concentrated in the lower tail of the distribution for younger workers and are especially large for those displaced in their fifties, a substantial fraction of whom never return to work after a displacement.

The findings indicate large-scale job displacements during recessions lead to a substantial loss in labor supply. Thereby, they are likely to increase the number of individuals with gaps in their earnings histories and hence reduce the earnings base for retirement benefits and total retirement wealth. They are also likely to lead to a rise in the number of individuals who may qualify for unemployment insurance and lower the opportunity cost in terms of foregone earnings of applying for SSDI.

THE EFFECT OF JOB DISPLACEMENT ON CUMULATED
YEARS WITH POSITIVE EARNINGS

In this section we adjust our comparisons between cumulated employment of displaced and nondisplaced workers for observable differences in preexisting characteristics. To do so, we estimate a series of linear regression models with total years worked (TYW_i) as the dependent variable of the form

$$TYW_i = \alpha + \beta D_i + \gamma X_i + v_i$$

where the main regressor of interest is a dummy for whether a worker i was displaced (D_i). We include a range of observable characteristics relating to the period in the late 1970s prior to the displacement date (X_i). The control variables include age at displacement, average earnings prior to displacement, eight dummies for major industries, growth in earnings prior to displacement, and firm size prior to displacement.[7]

The main coefficients on the displacement dummy are shown in Table 3.2. Results apply to workers with at least six years of tenure at displacement. Again we show estimates with work years up to age fifty-five and age seventy. The first column replicates the raw difference in total years worked between nondisplaced and displaced workers shown in Table 3.1, which amounts to 2.7 years. Column 2 confirms that accounting for age (a fourth order polynomial), that difference is reduced to about 1.5 years. The bottom panel shows the corresponding number for the longer time horizon. Again, accounting for age reduces the difference, but it leaves a considerable gap of 2.5 years. In both cases, the loss is slightly above 9 percent of the maximum potential total years worked for displaced workers shown in Table 3.1.

The remaining columns of the table show that those numbers are barely affected by any of the other control variables we include in the regression model. In total, all the characteristics combined further reduce the effect by about four percent (0.06 percentage points from a basic effect of −1.55). The results are also similar when we consider workers with at least three years of tenure (results not shown). Once we account for age differences among displaced and nondisplaced workers, the loss in total years worked is of similar magnitude. Those with lower job tenure are on average younger and hence have longer potential working lives and slightly larger losses.

The findings in Table 3.2 suggest the basic comparisons in age-adjusted averages of total years worked are robust to controlling for a range of predetermined worker characteristics. Clearly, we cannot exclude a potential role for differences in unobserved characteristics that may partly account for the findings. For example, the pool of high-tenured displaced workers might be composed disproportionately of workers with reduced health and hence low future employment potential. Because the incidence of onset of long-term adverse health should vary by age, the fact that our employment differences are reasonably robust across groups with different age of displacement speaks against such an interpretation. Moreover, *ex ante* differences in health characteristics seem unlikely because we consider workers of high job attachment and also control for both levels and trends in predisplacement wages.

TABLE 3.2

The effect of job displacement during a mass layoff between 1980 and 1986 on total years with positive earnings; by age at displacement for male workers in stable employment from 1974 to 1979 at firms with at least 50 employees in 1979

	COEFFICIENT ON INDICATOR FOR JOB DISPLACEMENT				
Specification	(1)	(2)	(3)	(4)	(5)
WORK UP TO AGE 55 (AGE 62 FOR 50–60)					
All displacements	−2.68	−1.55	−1.54	−1.50	−1.49
	(0.061)	(0.023)	(0.024)	(0.024)	(0.024)
Age at displacement 20–29	−1.90	−1.80	−1.75	−1.69	−1.71
	(0.119)	(0.120)	(0.122)	(0.123)	(0.124)
Age at displacement 30–39	−1.85	−1.90	−1.88	−1.83	−1.80
	(0.067)	(0.053)	(0.054)	(0.054)	(0.055)
Age at displacement 40–49	−1.48	−1.35	−1.34	−1.32	−1.32
	(0.052)	(0.026)	(0.026)	(0.026)	(0.027)
Age at displacement 50–60	−2.41	−1.27	−1.26	−1.22	−1.23
	(0.045)	(0.021)	(0.021)	(0.021)	(0.021)
WORK UP TO AGE 70					
All displacements	−3.92	−2.51	−2.51	−2.47	−2.38
	(0.059)	(0.039)	(0.039)	(0.039)	(0.040)
Age at displacement 20–29	−1.90	−1.80	−1.75	−1.69	−1.71
	(0.119)	(0.120)	(0.122)	(0.123)	(0.124)
Age at displacement 30–39	−2.26	−2.10	−2.09	−2.02	−1.95
	(0.070)	(0.070)	(0.071)	(0.071)	(0.073)
Age at displacement 40–49	−2.75	−2.50	−2.51	−2.48	−2.35
	(0.091)	(0.085)	(0.085)	(0.085)	(0.088)
Age at displacement 50–60	−3.99	−3.07	−3.05	−2.99	−2.99
	(0.063)	(0.056)	(0.056)	(0.056)	(0.057)

SOURCE: Authors' calculations using a 1 percent sample of Social Security Administration data.

NOTES: Includes only workers born after 1930. Control variables in regression specification in Column 1: Quartic polynomial in age in 1979 and indicators for deciles of mean annual earnings 1974–79. Column 2: (1) and indicators for 1-digit industry in 1979. Column 3: (2) and indicators for deciles of growth in annual earnings 1974–79. Column 4: (3) and indicators for deciles of size of employer in 1979.

Similarly, because our results are robust to controls for industry and firm size, it is unlikely that the findings are explained by the fact that displaced workers might be coming disproportionately from industries with high health risks.

Because few data sources contain information on total years of employment over such a long horizon, the effect of the control variables is of interest in itself. The coefficients of a variant of our main regression model are shown in Web Appendix Table A3.2, with column numbers matching the specifications described in Table 3.2. For ease of exposition, here we consider broader groups of mean earnings, earnings growth, and firm size (four instead of ten groups). The first row shows that coarser controls lead to slightly larger remaining effects. The second set of coefficients shows a mechanical effect on total years worked by age at displacement.

More interestingly, we see an inverse U-shaped effect of average earnings on life-years worked, with the middle two quartiles working more than the bottom and the top quartile (that the top quartile appears to work less than the bottom in specification 5 is likely to be an artifact of the particular specification and does not appear in the models underlying Table 3.2). A U-shape is sensible because a combination of substitution and income effects is likely at play, and those effects are likely to depress the labor supply of workers at the bottom and the top of the distribution of average earnings, respectively.[8] Yet the effects are not very large numerically.

No differences appear in total years worked across industries, with the exception of fewer years worked in mining. Interestingly, the growth in earnings also plays a role, even conditional on age; those with higher initial earnings growth rates tend to work more. Finally, it appears that workers initially employed in larger firms work longer. The effect is precisely estimated. Whether it is large depends on the benchmark. The effect is somewhat larger than the effect of average earnings and hence non-negligible. It is lower than the effect of earnings growth and substantially smaller than the effect of job displacement.

Overall, the findings in Web Appendix Table A3.2 suggest that observable characteristics can have substantial effects on total years worked over a long time horizon. Yet none of the observed characteristics come close to having as large an effect on total years worked as a job displacement. The effect of all the control variables is at most half as large, and most of the effects are a quarter as large. Hence, displacement appears to be an extraordinary event shaping workers' long-term cumulated earnings.

One concern is that some of the regressors in Web Appendix Table A3.2 may have different effects by age groups. To allow for this possibility, we estimated our regression model separately by age at displacement (Table 3.2). Controlling for age is again important, but none of the other control variables lead to a substantial reduction of the effect of job displacement on total years worked.

As suggested in the descriptive analysis, accounting for differences in initial age is particularly important for workers who were age fifty or above in 1979. (We exclude from the control group workers who voluntarily separate from their employers in circumstances other than layoff. Since this excludes most of nondisplaced workers age fifty or above who retire, it likely leads to a reduction in age of the control group relative to the mean age of displaced workers.) Once we account for the age differences, the *level* difference in total time worked declines somewhat with age if we consider employment only until age fifty-five. However, compared to the potential maximum years worked of displaced workers in Table 3.1, the percentage effects for the four age groups are increasing in age (6, 7, 8, and 10 percent for the four age groups in ascending order). If we follow workers until age seventy, both the level and the percentage effects are increasing in age from –1.7 years for the youngest to –3 years for the oldest (corresponding to percentage effects of 6, 7, 8, and 14 percent).

Overall, the findings suggest that job displacements of stable workers from midsize employers lead to a robust and sizeable reduction in total years worked relative to similar workers not displaced from similar employers. Relative to the maximum potential years worked indicated by initial age, the effects suggest a reduction ranging from 6 percent to 14 percent. None of the other observable characteristics predict effects close to that order of magnitude. Similarly, our rich set of covariates does not appreciably reduce the displacement effect we find. This suggests that if selection were to explain our results, it had to be entirely based on unobserved characteristics unrelated to workers' earnings histories and employer characteristics.

DISCUSSION

In this chapter we have used a large longitudinal administrative data source covering thirty years of information about workers' employment and their employers to study the effect of job displacement during mass layoffs on total cumulated years in employment. We find that male workers displaced from their stable jobs at a mid-sized employer experience a reduction in total years worked ranging from one and a half to three years, depending on the age at displacement and the number of years we follow workers after job loss. Relative to the maximum potential years of employment before displacement, losses range from 6 percent to 14 percent. Younger workers at the time of displacement experience smaller losses relative to potential years of work, whereas job loss later in the career has more severe consequences (also see Stevens and Moulton, "Effects of Late-Life Job Loss on Wealth and Labor Supply" in this volume). None of the predetermined characteristics we included had an effect of similar magnitude. While we find that the losses are concentrated in the lower tail, especially for younger workers, 45 percent of displaced workers have at least one spell of nonemployment of one year or more by age fifty-five. Those results point to substantial losses in years worked following job displacement. Given the definition of nonemployment based on absence of earnings in a given year, our effects may substantially understate the effect of job displacement on cumulated time worked.

Our results have potentially important implications for several public programs that are closely linked with nonemployment. Those programs include unemployment insurance, job training programs, and job search assistance. Similarly, a rise in the incidence of nonemployment enhances the potential eligibility of affected workers for SSDI and lowers the opportunity cost of an application. Finally, substantial gaps in years worked may reduce Social Security benefits because workers may not have enough time to accumulate thirty-five years of positive earnings. In that case, years lost due to a job loss may contribute zero earnings to the calculation of benefits. That effect comes in addition to the effect of reduced lifetime earnings on Social Security benefits. Given that we show the incidence of nonemployment is concentrated in the population, reduced lifetime earnings likely lead to both a reduction in average benefits and an increase in income inequality in old age.

NOTES

1. Note that the unit of analysis is the Employer Identification Number, or EIN, which may contain multiple establishments.

2. Given substantial worker mobility within a year, there is some inherent ambiguity in measuring firm size. Figures reported by the Census Bureau often refer to firm size at a given calendar date. This double counts workers with multiple jobs but does not count each job for workers switching jobs. We have

experimented with various ways of defining a worker-firm pair for generating estimates of firm size. See further detailed discussion in the Data Appendix of von Wachter, Song, and Manchester (2011).

3. Important exceptions here are survey data sets that have been linked with Social Security earnings records, such as the Health and Retirement Survey (HRS) and the Survey of Income and Program Participation (SIPP). Yet, the HRS covers only older workers and the matched SIPP has a restricted set of years.

4. For example, Farber (1999) shows that while the incidence of alternative employment arrangements, including self-employment, rises after job loss, it represents a temporary phenomenon. On the other hand, Sullivan and von Wachter (2009) show that job loss affects mortality, permanently affecting our measure of time worked. However, relative to the full sample of mature workers, the effective number of excess deaths is small.

5. The third group of workers—non-mass-layoff separators—is not shown here, because it contains both workers separating from their job voluntarily or exiting the labor force during the recession. Von Wachter, Song, and Manchester (2011) analyze the effects of including non-mass-layoff separators in the control group on estimates of the effect of job displacement and find them to be robust.

6. In separate tabulations, we examined the number of nonemployment spells. Among the 45.5 percent with at least one year of nonemployment, about 78 percent have one spell of nonemployment and about 17 percent have two spells, leaving 5 percent with more than two spells of nonemployment.

7. Given that the distribution of time worked is skewed to the right, other functional forms are worth exploring. Given space constraints, this is left for future work.

8. The cutoffs for the 25th, 50th, and 75th percentiles for average predisplacement earnings from 1974 to 1979 in 2000 prices are $30,000, $44,000, and $56,000, respectively. The same cutoffs for growth in predisplacement earnings from 1974 to 1979 are −0.01, 0.13, and 0.36 log-points, respectively. The three percentiles for employer size in 1979 are 380, 5,370, and 38,300.

REFERENCES

Abraham, Katharine G., and James L. Medoff (1984). "Length of Service and Layoffs in Union and Nonunion Work Groups." *Industrial Labor Relations Review* 38(1): 87–97.

Anderson, Patricia, and Bruce Meyer (1994). "The Extent and Consequences of Job Turnover." *Brookings Papers on Economic Activity* 1994:1.

Chan, Sewin, and Ann Huff Stevens (2001). "Job Loss and Employment Patterns of Older Workers." *Journal of Labor Economics* 19: 484–521.

Couch, Kenneth, and Dana W. Placzek (2010). "Earnings Impacts of Job Displacement Revisited." *American Economic Review* 100(1): 572–89.

Davis, Stephen J. (2008). "The Decline of Job Loss and Why It Matters." *American Economic Review Papers and Proceedings* 98(2): 263–67.

Elsby, Michael, Ryan Michaels, and Gary Solon (2009). "The Ins and Outs of Cyclical Unemployment." *American Economic Journal: Macroeconomics* 1(1): 84–110.

Farber, Henry S. (1999). "Alternative and Part-Time Employment Arrangements as a Response to Job Loss." *Journal of Labor Economics* 17(4): Part 2.

Friedman, Milton (1957). "The Permanent Income Hypothesis," in *A Theory of the Consumption Function*. Princeton, New Jersey: Princeton University Press, 20–37.

Jacobson, Louis, Robert LaLonde, and Daniel Sullivan (1993). "Earnings Losses of Displaced Workers." *American Economic Review* 83(4): 685–709.

Kopczuk, Wojciech, Emmanuel Saez, and Jae Song (2007). "Uncovering the American Dream: Inequality and Mobility in Social Security Earnings Data since 1937." National Bureau of Economic Research Working Paper No. 13345, http://www.nber.org/papers.

Ruhm, Christopher (1991). "Are Workers Permanently Scarred by Job Displacements?" *American Economic Review* 81: 319–23.

Shimer, Robert (2005). "The Cyclicality of Hires, Separations, and Job-to-Job Transitions." *Federal Reserve Bank of St. Louis Review* 87(4): 493–507.

Schoeni, Robert, and Michael Dardia (2003). "Estimates of Earnings Losses of Displaced Workers Using California Administrative Data." PSC Research Report No. 03-543, http://www.psc.isr.umich.edu/pubs/pdf/rr03-543.pdf.

Stevens, Ann Huff (1997). "Persistent Effects of Job Displacement: The Importance of Multiple Job Losses." *Journal of Labor Economics* 15(1): 165–88, Part 1.

Sullivan, Daniel, and Till von Wachter (2009). "Job Displacement and Mortality." *Quarterly Journal of Economics* 124(3): 1265–1306.

Topel, Robert, and Michael Ward (1992). "Job Mobility and the Careers of Young Men." *Quarterly Journal of Economics* 107(2): 439–79.

von Wachter, Till, Jae Song, and Joyce Manchester (2007). "Long-Term Earnings Losses due to Job Separation During the 1982 Recession: An Analysis Using Longitudinal Administrative Data from 1974 to 2004." Columbia University, Department of Economics, Discussion Paper No. 0708-16, http://hdl.handle.net/10022/AC:P:8330.

von Wachter, Till, Jae Song, and Joyce Manchester (2011). "Long-Term Earnings Losses due to Job Displacement During the 1982 Recession: An Analysis Using Longitudinal Administrative Data from 1974 to 2004." Available at http://www.columbia.edu/~vw2112/papers/mass_layoffs_1982.pdf.

CHAPTER FOUR

Effects of Late-Life Job Loss on Wealth and Labor Supply

Ann H. Stevens and Jeremy G. Moulton

INTRODUCTION

Job loss leads to persistent and substantial reductions in workers' earnings. For workers who lose jobs late in their working lives, with few working years left to replace lost earnings or savings, this earnings shock may also have large effects on wealth holdings and financial security in retirement. This study uses ten waves of the Health and Retirement Study (HRS) to examine the effects of job loss on the wealth and labor supply of older workers. Detailed longitudinal wealth data from the HRS combined with data on involuntary job changes over eighteen years of the survey produce a clear picture of the wealth effects of job loss.

Much of the private wealth accumulation among American households comes in the last decade of individuals' working lives, so a job loss in this period could have dramatic effects on private savings for retirement. While much is known about the effects of job loss on earnings, very few estimates exist of the effects of job loss on the wealth of older workers. Given estimated long-term earnings losses from displacement of 15 percent or more (Couch and Placzek 2010; Jacobson, LaLonde, and Sullivan 1993), it would be surprising if there were not substantial negative effects on wealth.

The large and lasting effects of job loss on earnings suggest a number of ways in which wealth could be affected. First, permanently reduced earnings during the years prior to retirement should result in reduced

---

We thank David Simon for excellent research assistance.

consumption spread across current and future periods. In addition, if job loss produces short-term credit constraints, some workers may reduce equity in their homes or borrow against other assets. Finally, as the last several years in the United States have demonstrated, job losses may be correlated with broader downturns in the local economy and with declines in housing values. These wealth reductions may not be caused by the individual worker's displacement, but if job loss is typically correlated with negative shocks in housing or other asset markets, the overall effects on wealth observed after job loss are likely to be even larger.

Given the expected reductions in wealth following late-life displacement, we also examine labor supply and retirement patterns of these older displaced workers. Economic theory suggests that negative shocks to wealth should lead workers to delay retirement. On the other hand, lasting difficulties in finding and keeping postdisplacement employment might ultimately lead displaced workers to earlier retirement. Understanding whether workers are able to respond to (and potentially mitigate) late-life wealth shocks by delaying retirement provides important context for interpreting any estimated wealth changes.

Modern economic models of retirement assume that workers forecast future earnings and other income. These models differ in the extent to which they emphasize, model, and quantify the role of uncertainty in earnings. Some recent work on retirement (Blau 2008; Hurd and Rohwedder 2006) has recognized an explicit role for shocks in altering retirement timing and related behavior. Because job loss is a clearly identifiable and well-defined shock to earnings, wealth, and retirement, a better understanding of job loss effects can inform both public policy and economic models of retirement.

This study follows much previous literature on displaced workers and uses the longitudinal data from the Health and Retirement Survey (HRS) to better control for differences between workers who do and do not lose jobs. This is done using individual fixed-effects models, so that we can compare wealth after job loss to the same worker's wealth levels several years prior to the job loss. A control group of workers not experiencing job loss allows us to estimate and adjust for expected evolution of wealth with age and across calendar years. In the analysis of labor supply and retirement, which does not lend itself as well to the fixed-effects approach, we instead make use of rich predisplacement information on workers' subjective retirement expectations and wealth to control for differences between displaced and not displaced workers.

Our findings point to substantial reductions in total assets in the years following job loss. Displacement reduces household wealth by approximately $28,000, or approximately 8 percent, seven or more years after job loss. For workers who lose jobs prior to age sixty, when many years remain before pension and Social Security eligibility and asset accumulation is still occurring, the effects of job loss are larger. Displacement between ages forty-five and sixty reduces total wealth seven or more years later by approximately $42,000, or 12 percent, on average. Effects of job loss on housing wealth measures are also substantial, and these appear to be driven by geographic mobility, reduction in homeownership, and correlated declines in housing values after displacement. Finally, displacement, on average, increases self-reported retirement for up to seven or more years. This overall effect may include heterogeneous effects, as we find some evidence that, once reemployed, some displaced workers are less likely to retire than nondisplaced peers over the next few years.

THE HRS DATA ON WEALTH AND JOB LOSS

Our analysis sample comes from HRS respondents from waves 1 through 10 of the survey, conducted between 1992 and 2010. The HRS originally interviewed individuals ages fifty to sixty-one and their spouses in 1992, and added new samples of the same age range in 1998 and 2004. We include all of these cohorts, subject to our other sample restrictions, so that our samples of displaced and not displaced workers reflect a broad range of birth cohorts. Individuals are asked about their labor market status and recent employment history in each wave. From these questions we are able to identify workers who have recently changed jobs and know the reason for the change. The HRS also collects detailed information on individual wealth holdings in different asset types. The use of brackets to elicit information on wealth values makes the responses to wealth questions in the HRS more complete than in some earlier surveys (Juster and Smith 1997).

Because of our focus on the effects of job loss, we need to construct a sample that includes workers at risk of job loss. The comparison group of not displaced workers should be otherwise similar to the displaced workers, and so we must impose restrictions with respect to labor-force attachment. Specifically, we require all individuals to be employed for at least the first year they are observed in the HRS survey data and not previously displaced. This gives us control (nondisplaced) and treatment (displaced) groups that start out the sample employed and at risk of displacement.

To define a job loss, we use responses to questions asked in each wave when a worker reports that he or she is no longer employed by the same employer as in the previous survey wave. We code an individual as displaced if he or she reports that the reason for leaving that job was "business closed" or "laid off or let go." Other responses available to workers answering this question include poor health, family care, better job, quit, or retired. This follows much previous literature in the approach to identifying involuntary separations based on self-reported reasons for leaving the job. A weakness of this definition is that the "laid off or let go" category may be especially likely to reflect workers dismissed for cause, who might have systematically lower wealth and lifetime earnings even in the absence of a displacement. Our use of fixed-effects models to identify displacement effects in the main analysis mitigates this concern.

The HRS collects several measures of wealth and its components and reports several different aggregations of this data. We take wealth data from the RAND version of the HRS files, in which wealth variables have been cleaned and imputed consistently across waves (St. Clair et al. 2010). Wealth is reported at the household level. To get as complete a measure of wealth across all waves as possible, we focus initially on total wealth, excluding the value of the second residence.[1] This measure includes the value of wealth held in housing and real estate, vehicles, IRAs, stocks and mutual funds, bonds, businesses, and checking or savings accounts. We also report some results for net housing wealth and for a very narrow definition of liquid financial wealth that includes only checking and savings accounts, CDs, stocks, bonds, and other nonretirement savings accounts. All wealth measures are converted to 2010 dollars.

One omission from all of these wealth measures is wealth held in employer-based pension accounts or entitlements. This is primarily due to data limitations. Only the self-reported pension wealth variables are available at each wave of the HRS, and much research suggests that these are noisy and incomplete measures of true pension wealth. (Gustman and Steinmeier 2004). Employer-reported pension data are available for a subset of workers at a point in time, but this would not allow us to capture changes in this pension wealth, if any, that occur with the job loss.

Our sample includes individuals who are considered displaced if they report leaving a job as the result of a layoff or business closing some time after their initial survey wave and before Wave 10 of the survey. We eliminate from the sample individuals who report losing a job prior to the first wave in which they enter the sample, since we have no predisplacement information for these individuals. At the initial wave displaced and not displaced workers are approximately fifty-five years old. Among the displaced workers a slightly larger fraction are female than among nondisplaced workers. Displaced workers are less educated on average, with only 44 percent having more than a high school education, compared to 48 percent of the not displaced. Displaced workers are also less likely to be married at the initial survey wave. By the end of the survey period, displaced workers are sixty-eight years old on average, while the not displaced sample has an average age of sixty-seven years. This may reflect the fact that individuals are more likely to experience a displacement the longer they are in the sample (and labor force) so the not displaced group includes a disproportionate number of individuals from cohorts that join the HRS in later waves. In the regressions below we control flexibly for age, so differences in the age profiles of wealth between displaced and not displaced individuals do not affect our estimated effects, presented in the following section.

Figure 4.1 summarizes mean wealth levels by year and displacement status. We show three different average wealth levels for each year in 2010 dollars: wealth levels of workers not displaced at any point in our sample, wealth levels prior to displacement for workers who are later displaced, and wealth levels after displacement. We drop the earliest years of the sample for the after-displacement average and the latest years of the sample for the before-displacement average to guarantee sufficiently large sample sizes for each year. The averages are adjusted for age differences, and the reported wealth levels represent average total wealth in each year for a worker at age sixty. For workers not experiencing a job loss, Figure 4.1 shows average wealth of approximately $600,000 that increases over most of the period up until 2006. After 2006, the

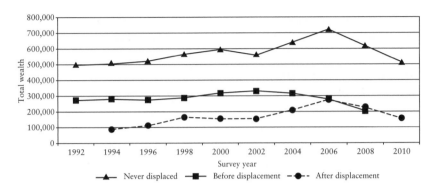

Figure 4.1   Total wealth by year

NOTES: Respondents to waves 1 through 10 of the Health and Retirement Study, ages 46 to 84. This figure depicts average wealth by survey year controlling for age-fixed effects.

recession, stock market, and housing market losses drive down average wealth levels even among those not losing jobs. Workers observed before job loss have average wealth just below $300,000 in 1992, substantially below that of never displaced workers. This points to the importance of controlling for predisplacement wealth levels to isolate the causal effect of job loss, as we do in the fixed-effects regressions below. Finally, the line showing wealth levels after displacement is lower still, providing the first evidence of substantial reductions in wealth following job loss.

EFFECTS OF DISPLACEMENT ON WEALTH AND LABOR SUPPLY

How Does Displacement Affect Wealth Holdings?

Our primary goal here is to measure the effects of job loss on total wealth holdings. Much previous research has measured the effects of displacement on earnings, and we begin with the basic approach used in that work, specifically:

$$(1) \qquad W_{it} = \alpha_i + \sum_k \beta^k D_{it}^k + X_{it}^{'}\gamma + \varepsilon_{it}$$

W_{it} is household wealth for person i observed in year t, and the main coefficients of interest are the β^ks, which are coefficients on a series of dummy variables for the periods just after displacement and for several years following. We also include a vector of controls, X_{it}, that comprises a full set of dummy variables for each year of age and each calendar year. Equation (1) also includes an individual-specific term, α_i, reflecting time-invariant ability or productivity differences across individuals. Because the individual-specific wealth effect is likely to be correlated with individuals' risk of displacement, we estimate fixed-effects regressions to avoid conflating the effects of these fixed characteristics of displaced workers with the effects of job loss. This also means that these characteristics, such as average lifetime earnings, race, or education, are eliminated from the equation. Because wealth is not normally distributed and has many extreme values in the upper part of the distribution, standard regression approaches can be very sensitive to a few extreme values. To address this concern, we trim the top and bottom one percent of wealth values and estimate some models using the natural log of wealth.[2]

Table 4.1 presents our regression estimates of the effect of job loss on wealth. Our standard specification includes four displacement-related dummy variables for having lost a job in the previous two years, two to four years ago, four to seven years ago, or seven or more years ago. There is no significant reduction in wealth in the four years immediately after job loss. Over the longer term, however, the wealth holdings of displaced workers deteriorate, and by seven or more years after job loss there is a sizeable and statistically significant reduction in total wealth from displacement of approximately $28,000. In column 4 we estimate a similar model for the log of total wealth and estimate approximately an 8 percent reduction in wealth seven or more years after the displacement.[3]

Because the literature on earnings reductions from displacement often shows deterioration in earnings prior to the job loss, it is possible that wealth reductions could also begin prior to the job loss. We tested for this possibility, however, and found no evidence of reductions in wealth prior to displacement.

As discussed above and shown in Figure 4.1, the typical individual saw large reductions in wealth as a result of the recession and housing market bust beginning in 2007, regardless of his or her labor market prospects. For this reason, we estimate displacement effects using the sample only through 2006, when most households were seeing positive returns on most assets. Columns 2 and 5 of Table 4.1 confirm that the

TABLE 4.1
Effect of job loss on wealth

	TOTAL WEALTH (TOP/BOTTOM 1% TRIMMED)			LN (TOTAL WEALTH)			HOUSING WEALTH	FINANCIAL WEALTH
	All displacements (1)	<= 2006 (2)	Displacements before age 60 (3)	All displacements (4)	<= 2006 (5)	Displacements before age 60 (6)	All displacements (7)	All displacements (8)
Displaced in current or previous year	-4,991 (8,010)	-8,831 (8,522)	-5,803 (10,990)	-0.00281 (0.0254)	0.0157 (0.0267)	0.00413 (0.0370)	-5,143* (2,651)	3,571 (4,758)
Displaced 2–4 years ago	2,866 (10,311)	-11,850 (11,402)	952.4 (13,286)	-0.0138 (0.0271)	-0.0610** (0.0295)	-0.0456 (0.0399)	-10,086*** (3,083)	-5,450 (5,558)
Displaced 4–7 years ago	-17,577 (11,739)	-18,645 (14,313)	-13,007 (16,949)	-0.0746** (0.0351)	-0.0477 (0.0360)	-0.0916*	-15,268***	-4,360
Displaced 7 or more years ago	-28,366** (11,994)	-42,902*** (14,723)	-41,744*** (16,077)	-0.0794** (0.0359)	-0.100** (0.0435)	-0.130*** (0.0486)	-18,712*** (4,293)	-13,350** (6,651)
N =	71,507	56,549	63,205	69,249	55,012	61,293	71,507	71,507

NOTES: Respondents to waves 1 through 10 of the Health and Retirement Survey, ages 46 to 84. Regressions include individual, age, and calendar-year fixed effects. Cluster-robust standard errors in parentheses.

*p < 0.1, **p < 0.05, ***p < 0.01.

years from 2007 to 2010 produce different effects of displacement on wealth than the earlier years. The long-term costs of job loss on wealth estimated using data prior to 2007 are substantially larger, at nearly $43,000, or around 10 percent. More detailed investigations confirm that the difference in wealth effect estimates is the result of the very large reductions in wealth experienced by never displaced workers between 2006 and 2010. During the period after 2006 when there were few investment gains to be had, the costs of earlier job losses on wealth holdings were reduced. Because our data end in 2010, we cannot speak to the long-term effects of displacements that occurred during the most recent recession.

The age at which displacement occurs may be important for a number of reasons, even within our sample of workers approaching retirement. We expect that job losses occurring close to standard retirement ages, or close to eligibility for Social Security or pensions, will have relatively small effects on earnings and wealth. Workers' asset accumulation plans almost certainly take into account their planned retirement dates, and eligibility for private pensions and Social Security upon retirement is likely to protect against asset losses once retirement age is reached. We thus repeat our main wealth regressions including only displacements that occur before the age of sixty, and show the results in columns 3 and 6 of Table 4.1. As expected, the reduction in assets among this group of displaced workers is larger, with long-run effects of nearly $42,000, or a 12 percent reduction in total wealth in the log specification. This confirms our expectations that the wealth of workers with the potential for another decade or more in the labor force is most strongly affected by job loss.

Another way in which age is an important part of the story here is that the estimated wealth effects of displacement can be sensitive to the specification of age controls. From ages fifty to fifty-five, for example, we would expect much more wealth accumulation in the absence of displacement than at ages sixty-five to seventy. Estimated age effects (not shown) from this fixed-effects specification point to increases in wealth up to approximately ages sixty-seven to sixty-nine and declines thereafter. Flexibly controlling for age in these regressions is quite important, as indicated by our sensitivity testing with respect to the age controls.

The details of how different age controls affect these estimates have meaning beyond econometric testing and point to an important interpretation of these results. Part of the reason that displacement produces reductions in wealth over time is that it disrupts the normal age-profile of asset accumulation, particularly for individuals in their fifties. If withdrawals or reduced contributions to savings in the decade just prior to retirement cannot be made up later, we should see long-term reductions in assets. Sensitivity to age controls highlights the importance of considering (and capturing in the econometric specification) the counterfactual scenario of asset accumulation in the absence of job loss.

The final two columns of Table 4.1 show the effect of job loss on two subcomponents of total wealth: net housing wealth and liquid financial wealth. Column 7 shows that much of the reduction in total wealth comes from a reduction in housing wealth, which is reduced by $10,000 a few years after job loss and by nearly $19,000 seven or more years after job loss. Further investigations show that most of this reduction comes from a reduction in individuals' reported value of their home, with little change in the amount of mortgage debt. This may reflect that job losses are often associated with declining local economies and so the shock of job loss may be correlated with negative shocks to housing values, which is especially true for job losses that occur when an entire business shuts down. Indeed, the effects on housing wealth are larger in all periods when we look only at job losses associated with business closings (not shown). After job losses from business closings, there is an immediate statistically significant reduction in housing values in the following two years of approximately $11,000.

Another mechanism that drives some of the reduction in housing wealth after job loss is increased residential mobility. When we estimate models for the probability of changing residences on the same set of regressors as in Table 4.1, we see that displacement results in an increase in the probability of moving of roughly 3.5 percentage points per year. We see slightly smaller effects of displacement on the probability of owning a home. This complicates the interpretation of our estimated effects of job loss on housing values or housing wealth. It is not simply that housing values are falling on workers' current homes, but also that the mix of homes is changing in the years after a job loss. While we find no evidence that reduced net housing wealth after job loss comes from increases in

debt on the value of fixed properties, understanding exactly how housing wealth changes in light of substantial increases in residential moves
deserves additional research. This is particularly true in light of the combination of historically high rates of job loss and plummeting property
values that occurred in the United States after 2007.

Finally, column 8 of Table 4.1 shows the effects of job loss on liquid,
nonfinancial wealth. Job loss reduces liquid wealth by approximately
$13,000 (around 10 percent) in the long run. Since this wealth is likely to
be the most accessible as a means of consumption smoothing, this may
suggest a source of consumption insecurity among older individuals who
have lost jobs in the past.

Do Wealth Effects of Displacement Vary by Worker Characteristics?

Job loss, like many economic shocks, is likely to have differential impacts
across the population. In this section we ask whether displacement effects
on wealth vary across workers with different demographic and socioeconomic characteristics, and also combine these characteristics with
whether the job loss occurred before age sixty. This will help to determine
which types of workers are best able to minimize or recover from some of
the effects of job loss on wealth. All of these characteristics are measured
in the individual's first wave of the survey, prior to any of the displacements. Because many of the subgroups differ substantially in their average levels of wealth, in this table we focus on results for log wealth to aid
in comparability across groups. The first two columns of Table 4.2 show
results separately for men and women. The long-run effects on wealth are
comparable for men and women when we look at all displacements; however, displacements occurring prior to age sixty reduce men's wealth more
than women's. For job losses that occur prior to age sixty, the effects are
larger for men, at roughly 15 percent compared to 9 percent for women.

The remaining columns of Table 4.2 show whether the effects of
displacement late in life are more severe (in terms of percentage reductions in wealth) for groups disadvantaged in terms of education or initial
wealth. Splitting the sample by the educational level of the respondent,
we find larger reductions in wealth among those with a high school education or less in some periods, but the long-term effects do not differ
systematically by education level. When we stratify the sample according

TABLE 4.2
Effect of job loss on wealth by gender, education, and initial wealth

Subgroup	Men	Women	<= High school	> High school	< Median W1 wealth	> Median W1 wealth
ALL DISPLACEMENTS						
Displaced in current or previous year	−0.0174 (0.0347)	0.0123 (0.0367)	0.0146 (0.0358)	−0.0184 (0.0359)	0.00811 (0.0372)	−0.0331 (0.0338)
Displaced 2–4 years ago	−0.0109 (0.0375)	−0.0124 (0.0389)	−0.0294 (0.0436)	0.00197 (0.0332)	−0.0408 (0.0408)	−0.00137 (0.0346)
Displaced 4–7 years ago	−0.0762 (0.0485)	−0.0708 (0.0500)	−0.0987* (0.0529)	−0.0445 (0.0460)	−0.124** (0.0559)	−0.0510 (0.0391)
Displaced 7 or more years ago	−0.0825* (0.0497)	−0.0706 (0.0510)	−0.0392 (0.0497)	−0.107** (0.0520)	−0.128** (0.0570)	−0.0706* (0.0421)
N =	32,199	37,050	35,554	33,695	34,854	34,395
DISPLACEMENTS BEFORE AGE 60						
Displaced in previous 2 years	−0.0733 (0.0574)	0.0661 (0.0479)	0.0355 (0.0552)	−0.0190 (0.0496)	0.0290 (0.0507)	−0.0626 (0.0529)
Displaced 2–4 years ago	−0.0712 (0.0600)	−0.0208 (0.0536)	−0.0380 (0.0676)	−0.0432 (0.0464)	−0.0766 (0.0573)	−0.0455 (0.0536)
Displaced 4–7 years ago	−0.153** (0.0754)	−0.0423 (0.0665)	−0.140* (0.0809)	−0.0276 (0.0597)	−0.164** (0.0789)	−0.0555 (0.0506)
Displaced 7 or more years ago	−0.162** (0.0716)	−0.0997 (0.0655)	−0.0969 (0.0678)	−0.135* (0.0710)	−0.187*** (0.0722)	−0.135** (0.0596)
N =	28,274	33,019	31,316	29,977	30,548	30,745

NOTES: Respondents to waves 1 through 10 of the Health and Retirement Survey, ages 46 to 84. Regressions include individual, age, and calendar-year fixed effects. Cluster-robust standard errors in parentheses.
*p < 0.1, **p < 0.05, ***p < 0.01.

to whether the individual's initial wealth is above or below the median, there are larger effects on wealth holding for those initially below the median. Job loss among workers with initial wealth below the median results in a long-term effect on wealth of 13 to 19 percent. For those starting out with above median wealth accumulation the long-term reduction is smaller, at 7 to 13 percent. We note, however, that few of these differences across groups are statistically significant.

Do Displacement-Induced Wealth Changes Alter Retirement or Labor Supply?

The substantial reductions in wealth following displacement may reflect several years of reduced employment prospects or earlier than planned retirement. Previous work (Chan and Stevens 2001; Farber; and von Wachter, Song, and Manchester in this volume) shows high rates of non-employment following job loss among older workers. For older workers, the employment and retirement changes resulting from job loss are both a *cause* of the wealth and income losses and an *effect* of the wealth losses, and they serve to mitigate or exacerbate them. Older workers may struggle to find initial reemployment after job loss, but then may respond to the negative wealth shock by working longer. In this section, we explore the employment and retirement patterns of displaced workers. To do this, consider a modification of Equation 1 for wealth effects of displacement

(2) $$Prob(work)_{it} = \alpha_i + \sum_k \beta^k D_{it}^k + X_{it}'\gamma + \varepsilon_{it}.$$

Unfortunately, when focusing on models of work or retirement, it is not practical to estimate fixed-effects regressions. There is no variation in predisplacement work status (because all individuals must be working prior to displacement) that can help to identify a fixed-effects model. Instead we make use of a rich set of observable characteristics from the initial wave of the HRS to control for worker characteristics that might differ between displaced and nondisplaced workers and be associated with work or retirement behavior. We estimate logit models for the probability of working, and the probability of self-reporting one's status as fully or partially retired. The individual effect, α_i is modeled as a function of these initial period observables (Z_{i0}), or:

(3) $$Prob(work)_{it} = Z_{i0}'\alpha + \sum_k \beta^k D_{it}^k + X_{it}'\gamma + \varepsilon_{it}.$$

Empirically, Z_{i0} includes individuals' level of wealth in their initial survey wave, marital status in the initial wave, and subjective probabilities of working beyond age 62 reported in the initial wave. In this specification, the additional worker characteristics (represented by Z_{i0}) play a similar role as the fixed effects in the wealth regressions, insuring that the implied comparisons between displaced and not displaced workers control as fully as possible for preexisting differences between the groups.

Table 4.3 shows the marginal effects of displacement (computed from estimated coefficients from the logit models) on three measures of late life labor supply: the probability of employment and the probabilities of self-reported full and partial retirement. Given differences in the labor

TABLE 4.3
Effect of job loss on employment and retirement

	FULL SAMPLE			NOT DISPLACED & RE-EMPLOYED DISPLACED
	Working	Self-reported "fully retired"	Self-reported "partially retired"	Self-reported "fully retired"
ALL MEN				
Displaced in current or previous year	−0.140*** (0.018)	0.032* (0.017)	0.053*** (0.016)	
Displaced 2–4 years ago	−0.013 (0.019)	0.054*** (0.018)	0.092*** (0.017)	−0.093*** (0.027)
Displaced 4–7 years ago	−0.036* (0.022)	0.028 (0.018)	0.083*** (0.019)	−0.045** (0.199)
Displaced 7 or more years ago	−0.032 (0.020)	0.020 (0.018)	0.064*** (0.022)	−0.023 (0.019)
N =	21,702	21,702	21,702	20,188
ALL WOMEN				
Displaced in current or previous year	−0.176*** (0.014)	−0.014 (0.013)	0.048*** (0.014)	
Displaced 2–4 years ago	−0.060*** (0.017)	0.035** (0.014)	0.083*** (0.015)	−0.093*** (0.023)
Displaced 4–7 years ago	−0.052*** (0.017)	0.017 (0.160)	0.062*** (0.017)	−0.051** (0.019)
Displaced 7 or more years ago	−0.058*** (0.016)	0.022 (0.014)	0.073*** (0.016)	−0.031** (0.015)
N =	27,165	27,165	27,165	25,916

NOTES: Respondents to waves 2 through 10 of the Health and Retirement Survey, ages 46 to 84. Marginal effects from logit models controlling for a step function in age and education, calendar-year fixed effects, and first wave total wealth, financial wealth, marital status, widow status, and self-reported expectation of working beyond age 62. Cluster-robust standard errors in parentheses.

*p < 0.1, **p < 0.05, ***p < 0.01.

force attachment of older men and women, we show separate results by gender. Men's employment probabilities are reduced by approximately 14 percentage points, and women's by 18 percentage points, for up to two years after displacement. There is substantial convergence in the employment rates of displaced and not displaced workers during the next several years, but displaced women remain between 6 and 8 percentage points less likely to be employed over the next several years than their nondisplaced counterparts. Among men, employment rates are

1 to 3 percentage points lower three or more years after job loss, and these reductions are statistically significant only for years four through seven.

The second column of Table 4.3 reports the effect of job loss on the probability that workers report themselves as "fully retired" in subsequent years. For men, rates of retirement increase by much less than the employment decline initially, with just a 3 percentage point increase in the fraction reporting themselves fully retired in the two years after job loss. In later years, however, the effects on retirement are roughly opposite the employment effects. Among women, there is little evidence of statistically significant increases in full retirement following job loss.

The third column of Table 4.3 shows the effect of displacement on the probability that workers report themselves as "partially retired." Here, the effects of job loss for men are larger than the effects on employment. Men are 5 to 9 percent more likely to report that they are partially retired following a job loss. This, combined with smaller effects on employment, suggests that men may be employed in jobs that they do not consider "career jobs" following displacement, and so even those returning to employment may view themselves as transitioning to retirement. For women, the patterns of partial retirement after job loss are similar to those for men, and suggest a lasting change in labor force attachment or in how workers view their levels of labor force attachment.

While employment rates fall and self-reported retirement rates rise as a result of displacement, most displaced individuals, even among our group of older workers, do return to employment after job loss. Among those who are able to return to employment, what happens to their subsequent retirement patterns? These are workers who do not face immediate barriers to employment but have experienced the income and wealth shocks of displacement. Do such workers prolong their careers in the face of this negative wealth shock?[4] This question is difficult to answer because postdisplacement employment is itself a function of worker choices, the constraints they face after job loss, underlying wealth holdings, preferences, and other worker characteristics. Even if the initial job loss is exogenous (after conditioning on worker fixed effects), reemployment after job loss may not be. Nonetheless, it is informative to consider the retirement patterns of *reemployed* displaced workers. In a purely descriptive sense, this will show the extent of heterogeneity in long-term effects on labor supply and whether there is any potential for some workers to mitigate the initial shock by delaying retirement.

We next estimate logit models for full retirement using displaced workers who return to employment and the never displaced group. For these displaced workers, we drop the years immediately after job loss before they become reemployed. These results are shown in the final column of Table 4.3. Once reemployed, displaced workers do have small increases (relative to the never displaced) in the probability of being fully retired four or more years after job loss. This may reflect true delayed retirement by some displaced workers, but could also simply reflect that these workers would have remained in the labor force longer than the never displaced independent of the job loss. These models control for workers' stated expectations of continuing to work beyond age 62 (elicited prior to any job losses), but even this may not control completely for unobserved differences in workers' labor force attachment that may also drive reemployment status. Despite the caveat, this finding speaks to the tension between employment constraints and limitations for older workers (which should reduce their long-run labor supply) and the negative wealth shocks that result from displacement (which should encourage increased labor supply to mitigate the wealth losses). Even this possibly upward biased estimate of the extent of delayed retirement is limited; by seven or more years after job loss, there is no evidence of significant positive effects of a prior displacement on full retirement after reemployment.

CONCLUSION

Job loss near the end of workers' careers brings with it substantial reductions in accumulated wealth just as these workers are preparing for retirement. A typical displaced worker will have total wealth that is roughly 8 percent lower, or nearly $28,000 on average, than might have been the case had the individual not lost his or her job. Among those with initially lower wealth levels, these effects are even larger, roughly 12 percent. For workers between ages forty-six and fifty-nine, when most individuals in the labor force are accumulating wealth for retirement, the consequences are even more severe. These workers see wealth holdings reduced by

12 percent, with men and those with lower initial wealth seeing still larger percentage effects, 16 and 19 percent, respectively.

Because employment remains significantly lower for up to seven years after these job losses, it is not surprising that displaced workers fail to accumulate the expected wealth in the final years before retirement. Evidence here suggests that difficulty finding postdisplacement employment, or perhaps dissatisfaction with available employment options after job loss may dominate these wealth losses in determining later employment and retirement patterns. Despite the negative wealth shocks, we find only limited, suggestive evidence that older displaced workers work longer or delay retirement to make up some of this lost ground. In addition, we find that a large portion of the wealth loss is due to falling housing wealth. This, in turn, reflects a combination of reductions in house values and the tendency of displaced workers to relocate to lower-priced housing.

What should we conclude about the effects of labor market shocks on wealth and well-being of older workers? One source of context for this question is to recognize that labor market shocks, particularly in recent years, have often occurred simultaneously with major declines in the stock market. Relatively more attention has been paid by researchers to reductions in retirement wealth produced by recent stock market declines than to the potential role of job loss on wealth, but most research suggests the effects of stock market shocks are small. Gustman and Steinmeier (2011), for example, find that the 2007 stock market decline produced only modest reductions in the overall wealth of near-retirees, primarily because a relatively small fraction of that wealth was held in stocks, a finding corroborated by Coile and Levine (2010). Our work points to differences in the effects of labor market shocks and broader-based economic shocks, such as stock market declines. Job loss does not affect all older workers, but the consequences for those it hits may be more severe than recently observed reductions in the value of stock holdings. Private wealth holdings, including housing wealth, of workers experiencing job loss in the decade prior to retirement are substantially reduced. Such losses are likely to further increase the dependence of these workers on public and private pension income, which, of course, faces an uncertain future as well.

NOTES

1. The value of the second residence was subject to some survey errors in the third wave of the HRS and so total wealth including this measure is not available in that wave.

2. Some additional testing indicates that this simple approach produces robust estimates of job loss on wealth. Another standard approach here is the use of median regressions, but this method cannot easily accommodate individual fixed effects. We have compared OLS and median regression results without fixed effects, and find that after trimming the sample our results are quite stable.

3. The log specification requires that we drop a small number of observations with zero or negative wealth, but may provide a better fit for the wealth data. In the log specification, the exact percentage effect on wages is given by $(e^{\beta}-1)$ where β is the coefficient from Table 4.2.

4. See Hurd and Rohwedder (2010) for evidence that older workers responded to the economy-wide wealth shock of 2007–8 with increased expectations of working into their sixties.

REFERENCES

Blau, David (2008). "Retirement and Consumption in a Life Cycle Model." *Journal of Labor Economics* 26(1): 35–71.

Coile, Courtney C., and Phillip B. Levine (2010). *Reconsidering Retirement: How Losses and Layoffs Affect Older Workers*. Washington, DC: The Brookings Institution.

Couch, Kenneth A., and Dana Placzek (2010). "Earnings Losses of Displaced Workers Revisited." *American Economic Review* 100(1): 572–89.

Chan, Sewin, and Ann H. Stevens (2001). "Job Loss and Employment Patterns of Older Workers." *Journal of Labor Economics* 19(2): 484–521.

Gustman, Alan, and Thomas Steinmeier (2004). "What People Don't Know About Their Pensions and Social Security." In William G. Gale, John B. Shoven, and Mark J. Warshawsky (Eds.) *Private Pensions and Public Policies*. Washington, DC: The Brookings Institution.

Gustman, Alan, and Thomas Steinmeier (2011). "Stock Market Fluctuations and Retirement Decisions." Working Paper No. 15435, National Bureau of Economic Research, Cambridge, MA.

Hurd, Michael D., and Susann Rohwedder (2006). "Some Answers to the Retirement-Consumption Puzzle." Working Paper No. 12057, National Bureau of Economic Research, Cambridge, MA.

Hurd, Michael D., and Susann Rohwedder (2010). "The Effects of the Economic Crisis on the Older Population." Working Paper No. 2010–231, Michigan Retirement Research Center.

Jacobson, Louis, Robert LaLonde, and Daniel Sullivan (1993). "Earnings Losses of Displaced Workers." *American Economic Review,* 83:685–709.

Juster, Thomas, and James P. Smith (1997). "Improving the Quality of Economic Data: Lessons from the HRS and AHEAD." *Journal of the American Statistical Association,* 92(440): 1268–78.

St. Clair, Patricia, Darlene Blake, Delia Bugliari, Sandy Chien, Orla Hayden, Michael Hurd, Serchii Ilchuk, Fuan-Yue Kung, Angela Miu, Constantijn Panis, Philip Pantoja, Afshin Rastegar, Susann Rohwedder, Elizabeth Roth, Joanna Carooll, Julie Zissimopoulos (2010). "RAND HRS Data Documentation, Version J." Santa Monica, CA: RAND Center for the Study of Aging.

CHAPTER FIVE

Involuntary Job Transitions and Subjective Well-Being

Ariel Kalil and Thomas DeLeire

INTRODUCTION

Older adults in the United States are living longer and working harder. Workers ages fifty-five years and older are unique in experiencing strong growth in their participation rates in the labor market during the last two decades; their labor force participation rates are likewise projected to have the fastest growth among all age groups in the decade ahead (Toossi 2007). However, increased exposure to the labor market brings increased exposure to its vicissitudes, including involuntary transitions out of work. Since the start of the "Great Recession" in December 2007, the unemployment rate for persons age fifty-five and older rose from 3.1 percent to 7 percent in February 2010—a level just shy of the record high of 7.2 percent in December 2009 (Sok 2010). The duration of unemployment has also increased for older workers.

Older workers are also having increasingly diverse employment experiences toward the end of their careers. Quickly disappearing is the prescribed path whereby older workers wrap up long career stints with a single employer and make a seamless transition to a nonworking retirement. In fact, long-term employment relationships have declined in the United States since the mid-1970s, particularly among workers older than fifty (Farber 2007; Farber, in this volume). Workers ages fifty to sixty-four are twice as likely to be employed in "new" jobs (e.g., ones they have held for less than one year) than workers of that age were thirty years ago (Farber 2007). These facts suggest far more fluidity in end-of-career employment than has historically been true, with unknown implications for older workers' well-being.

To date, we know little about how involuntary job transitions affect psychological well-being among older adults. Why should we care about positive dimensions of psychological well-being in an older population? First, psychological well-being correlates positively with longevity and negatively with all-cause mortality (Lyubomirsky, King, and Diener 2005; Ryff, Singer, and Love 2004). Second, social scientists and government leaders are increasingly calling for the establishment of a "national index" of positive well-being as a key indicator of a nation's wealth and health (Diener 2000; Krueger et al. 2008). Indeed, former French president Nicolas Sarkozy proposed replacing gross domestic product (GDP) with a "happiness index" and urged the rest of the world to do the same. Sarkozy's proposal followed a report he received from Nobel Prize–winning economists Joseph Stiglitz and Amartya Sen (Stiglitz, Sen, and Fitoussi 2009) arguing for such an index.

Our chapter examines the question of whether and how job loss and involuntary retirement are related to subjective well-being using newly available data from a large nationally representative U.S. data source, the Health and Retirement Survey (HRS). The chapter is structured as follows: the next section reviews the existing evidence on involuntary job transitions and subjective well-being and outlines the main contributions of our analysis. The next outlines the data and our analytic model, followed by the results of our estimation and concluding remarks.

INVOLUNTARY JOB TRANSITIONS AND SUBJECTIVE WELL-BEING

In this section, we discuss the relevant literature on involuntary job transitions and subjective well-being and the contributions of our study. First, however, we discuss the measurement of subjective well-being and the contributions of our chapter on this point.

What Is Subjective Well-Being?

Well-being has been studied extensively by social psychologists (Campbell 1981; Ryan and Deci 2001) and research in this area has flourished in recent decades. Although the distinct dimensions of well-being have been debated, the general quality of well-being refers to optimal psychological functioning and experience. Ryan and Deci's 2001 integrative review organized the field of well-being into two broad traditions: one dealing with happiness (hedonic well-being) and one dealing with human potential (eudaimonic well-being). Keyes, Shmotkin, and Ryff (2002) elaborate on the meaning of these two traditions and their respective empirical indicators. The hedonic (or subjective well-being) view equates well-being with happiness or life satisfaction and is often operationalized as the balance between positive and negative affect (Diener et al. 1999; Ryan and Deci 2001; Ryff 2008). Among valued life goals, subjective well-being is the highest-ranked across many countries and among many different demographic groups (Diener 2000). The eudaimonic (or psychological well-being) perspective, on the other hand, assesses how well people are living in relation to their true selves (Ryff and Singer 2006). Scholars have pointed to the multidimensionality of well-being and believe that measures should encompass both hedonic and eudaimonic well-being (Ryan and Deci 2001; Ryff 2008; Ryff and Singer 2006).

For those who study aging, the distinction between hedonic and eudaimonic well-being is critical: Hedonic aspects of well-being in much longitudinal research have been shown to rise, on average, until very late in life. In contrast, eudaimonic well-being, which centers on whether one feels one's life has purpose and meaning and that one is continuing to learn new things and realize one's potential, declines with age according to both cross-sectional and longitudinal studies (Ryff 2008).

According to Ryff (2008), a key reason that the distinction between hedonic and eudaimonic well-being is relevant for the study of later-life involuntary job transitions is because older persons show a significant decline in purpose in life partly because the surrounding social structure provides too few opportunities for meaningful engagement. Thus, understanding employment transitions and well-being among older Americans is potentially critical for understanding life-course changes in well-being, especially as the number of older workers continues to grow. Moreover, the distinction between the two types of well-being is the focus of intense study among biopsychosocial researchers who are probing the underlying biological determinants of well-being (Ryff, Singer, and Love 2004).

Consequently, we aim to understand whether the impact of involuntary employment transitions differs for hedonic and eudaimonic well-being (i.e., satisfaction with life versus purpose in life), thus helping to clarify the extent to which such measures tap distinct or overlapping aspects of well-being. Our analysis is the first, to our knowledge, to address this question.

Many theoretical models in the economics literature have sought to incorporate measures of subjective well-being into a utility-maximizing framework, with some going so far as to treat subjective well-being as a measure of "utility" (e.g., Oswald 1997; Clark and Oswald 1996). Treating subjective well-being as utility is potentially limited in that it does not allow for behavior in which individuals may trade off their "happiness" for other measures of well-being, such as purpose in life. In other words, these models do not appear to allow for distinctions between a happy life and a meaningful life. By broadening the scope of well-being measures to include psychological (eudaimonic) well-being, our work can also contribute to the developing field of the economics of happiness and well-being (Di Tella and MacCulloch 2006).

Literature Review and Theoretical Framework

To date, the empirical evidence on the linkages between employment and well-being has most often studied hedonic aspects of well-being in relation to involuntary unemployment. Much of this work has focused on individuals' responses to the single question, How satisfied are you at present with your life as a whole?, which has been included in the German Socio-Economic Panel Study; the Household, Income and Labour Dynamics in Australia Survey; and the British Household Panel Survey. Despite the brevity of the outcome measure, one of the most robust results from this literature is that unemployment has long-lasting negative impacts on life satisfaction (Lucas et al. 2004). Similarly, using the Day Reconstruction Method, Krueger and Mueller (2008) compare the emotional well-being of employed and unemployed persons during similar activities and find that the unemployed report feeling more sadness, stress, and pain than the employed.

The adverse impacts of involuntary job loss on older workers' well-being have also been established, although most existing studies have tended to focus on depression and poor health (versus positive states of mind). This distinction is important because research shows that the effects of positive mental states are often more important than the absence of negative states in the prediction of subsequent morbidity and mortality (Danner, Snowdon, and Friesen 2001). Two studies compared changes over time in physical functioning and depressive symptoms between older workers who experienced involuntary job loss and comparison groups of continuously employed workers in the HRS. These studies found statistically significant adverse impacts of job loss on depressive symptoms and physical health functioning following the job loss (Gallo et al. 2000; Gallo et al. 2006).

Shields and Wheatley Price (2005) review many existing studies and argue that the causal link between unemployment and lower levels of self-reported subjective well-being has been convincingly demonstrated by using panel data and appropriate econometric techniques. Using the same data, Lucas et al. (2004) also find that unemployment substantially reduces subjective well-being and that, although life satisfaction shifts back toward its baseline level, those who experience a spell of unemployment do not completely return to their former level of life satisfaction. Similarly, Lucas (2007) found that the onset of a disability is associated with diminished satisfaction with life and that the effects do not dissipate with time. Thus, these studies refute the idea of "hedonic adaptation," the process by which individuals return to baseline levels of happiness following a change in life circumstances.

Theoretically, the linkages between involuntary job losses and reduced well-being could arise from a variety of mechanisms. Warr (1987) suggests that unemployment leads to negative psychological outcomes because unemployed individuals do not experience the many benefits associated with employment, including the opportunity for control, skill use, and interpersonal contact; variety; availability of money; and valued social position. Jahoda (1982) also suggested that employment imposes a time structure on the day, affords opportunities to socialize with others, provides a sense of purpose, increases status, and encourages activity. In fact, a recent nationwide survey found that financial concerns were not the primary factor compelling older workers to remain in the labor force (Pew Research Center 2009). Only 17 percent of workers ages sixty-five and older stated in that survey that they were working just "because they needed the money" (the comparable figure for workers ages sixteen to sixty-four was 49 percent). Instead, these older workers emphasized psychological and social factors as "big reasons" for their continued employment—chiefly, that they wanted to "feel useful," "have something to do," and "be with other people." This suggests that job loss could lower well-being in later life through the loss of social connections. Winkelmann and Winkelmann (1998), who used the German Socio-Economic Panel Study, concluded that there is causal evidence that unemployment worsens future life satisfaction, that its adverse impact is much larger than the effect of bad health, and that the effect does not operate through income loss. The authors concluded that the main channel linking unemployment to decreased life satisfaction is the loss of the social rewards of employment.

DATA AND ANALYTIC MODEL

This section provides a detailed description of the data set we use for the empirical analysis, the particular measures we use from those data, and the empirical methods we employ to address our key research questions.

Data

We use the HRS, a data effort funded primarily by the National Institute on Aging and collected by the University of Michigan. The HRS has been an interdisciplinary and international scientific project of major importance both for basic science and for public policy. The HRS began as two distinct though closely related surveys that were merged in 1998; 2008 is the most recent year for which data are available. Data from the HRS are also used in this volume by Daly and Gardiner and by Stevens and Moulton.

The HRS contains a core survey, which includes detailed questions on employment, income, health, family structure, and wealth and is asked of all participants in every round. In addition, the HRS supplements the core survey with data from "modules" that collect data on a wide variety of other measures. Our measures of psychological and subjective well-being come from one of these modules (the Participant Lifestyle Questionnaire), first administered as a pilot to a subset of HRS respondents in 2004 and subsequently to half the survey sample in 2006 and to the other half in 2008. The chapter by Daly and Gardiner in this volume also uses a measure of subjective well-being from the Participant Lifestyle Questionnaire.

Our analyses use a cross-sectional sample and a panel sample. The cross-sectional sample pools responses from the 2006 and 2008 waves and examines how subjective well-being at the time of the survey is associated with measures of recent job loss and involuntary transitions to retirement (described below). The sample size for this analysis is 9,965 respondents. The panel sample examines job losses and involuntary transitions to retirement that occurred between 2004 and either 2006 or 2008 to see how these phenomena relate to change in subjective well-being between 2004 and 2006/08. The sample size for this analysis is 1,453 respondents.

We arrive at these sample sizes as follows: First, in the 2006/2008 data, we initially have 14,743 respondents who completed either the 2006 or 2008 Participant Lifestyle Questionnaire. After dropping category 4 responses to subjective well-being in 2008 (as described below) and dropping those respondents younger than age fifty, we are left with a sample of 11,819. Then we have 9,755 after dropping those who have missing data on the control variables (of these, 4,138 were employed in 2004). Our panel sample comprises those in the cross-sectional data who also have data from the 2004 questionnaire. There are 3,165 respondents in the 2004 questionnaire, of whom 2,447 also completed either the 2006 or 2008 questionnaire. This figure falls to 1,645 after dropping the category 4 responses to subjective well-being and to 1,471 after dropping those with missing values on the control variables. (Of these, 665 were employed in 2004.)

Measures

Outcomes. We consider two overlapping but distinct measures of subjective well-being as our key outcomes in our empirical analysis: "life satisfaction" and "purpose in life." These measures are among the most commonly used in studies of subjective well-being (Keyes, Shmotkin, and Ryff 2002).

Purpose in Life. Ryff (1989) outlines a six-dimensional model of psychological well-being. Each dimension represents different challenges individuals encounter as they strive to function positively (Ryff 1989; Ryff and Keyes 1995). In the 1989 formulation of Ryff's scales, the six measures described were self-acceptance, environmental mastery, positive relations with others, personal growth, purpose in life, and autonomy.

In the HRS participant lifestyle questionnaires, only the measure of purpose in life is assessed both in 2004 and in 2006/08, and the scale differs between 2004 and 2006/08. Seven items tap purpose in life in 2006 and 2008, but only four of these items are available in the 2004 survey. Sample items include "I enjoy making plans for the future and working to make them a reality"; "I live life one day at a time and don't really think about the future" (reverse coded); "I sometimes feel as if I've done all there is to do in life" (reverse coded); and "I have a sense of direction and purpose in my life." The scale represents the average of the item scores, where 1= "strongly disagree" and 6= "strongly agree."

Satisfaction with Life. Life satisfaction reflects individuals' perceived distance from their aspirations. Satisfaction is a judgmental, long-term cognitive evaluation of one's life, whereas happiness, a related and often-used concept in this literature, is a reflection of pleasant and unpleasant affect in one's immediate experience (Keyes, Shmotkin, and Ryff 2002).

Life satisfaction is measured with the well-known "satisfaction with life scale." Specifically, respondents are asked to rate how much they agree or disagree with the following five statements: "In most ways my life is close to ideal"; "The conditions of my life are excellent"; "I am satisfied with my life"; "So far, I have gotten the important things I want in life"; and "If I could live my life again, I would change almost nothing." The scores from these five items are averaged to create the scale, one of the most frequently used measures of subjective well-being, which also exhibits good psychometric properties (alpha of 0.89 in the HRS data). Measuring life satisfaction in this manner follows Diener et al. (1999).

This five-item measure is available both in the 2004 and the 2006/08 participant lifestyle questionnaires, although the responses are reverse-coded in 2004. In addition, answers are recorded on a seven-point scale in 2004 and 2008, but use a six-point scale in 2006, making longitudinal comparisons difficult. In 2004 and 2008, response 4 is "neither agree nor disagree," and it is not included in 2006. In order to make the measures more comparable across waves of the survey, we treat the category 4 responses as nonresponses for 2004 and 2008. Doing so allows us to compare this scale across time, with the assumption that the other six categories are comparable across surveys. We then rescale the variables for 2004 and 2008 to a 1-to-6 scale, where 1= "strongly disagree" and 6= "strongly agree." Excluding these individuals and rescaling do not change our results drastically and in fact sharpen the results, suggesting that these category 4 responses are merely adding noise to the measure. Daly and Gardiner (this volume) adopt a similar approach.

In our sample, the correlation between the measures of purpose in life and of life satisfaction is 0.36. Thus, while correlated, these two measures appear to be measuring distinct aspects of subjective well-being.

Control Variables. The HRS also allows us to control for a rich set of control variables. These include 2004 measures of age, gender, marital status, race, education, income, assets, self-reported health, and employment. We also control for whether an individual received the Participant Lifestyle Questionnaire in 2006 or in 2008. Measures of personality are available in the 2006/08 surveys and can also be employed as controls. The Midlife Development Inventory (MIDI) is a 26-item scale that measures the "Big 5" personality items using self-descriptive adjectives (Neuroticism, Extraversion, Openness to Experience, Agreeableness, and Conscientiousness; see Lachman and Weaver 1997). Items reflecting extraversion, for example, include being outgoing, friendly, lively, active, and talkative. Conversely, items for neuroticism include being moody, worrying, nervous, and calm [reverse scored]. Higher scores reflect higher standing on each dimension. Although the measures of personality were not included in the HRS until 2006, there is evidence that such traits are stable in adulthood (Costa and McCrae 1986).

Measures of Job Loss and Involuntary Retirement. Our measure of job loss comes from the Participant Lifestyle Questionnaire. A single item in this questionnaire asks respondents whether they have had an involuntary job loss in the previous five years and, if so, in which year. This question is included in a set of questions about stressful life events. For our analysis, we examine the specific year of the job loss and limit the analysis to losses that occurred between 2004 and 2008.

Our measure of involuntary retirement comes from the core survey and is measured with the question posed to all respondents who identify themselves as retired for the first time in that survey wave: "Thinking back to the time you [partly/completely] retired, was that something you wanted to do or something you felt you were forced into? Response options include (1) Wanted; (2) Forced Into; (3) Part Wanted; and (4) Part Forced. We create a dummy indicator of "voluntary retirement" for each wave of survey where (1) Wanted is coded as "voluntary" and all other options are coded as "involuntary" and again we identify the year in which an involuntary retirement occurred and focus on those that occurred between 2004 and 2008.

The frequencies of job loss and involuntary retirement in our sample are reported in Web Appendix Table A5.1. Roughly 4.3 percent of respondents in the cross-sectional sample and 4.2 percent of respondents in the panel sample experienced either a job loss or involuntary retirement during this period. One limitation of these data, however, is that they limit our exploration to job loss and involuntary retirements that occur at older ages, given the age of the HRS respondents and the relatively late date at which the measures of subjective well-being were added to the survey.

Analytic Approach

We estimate two sets of analyses on both measures of well-being: a cross-sectional analysis and a fixed-effects analysis. Our basic cross-sectional analysis takes this form,

(1) $$y_{i,06/08} = \gamma Loss_i + X_i B + \varepsilon_{i,06/08},$$

where: $y_{i,06/08}$ is the measure of subjective well-being in either 2006 or 2008 (alternatively life satisfaction or purpose in life); $Loss_i$ is the measure of involuntary job transitions (coded as either a job loss or an involuntary retirement between 2004 and 2008); and X_i is the set of demographic control variables described above (most of which are measured in 2004), including age, education (less than high school, GED, high school [omitted], some college, and college), female, non-white, married in 2004, a cubic in 2004 income, a cubic in 2004 wealth, the Big-5 personality measures (measured in 2006/08), employment in 2004, and whether the respondent received the Participant Lifestyle Questionnaire in 2006 or in 2008. We also estimate Equation (1), restricting our sample to those who were employed in 2004.

We also use two other methods to specify involuntary job transitions in this model. First, we include separate controls for job losses and involuntary retirements. Second, we include measures for whether the loss occurred in the past year, two years prior, three years prior, four years prior, or five years prior to the interview.

The cross-sectional models, while informative in a descriptive sense, are limited in that job loss and involuntary retirement may be correlated with unobserved determinants of life satisfaction and purpose in life. For example, individuals who report having lower levels of purpose in their lives may be more likely to subsequently lose their jobs than others. Because of the panel nature of our data, however, we can eliminate time-invariant characteristics of individuals that may be biasing our cross-sectional models by estimating fixed-effects models.

These models take the form,

$$(2) \qquad\qquad y_{i,t} = \gamma Loss_{i,t} + \varphi_i + \varepsilon_{i,t},$$

where: $y_{i,t}$ is the measure of well-being in year t (either 2004 or 2006/08), with well-being measured alternatively by life satisfaction or purpose in life; $Loss_{i,t}$ is the measure of involuntary job transitions, coded as zero in 2004 and as one in 2006/08 if a job loss or an involuntary retirement occurred between 2004 and 2008; and φ_i is an individual fixed effect.

While the fixed-effects models are likely superior to the cross-sectional models described by Equation 1, they still may not yield causal estimates of the effect of job loss and involuntary retirements on subjective well-being if involuntary employment transitions occur simultaneously with changes in unobserved determinants of life satisfaction or purpose in life. Thus, despite the relative strength of these models, we advise caution in interpreting our results as causal.

Because of the way our panel sample is constructed (the intersection between the subsample of respondents given the 2004 pilot Participant Lifestyle Questionnaire and each half-sample given the 2006 and 2008 Participant Lifestyle Questionnaire), it is not obvious what the proper weighting scheme for the analysis should be. As a result, all analyses we report are unweighted. However, the results do not change appreciably if we use the 2004 household analysis weight.

DESCRIPTIVE STATISTICS AND RESULTS

The average age of the HRS respondents in our sample is about sixty-five (in 2004). Almost 60 percent of respondents are female, 14 percent are non-white, and in 2004 almost 70 percent are married. Roughly 20 percent of the sample reports being in bad health. The sample characteristics are fairly similar across the two samples. Web Appendix Table A5.2 contains these and other summary statistics for the cross-sectional and panel samples.

On average, respondents in the HRS report high levels of subjective well-being. Scores on both satisfaction with life and purpose in life cluster about halfway between 4 "slightly agree" and 5 "somewhat agree." The scales run from 1, "strongly disagree," to 6, "strongly agree.

The results from the cross-sectional regressions of life satisfaction on job loss and involuntary retirement (Equation 1) are presented in Table 5.1. Columns 1 to 3 are run on the full sample without controls, columns 4 to 6 are run on the sample of respondents who were employed in 2004 (42 percent of the sample), and columns 7 to 12 are identical but include demographic controls. We present results from the three specifications of Equation 1 described above: first, the specification that measures "any loss" (job loss or involuntary retirement); second, the specification that separates job losses from involuntary retirements; and third, the specification that examines the timing of the losses prior to 2008. In this specification the share (approximately 60 percent) of the sample that received the Participant Lifestyle Questionnaire in 2006 only contributes to the observations of job losses that occurred one, two, or three years prior to the interview.

We see that any loss (either a job loss or an involuntary retirement) is associated with statistically significant and sizably lower levels of life satisfaction in the cross-sectional sample whether or not we include demographic controls and in both the full sample and the portion who were working in 2004. In particular, a loss is associated with about a 0.6 point lower level of life satisfaction when we do not control for 2004 demographic characteristics and with about a 0.35 point lower level of life satisfaction when we do control for these characteristics. The size of this association relative to the standard deviation of life satisfaction in 2006/08 (1.24) is about 48 percent in the models without controls and

TABLE 5.1

Cross-sectional models of job loss, involuntary retirement, and life satisfaction

	(1)	(2)	(3)	(4)	(5)	(6)	(7)	(8)	(9)	(10)	(11)	(12)
Job loss or involuntary retirement	-0.575*** (0.0695)			-0.611*** (0.0789)			-0.358*** (0.0614)			-0.371*** (0.0687)		
Job loss, 2004–2008		-0.644*** (0.0846)			-0.685*** (0.0953)			-0.465*** (0.0729)			-0.506*** (0.0808)	
Involuntary retirement, 2004–2008		-0.334*** (0.110)			-0.351*** (0.122)			-0.104 (0.0974)			-0.0688 (0.109)	
Either in prior year			-0.500*** (0.147)			-0.445*** (0.157)			-0.336** (0.132)			-0.258* (0.140)
Either two years prior			-0.449*** (0.105)			-0.495*** (0.118)			-0.242*** (0.0888)			-0.247** (0.0982)
Either three years prior			-0.569*** (0.133)			-0.602*** (0.152)			-0.381*** (0.114)			-0.419*** (0.133)
Either four years prior			-0.962*** (0.233)			-1.229*** (0.260)			-0.616*** (0.209)			-0.870*** (0.228)
Either five years prior			-0.454* (0.241)			-0.360 (0.260)			-0.301 (0.227)			-0.192 (0.234)
Constant	4.435*** (0.0160)	4.435*** (0.0160)	4.434*** (0.0160)	4.452*** (0.0239)	4.451*** (0.0239)	4.448*** (0.0240)	2.833*** (0.171)	2.834*** (0.171)	2.832*** (0.171)	3.215*** (0.263)	3.214*** (0.263)	3.226*** (0.264)
Observations	9,755	9,755	9,755	4,138	4,138	4,138	9,755	9,755	9,755	4,138	4,138	4,138
Sample	Full	Full	Full	Work	Work	Work	Full	Full	Full	Work	Work	Work
Demographic controls?	No	No	No	No	No	No	Yes	Yes	Yes	Yes	Yes	Yes
R-squared	0.009	0.009	0.009	0.019	0.022	0.023	0.234	0.235	0.234	0.206	0.209	0.208
P-value from F-test of equality of coefficients	0.009	0.0304	0.399		0.0382	0.100		0.00447	0.580		0.00199	0.138

SOURCE: Authors' calculations based on data from the Health and Retirement Survey.

NOTES: Robust standard errors in parentheses. *$p < 0.1$, **$p < 0.05$, ***$p < 0.01$.

The dependent variable is life satisfaction. The mean (standard deviation) of the dependent variable is 4.42 (1.24).

Controls include a dummy for whether the observation was from the 2008 wave, age, education, gender, marital status, a cubic in income, and a cubic in wealth—all measured in 2004—and measures of the "Big 5" personality characteristics measured in either 2006 or 2008. The specifications on the full sample also include an indicator for working in 2004.

In columns 2, 5, and 8, we conduct an F-test of whether the coefficients on job loss and involuntary retirement are equal. In columns 3, 6, and 9, we conduct an F-test of whether the five coefficients on the timing of job loss/involuntary retirement are equal.

about 28 percent in the models with controls. While the effect size drops considerably with the addition of the demographic controls, it is roughly similar between both the full and work samples.

The association between job loss and life satisfaction is consistently larger than (and is always statistically different from) the association between involuntary retirement and life satisfaction (see columns 2, 5, and 8). The results also show no evidence that the timing of the association between job loss/involuntary retirement and life satisfaction matters, at least in the first five years following a loss (see columns 3, 6, and 9). In a separate set of models (not shown), we allow for time effects separately for job loss and involuntary retirement and also do not find evidence that timing matters within the first five years following an involuntary employment transition.

Table 5.2 presents the cross-sectional models of purpose in life on involuntary job loss. This table follows the same format as Table 5.1. These models also show a statistically significant and sizeable association between job loss or involuntary retirement and purpose in life. Relative to the standard deviation in purpose in life (0.93), experiencing either a job loss or an involuntary retirement is associated with lower reported levels of purpose in life of about 14 percent. These associations are of about the same size in the full sample as they are in those working in 2004 and are not affected by whether or not we control for demographic characteristics.

When we control for demographic characteristics, only job losses (as opposed to involuntary retirements) are associated with lower levels of purpose in life. As with life satisfaction, we see no evidence that timing matters within the first five years of a loss.

In Table 5.3, we present the results of our fixed-effects models using our panel samples. Because the dependent variables in these models are essentially the difference between 2004 and 2006/08 levels of well-being, they are less subject to the concern of reverse causality (i.e., that having low levels of well-being leads to an increased risk of job loss). The results for life satisfaction are presented in columns 1 and 2 and the results for purpose in life are presented in columns 3 and 4. Columns 1 and 3 present results from the full sample and columns 2 and 4 present results from the work sample. The results of these models, which control for all time-invariant individual characteristics, are similar to those

TABLE 5.2
Cross-sectional models of job loss, involuntary retirement, and purpose in life

	(1)	(2)	(3)	(4)	(5)	(6)	(7)	(8)	(9)	(10)	(11)	(12)
Job loss or involuntary retirement	-0.122**			-0.274***			-0.143***			-0.126***		
	(0.0495)			(0.0555)			(0.0407)			(0.0456)		
Job loss, 2004–2008		-0.116**			-0.269***			-0.198***			-0.210***	
		(0.0590)			(0.0659)			(0.0491)			(0.0544)	
Involuntary retirement, 2004–2008		-0.101			-0.200**			-0.00479			0.0539	
		(0.0797)			(0.0875)			(0.0622)			(0.0680)	
Either in prior year			-0.0903			-0.289**			-0.147			-0.161
			(0.111)			(0.120)			(0.0954)			(0.103)
Either two years prior			-0.115			-0.271***			-0.130**			-0.118*
			(0.0755)			(0.0847)			(0.0575)			(0.0646)
Either three years prior			-0.149*			-0.252**			-0.184**			-0.169*
			(0.0895)			(0.0966)			(0.0772)			(0.0888)
Either four years prior			-0.134			-0.365**			0.00392			-0.0471
			(0.156)			(0.174)			(0.123)			(0.131)
Either five years prior			-0.107			-0.0260			-0.178			-0.0175
			(0.182)			(0.201)			(0.128)			(0.134)
Constant	4.583***	4.582***	4.583***	4.753***	4.752***	4.754***	2.256***	2.258***	2.252***	2.190***	2.192***	2.185***
	(0.0124)	(0.0124)	(0.0124)	(0.0179)	(0.0179)	(0.0179)	(0.121)	(0.121)	(0.121)	(0.182)	(0.181)	(0.182)
Observations	9,755	9,755	9,755	4,138	4,138	4,138	9,755	9,755	9,755	4,138	4,138	4,138
Sample	Full	Full	Full	Work	Work	Work	Full	Full	Full	Work	Work	Work
Demographic controls?	No	No	No	No	No	No	Yes	Yes	Yes	Yes	Yes	Yes
R-squared	0.007	0.007	0.007	0.018	0.018	0.019	0.370	0.370	0.370	0.341	0.342	0.341
P-value from F-test of equality of coefficients		0.888	0.996		0.563	0.764		0.0226	0.756		0.005	0.861

SOURCE: Authors' calculations based on data from the Health and Retirement Survey.

NOTES: Robust standard errors in parentheses. * p < 0.1, ** p < 0.05, *** p < 0.01.

The dependent variable is purpose in life. The mean (standard deviation) of the dependent variable is 4.64 (0.93).

Controls include a dummy for whether the observation was from the 2008 wave, age, education, gender, marital status, a cubic in income, and a cubic in wealth—all measured in 2004—and measures of the "Big 5" personality characteristics measured in either 2006 or 2008. The specifications on the full sample also include an indicator for working in 2004.

In columns 2, 5, and 8, we conduct an F-test of whether the coefficients on job loss and involuntary retirement are equal. In columns 3, 6, and 9, we conduct an F-test of whether the five coef-

TABLE 5.3

Fixed-effects models of job loss and involuntary retirement on subjective well-being

	LIFE SATISFACTION		PURPOSE IN LIFE	
Outcome	*(1)*	*(2)*	*(3)*	*(4)*
Job loss, 2004–2008	–0.338*	–0.524**	–0.217	–0.290
	(0.178)	(0.206)	(0.160)	(0.199)
Involuntary retirement,	0.0170	0.225	0.0930	0.0377
2004–2008	(0.294)	(0.309)	(0.222)	(0.235)
Constant	–0.909***	–0.865***	0.167***	0.201***
	(0.0454)	(0.0549)	(0.0296)	(0.0433)
Observations	1,471	665	1,471	665
Sample	Full	Work	Full	Work
R-squared	0.003	0.014	0.009	0.012
P-value from F-test of equality of coefficients	0.328	0.050	0.260	0.311

SOURCE: Authors' calculations based on data from the Health and Retirement Survey.

NOTES: Robust standard errors in parentheses. *p < 0.1, **p < 0.05, ***p < 0.01.

The dependent variables are life satisfaction in columns 1 and 2 and purpose in life in columns 3 and 4. The mean (standard deviation) of life satisfaction in this sample is 4.58 (1.22), and the mean of purpose in life is 4.75 (0.92).

In all columns, we report the p-value from an F-test of whether the coefficients on job loss and involuntary retirement are equal.

based on the cross-sectional samples (Equation 1) in terms of the point estimates, but standard errors are larger and thus some of the coefficients are not statistically significant. In the full panel sample as well as those who were working in 2004, we find that experiencing a job loss leads to a sizeable and statistically significant decline in life satisfaction of roughly 0.34 to 0.52 units. These results are roughly comparable in size to those from the cross-sectional regressions that included the controls (columns 8 and 11 of Table 5.1). Relative to the standard deviation of life satisfaction in 2006/08 (1.22 in this sample), these effects are large (as high as 42 percent of a standard deviation). As with the cross-sectional models, we see little effect of involuntary retirement on life satisfaction. We do not know why the effects of job loss are so much greater than the effects of involuntary retirement.

Turning to the fixed-effects models predicting purpose in life (columns 3 and 4), we see that once we control for time-invariant individual characteristics, we do not observe any statistically significant effect of job loss or involuntary retirement on purpose in life. The effect sizes for job loss remain sizeable, however, being comparable in magnitude to those reported in the cross-sectional models in Table 5.2. Thus, together, these results suggest that whereas unobserved individual fixed effects were not biasing the associations between job loss and life satisfaction, we can be less confident that they do not play a role in the associations between job loss and purpose in life observed in the cross-sectional models.

CONCLUSIONS

Psychologists and economists have suggested that national indicators of subjective well-being should be collected and that these indicators should be used to guide public policy (Diener 2000; Krueger et al. 2008). Yet, as Lucas (2007) argued, for subjective well-being to be used in this way, the construct and its measures must be responsive to changing life circumstances. Moreover, measures of people's long-term levels of well-being would provide little information about basic human needs if people quickly adapted to external conditions, what psychologists call "hedonic adaptation." In this case, steady-state measures of subjective well-being might instead merely reflect individual differences in personality.

Overall, our results support the view that measures of subjective well-being are responsive to changing life circumstances and are amenable to policy intervention. We find compelling—though certainly not definitive nor necessarily causal—evidence that involuntary job losses lead to declines in subjective well-being and that the size of these associations is relatively constant over the five years following the loss. The size of these associations is relatively large, equivalent to as much as 40 percent of a standard deviation. Our panel approach helps to rule out the possibility that our results were reached because of individuals with low levels of subjective well-being being more likely to lose their jobs. Moreover, our data allow us to control for individual differences in personality, an important potential confounder in this area of investigation.

Thus, because the association between involuntary job loss and declines in life satisfaction is sizeable, does not decline over time, and does not change when we control for individual fixed effects, we believe there is promise in using measures of subjective well-being in public policy.

Our results show weaker and less robust associations between involuntary job losses and declines in purpose in life. This is good news from a population health perspective, insofar as new research by Constanzo et al. (2012) suggests that people who maintain a sense of purpose as they age are more likely to remain cognitively intact, have better mental health, and even live longer than people who focus on achieving feelings of happiness. Thus, the fact that job losses and involuntary retirements do not seem to diminish older adults' purpose in life could be taken as a good sign, especially given the recent economic downturn and slow recovery.

Due to sample size limitations and the low rate of job losses and involuntary retirements, we were unable to examine many interesting questions in this research area. For example, the association between involuntary employment transitions and lower levels of psychological and subjective well-being is undoubtedly not uniform but rather differs for individuals with different characteristics. Two sets of factors may be especially relevant: social connections and financial security. As suggested earlier, an important pathway leading from job loss to lower well-being in later life could be the loss of social connections. Social connections are increasingly viewed as the foundation of numerous dimensions of physical and mental health (Cacioppo et al. 2007). Analytically, this suggests that an involuntary transition out of work changes (i.e., diminishes) social connections and that this change accounts for the impact on well-being. Alternatively, one's "stock" of social connections may moderate the association between involuntary transitions out of work and well-being. Dehejia, DeLeire, and Luttmer (2007), for instance, find evidence that religious participation helps insure happiness against negative income shocks.

Financial security may also play a role in mediating or moderating the effect of employment experiences on well-being in later life. Involuntary transitions out of employment are associated with lost wages and family income and may increase debt and perceived financial distress, which is known to affect psychological well-being and reduce happiness (Cacioppo et al. 2007). Analytically, this suggests that an involuntary transition out of work changes (i.e., diminishes) financial security and that this change accounts for the impact on well-being. Alternatively, one's "stock" of financial security may moderate the association between involuntary transitions out of work and well-being. It seems self-evident that those with higher levels of savings or wealth will be better able to weather a spell of involuntary unemployment and that this may buffer any adverse effects on well-being.

Economists have identified a number of important trends in the employment experiences of older workers during the period captured by our data. However, many fewer studies have examined the implications of these trends for older workers' well-being. The effects on well-being remain uncertain for older workers when they follow different pathways to retirement. Credible estimates, reflecting multidisciplinary perspectives, can help guide appropriate policy responses to these ongoing labor market trends. Although our estimates are not necessarily causal, we believe they are credible. Our results may therefore be instructive in shaping decisions about the need for multiple kinds of policy solutions. For example, national policy for involuntarily unemployed workers currently focuses on economic solutions (e.g., extended unemployment insurance, job retraining, or temporary reemployment accounts). In contrast, our work may illustrate the merit of developing interventions that also attend to older workers' psychological health and well-being.

REFERENCES

Cacioppo, J., L. Hawkley, A. Kalil, M. Hughes, L. Waite, and R. Thisted. "Happiness and the Invisible Threads of Social Connection: The Chicago Health, Aging, and Social Relations Study." In *The Science of Subjective Well-Being*, M. Eid and R. Larsen (Eds.). New York: Guilford Publications, 2007, 195–219.

Campbell, A. *The Sense of Well-Being in America: Recent Patterns and Trends*. New York: McGraw-Hill, 1981.

Clark, A., and A. Oswald. "Satisfaction and Comparison Income." *Journal of Public Economics* 61 (1996): 359–81.

Constanzo, E. S., R. S. Stawski, C. D. Ryff, C. L. Coe, and D. M. Almeida. "Cancer Survivors' Responses to Daily Stressors: Implications for Quality of Life." *Health Psychology* 31, no. 3 (2012): 360–70.

Costa, P. T., and R. R. McCrae. "Personality Stability and its Implications for Clinical Psychology." *Clinical Psychology Review* 6 (1986): 407–23.

Danner, D. D., D. A. Snowdon, and W. D. Friesen. "Positive Emotions in Early Life and Longevity: Findings from the Nun Study." *Journal of Personality and Social Psychology* 80 (2001): 804–13.

Dehejia, R., T. DeLeire, and E. Luttmer. "Insuring Consumption and Happiness through Religious Organizations." *Journal of Public Economics* 91 (February 2007): 259–79.

Di Tella, R., and R. MacCulloch. "Some Uses of Happiness Data in Economics." *Journal of Economic Perspectives* 20 (2006): 25–46.

Diener, E. "Subjective Well-Being: The Science of Happiness and a Proposal for a National Index." *American Psychologist* 55 (2000): 34–43.

Diener, E., E. M. Suh, R. E. Lucas, and H. L. Smith. "Subjective Well-Being: Three Decades of Progress." *Psychological Bulletin* 125 (1999): 276–303.

Farber, H. "Job Loss and the Decline in Job Security in the United States." Working Paper No. 520. Princeton University Industrial Relations Section, Princeton, NJ, 2007.

Gallo, W., E. Bradley, J. Dubin, R. N. Jones, T. A. Falba, H. M. Teng, and S. V. Kasl. "The Persistence of Depressive Symptoms in Older Workers Who Experience Involuntary Job Loss: Results from the Health and Retirement Survey." *Journal of Gerontology: Social Sciences* 61B (2006): S221–28.

Gallo, W., E. Bradley, M. Siegel, and S. Kasl. "Health Effects of Involuntary Job Loss Among Older Workers: Findings from the Health and Retirement Survey." *The Journals of Gerontology Series B: Psychological Sciences and Social Sciences* 55 (2000): S131–40.

Jahoda, M. *Employment and Unemployment: A Social-Psychological Analysis*. Cambridge: Cambridge University Press, 1982.

Keyes, C. L., D. Shmotkin, and C. D. Ryff. "Optimizing Well-Being: The Empirical Encounter of Two Traditions." *Journal of Personality and Social Psychology* 82 (2002): 1007–22.

Krueger, A. B., and A. Mueller. "The Lot of the Unemployed: A Time Use Perspective." IZA Discussion Paper No. 3490, May 2008.

Krueger, A., D. Kahneman, D. Schkade, A. Stone, and N. Schwarz. "National Time Accounting: The Currency of Life." In *Measuring the Subjective Well-Being of Nations: National Accounts of Time Use and Well-Being*, A. B. Krueger (Ed). Chicago: University of Chicago Press, 9–86.

Lachman, M. E., and S. L. Weaver. "Midlife Development Inventory (MIDI) Personality Scales: Scale Construction and Scoring." Unpublished technical report, Brandeis University, Waltham, MA, 1997, http://www.brandeis.edu/projects/lifespan/scales.html.

Lucas, R. E. "Long-Term Disability Is Associated with Lasting Changes in Subjective Well-Being: Evidence from Two Nationally Representative Longitudinal Studies." *Journal of Personality and Social Psychology* 92, no. 4 (2007): 717–30.

Lucas, R. E., A. E. Clark, Y. Georgellis, and E. Diener. "Unemployment Alters the Set-Point for Life Satisfaction." *Psychological Science* 15 (2004): 8–13.

Lyubomirsky, S., L. King, and E. Diener. "The Benefits of Frequent Positive Affect: Does Happiness Lead to Success?" *Psychological Bulletin* 131 (2005): 803–55.

Oswald, A. "Happiness and Economic Performance." *Economic Journal* (1997): 1815–31.

Pew Research Center. *America's Changing Workforce: Recession Turns a Graying Office Grayer.* Washington, DC: Pew Research Center. September 9, 2009, http://pewsocialtrends.org/assets/pdf/americas-changing-workforce.pdf.

Ryan, R., and E. Deci. "On Happiness and Human Potentials: A Review of Research on Hedonic and Eudaimonic Well-Being." *Annual Review of Psychology* 52 (2001): 141–66.

Ryff, C. D. "Beyond Ponce de Leon and Life Satisfaction: New Directions in Quest of Successful Aging." *International Journal of Behavioral Development* 12 (1989): 35–55.

Ryff, C. D. "Challenges and Opportunities at the Interface of Aging, Personality, and Well-Being." In *Handbook of Personality: Theory and Research*, 3rd ed., O. P. John, R. W. Robins, and L. A. Pervin (Eds.). New York: Guilford Press, 2008, 399–416.

Ryff, C. D., and C. L. M. Keyes. "The Structure of Psychological Well-Being Revisited." *Journal of Personality and Social Psychology* 69 (1995): 719–27.

Ryff, C. D., and B. Singer. "Know Thyself and Become What You Are: A Eudaimonic Approach to Psychological Well-Being." *Journal of Happiness Studies* 9 (2006): 13–39.

Ryff, C. D., B. Singer, and G. D. Love. "Positive Health: Connecting Well-Being and Biology." *Philosophical Transactions of the Royal Society of London* B 359 (2004): 1383–94.

Shields, M., and S. Wheatley Price. "Exploring the Economic and Social Determinants of Psychological Well-Being and Perceived Social Support in England." *Journal of the Royal Statistical Society* A 168 (2005): 513–37.

Sok, E. "Record Unemployment Among Older Workers Does Not Keep Them Out of the Job Market." *Issues in Labor Statistics*, U.S. Department of Labor, U.S. Bureau of Labor Statistics, 2010.

Stiglitz, J., A. Sen, and J. P. Fitoussi. *Report by the Commission on the Measurement of Economic Performance and Social Progress.* Paris: Commission on the Measurement of Economic Performance and Social Progress, 2009, www.stiglitz-sen-fitoussi.fr.

Toossi, M. "Labor Force Projections to 2016: More Workers in Their Golden Years." *Monthly Labor Review* (November 2007): 33–52.

Warr, P. *Work, Unemployment and Mental Health.* Oxford: Oxford University Press, 1987.

Winkelmann, L., and R. Winkelmann. "Why Are the Unemployed So Unhappy? Evidence from Panel Data." *Economica* 65 (1998): 1–15.

CHAPTER SIX

Job Loss

A Discussion

Michael D. Hurd

The common theme of these chapters is their discussion of the effects of unemployment, particularly that caused by labor-force displacement in times of recession. Henry Farber uses data from the Displaced Workers Survey to examine the record of job losses over time, suggesting that the recent Great Recession resulted in a higher rate of job loss than any other period in the past 30 years. Till von Wachter, Jae Song, and Joyce Manchester examine how jobless spells in one recession may lead to other subsequent spells of reduced hours. Ariel Kalil and Thomas DeLeire use cross-sectional and longitudinal data from the Health and Retirement Study to assess how involuntary job transitions can subsequently affect subjective well-being, even years after the displacement. Ann H. Stevens and Jeremy G. Moulton explore how late-life job loss, the period in which many workers are most likely to accumulate assets for retirement, can subsequently affect wealth.

All of these essays are timely because of the recent recession. However, the Great Recession is unlike other recessions in that it led not to just an increase in unemployment but it also affected the housing and stock markets. Thus, the consequences of unemployment in prior recessions may not provide good predictions of the consequences from unemployment in the Great Recession.

The 1981–82 recession saw the civilian unemployment rate increase by about 3.5 percentage points, and the value of the stock market decrease by about 15 percent, but housing prices during that recession held stable or decreased only slightly. The 1990–91 recession saw the civilian unemployment rate increase by about 2 percentage points, but housing prices were stable or decreased only slightly, while the value of the stock market increased. The 2001–02 recession saw the civilian unemployment rate increase by about 2 percentage points and the stock market decrease in value by about 25 percent, but housing prices increased and the recession's effects on unemployment were mitigated by a low prior rate of 4 percent.

By contrast, the Great Recession of 2008–09 adversely affected unemployment, housing prices, and stock market value. Unemployment increased by about 5 percentage points. Housing prices decreased by about 10 percent (continuing a trend that began in 2006), with some areas, such as the Phoenix metropolitan area, seeing decreases of more than 50 percent. The value of the stock market decreased by about 40 percent.

In addition, loose lending practices had permitted some to enter the housing market who normally would have been excluded due to lack of down payment, low income, or bad credit history. As unemployment increased, these persons were at greater risk of unemployment because of the correlation between socioeconomic status and unemployment that is evident during normal times. (See Farber, in this volume, for further discussion of the relationship between education and unemployment.) In particular, younger or lower-paid workers were admitted to the housing market during boom years, but were more likely to be subsequently unemployed. The combination of decreasing housing prices and low or zero down payments led to negative equity and an inability to make mortgage payments, resulting in loss of housing. These effects were compounded by the use of balloon loans for houses, increasing mortgage payments even as homeowners found themselves with negative equity. Many homeowners not able to make payments saw their properties foreclosed.

The adverse effects of the Great Recession have been compounded by other developments. The greater prevalence of defined-contribution pensions with more retirement assets held in stocks have made more workers' retirement plans subject to changes in the stock market. The retirement assets of older workers have been most affected by these changes. The decline in the stock market reduced the buffer that it might otherwise have afforded against distress in the housing and labor markets.

The combination of increased unemployment, decreased housing value, and decreased stock market value demonstrates the need to study interactions in the effects of the Great Recession. These four essays offer a start to reaching this goal, which I augment with some results from our ongoing monthly survey in the RAND American Life Panel (ALP).[1] The RAND ALP is an Internet survey (with Internet access supplied to those lacking it). It currently has about 2,500 respondents but is expanding. Its first questions on the financial crisis were asked in November 2008, with questions again asked in March 2009 and monthly thereafter. These panel surveys follow individuals and households as they experience unemployment or housing changes. The most innovative part of the survey is a series of questions that asks respondents about total spending in more than three-dozen categories. These totals have aggregated closely to the Consumer Expenditure Survey. The ALP also asks respondents their subjective probabilities of different economic events.

RECESSIONS AND DISPLACED WORKERS

Henry Farber uses data from the Displaced Workers Survey to investigate the incidence and consequence of job loss in recent decades, particularly during recessionary periods. He finds that unemployment resulting from the Great Recession has remained stubbornly high for an extended period of time. In particular, he finds that nearly one in six workers reported losing a job at some point during the Great Recession. The consequences of job loss for those suffering it include difficulties in finding new employment, especially in full-time positions, and subsequent and substantial loss of earnings.

Farber's findings rely on survey questions asking respondents to recall job separation over a three- or five-year period. This introduces several methodological difficulties. Respondents may forget some spells of unemployment, especially short ones. Indeed, results from the ALP suggest that results based on the Displaced Worker Survey understate the rate of job loss during the Great Recession. While Farber's results suggest 16 percent lost a job between 2007 and 2009 inclusive, the ALP, with its more frequent queries regarding employment status (and other variables), found that more than 19 percent of respondents reported job loss between November 2008 and October 2009 alone. By either survey, the extent of job loss during the Great Recession has been very high.

Furthermore, recall bias associated with the Displaced Worker Survey may lead to the misclassification of some causes of unemployment. Farber wishes to exclude from his analysis cases in which respondents were fired for cause. Yet respondents may misremember (or misstate) the cause of their termination, leading to questions of how well the data reflect only those terminated for reasons other than cause. Beyond that, the chances for reemployment among those fired for cause are likely to be even lower in the Great Recession than they have been in other recessions—an additional cost of the Great Recession that deserves analysis.

Nevertheless, I certainly agree with Farber's central conclusion: Job loss is at the core of the Great Recession. Those with lower levels of educational attainment are much more likely to have become unemployed. And interactions between job loss and housing problems, with many workers who have lost their jobs losing their homes as well, point to compounding effects of the Great Recession.

LIKELY LONGSTANDING EFFECTS OF JOB LOSS

Von Wachter, Song, and Manchester vividly point out that the effects of the Great Recession will be long-lasting for many individuals. Those who suffered job losses during the Great Recession will likely see a substantial reduction in their lifetime hours of work and hence in their lifetime income. Their longitudinal analysis of administrative data suggests that, relative to the maximum number of years before displacement, those losing jobs will ultimately work 6 percent to 14 percent fewer lifetime hours of work than others. Such losses are concentrated among younger workers and those who suffered at least one spell of nonemployment lasting a year or more before age fifty-five. Documenting such losses, which exceed the time one might lose from any given spell of unemployment, is especially pertinent for ascertaining the long-term costs of the Great Recession.

There is a caveat to these results, albeit one that is unlikely to greatly affect their implications. Some of the reductions in lifetime hours worked that von Wachter, Song, and Manchester find may be due to the effects of personal characteristics such as health differences. Those in worse health may work fewer hours and have a greater chance of suffering even worse health, further reducing their hours. Those whose health becomes bad similarly might be more likely to suffer unemployment, but also be more likely to work fewer hours anyway because of their health. In the data available to the authors, information on preexisting health conditions is not available but controlling for them would be likely to attenuate the observed impacts.

JOB LOSS AND WELL-BEING

The evidence about the way that unemployment affects income and wealth is substantial and growing. It can also, as Kalil and DeLeire suggest, have sociopsychological effects, such as that on life satisfaction. Kalil and DeLeire suggest in particular that involuntary job loss can lead to a measurable reduction in life satisfaction and that this effect persists over time. While this certainly seems plausible, quantifying such effects can be challenging.

Problems with quantifying the effects of job displacement on life satisfaction begin with the data used for such analysis. Kalil and DeLeire draw their main data from the 2006 and 2008 waves of the Health and Retirement Survey (HRS). The HRS administered questions about subjective well-being to random half-samples in each of those years. Thus, for these questions from these two waves of the HRS, we have only cross-sectional data (albeit from large samples).

Analyses of cross-sectional effects of unemployment on life satisfaction can pick up correlated personal characteristics or those related to the economic situation. This is evident in ALP questions about satisfaction with life, income, economic situation, self-rated health, difficulty sleeping, and feelings of sadness, depression, or happiness. Like the HRS, the ALP indicates an increase in dissatisfaction with life for those becoming unemployed. Specifically, it finds that, on a five-point scale about life satisfaction (1 = very dissatisfied and 5 = very satisfied), those who transition from employment to unemployment see their life satisfaction go from a mean score of 3.55 to 3.35. This change of 0.20 is 21 percent of the standard deviation for this measure. At the same time, those who remain employed have an unchanging mean life-satisfaction score of 3.85. Put another way, the cross-section variation between those employed who will remain employed and those who are employed but will become unemployed is greater than the panel variation. As a result, cross-section regression will substantially overestimate the effects of unemployment on subjective well-being.

Kalil and DeLeire use a small panel component for their analysis. In 2004, the HRS had an experimental self-administered paper-and-pencil questionnaire that was offered to about 4,000 HRS respondents. The Participant Lifestyle Questionnaire had items concerning subjective well-being. The panel component is the respondents from the 2004 survey who were also in the 2006 or 2008 survey. But a change in scaling makes a direct comparison between 2004 (seven-point scale) and 2006 (six-point scale) impossible, leading to the deletion of some observations. The sample size rapidly becomes small: Kalil and DeLeire have 665 persons who were employed in 2004 and were in either the 2006 or 2008 surveys with the necessary data.[2] In the entire panel sample of 1,471 there were just 45 instances of job loss and 21 instances of involuntary retirement, so the number of transitions among the 665 persons working in 2004 is quite small. Indeed, as the authors say, the extent of the analysis is, of necessity, limited. Nonetheless, they find significant reduction in life satisfaction associated with job loss over the sample working in 2004.

The results do indicate that unemployment can adversely affect subjective well-being. Nevertheless, the extant data are not quite adequate for quantifying this effect. In addition to the problems noted above, I imagine that the data, like the Displaced Worker Survey, may be subject to recall error about unemployment. The data are also subject to problems caused by the varying length of time (up to four years) from unemployment to a second observation on subjective well-being—a period of time in which some who lost employment may have regained satisfactory employment.

THE EFFECT OF LATE-LIFE JOB LOSS ON WEALTH

Job loss, as Stevens and Moulton note, can affect not only workers' earnings but their wealth as well. These changes, they suggest, may be particularly profound for workers in their late career years, the period in which many are rapidly accumulating assets for retirement.

The equation of motion of wealth, accounting for changes in income, spending, and capital gains, is

(1) $$\frac{dw_t}{dt} = income - spending + capital\ gains.$$

Clearly, job loss affects income, and panel data can help estimate the extent of the loss. What is less clear is how much spending will change in the wake of job loss, whether those suffering job loss also suffered capital gains or losses (e.g., in the housing or stock markets), and whether these gains affected spending as well. The effects of job loss, particularly in late life, are further complicated by likely lifecycle changes in spending, especially for families with children. As children leave the household and educational expenses cease, spending can diminish to levels that increase savings.

The ALP provides some insights on the dynamic relationship among income, spending, and wealth, including by how much spending is reduced following a loss of employment income. Should spending remain unchanged for households experiencing income loss but not experiencing capital gains, then wealth will diminish by the amount of income lost. But changes in spending are neither zero nor equal to the amount of the income loss following unemployment, so that the effects of unemployment on wealth cannot be found directly from changes in income. The ALP monthly data on spending, income, and employment status, for example, indicate that, subsequent to unemployment, spending decreases by about 20 percent while income decreases by about 50 percent. The implication is that wealth will change by less than the loss in income. Thus, to find the effects of unemployment on wealth, examining wealth change directly, as Stevens and Moulton have done, is required.

The manner in which capital gains or losses affect wealth change also needs to be addressed. Stevens and Moulton examine the period of 1992 to 2006, a time in which the value of the stock market appreciated greatly. In real terms, the value of the Standard & Poor's 500-stock index (S&P 500) more than doubled in this time, and the annual real rate of return on equities was 5.2 percent. If those who became unemployed were less likely to have held stocks, which is plausible, then some of the differential wealth change for those losing employment may be a result of holding fewer stocks. This illustrates a general problem in estimating effects on wealth from loss of employment: If those who become unemployed have characteristics that affect the rate of wealth change (rather than the level) regardless of their employment status, then fixed-effects models such as Stevens and Moulton use will not be adequate for analysis.

SUMMARY

Farber shows the Great Recession to be more severe than other recent recessions in its effects on unemployment. As a result, the effects of unemployment on work later in life, well-being, and wealth are likely greater than what is found in the other chapters, all of which use data prior to the Great Recession. It is also beyond the scope of these chapters to consider other aspects of the Great Recession that interact with unemployment.

Nevertheless, of particular interest in studying the effects of the Great Recession may be how the crisis in the housing sector has interacted with unemployment. For example, in the ALP, the unemployed are less likely, by 18 percentage points, than the employed to be homeowners but, conditional on being a homeowner, they are more likely to have a mortgage, by 5 percentage points. Among mortgage-holders, 9 percent of the unemployed but just 2 percent of the employed are more than two months in arrears on their mortgage payments. Furthermore, among those holding mortgages, 20 percent of the unemployed but only 12 percent of the employed have properties that are "underwater," or are worth less than the balance of their mortgage. Had the housing market remained firm, unemployed homeowners would have had home equity to buffer the loss of income. Instead, a significant fraction of the unemployed face the loss of their homes, exacerbating the lifetime effect of unemployment.

These four chapters, together, provide many insights on how decreases in employment, income, and wealth resulting from the Great Recession may affect individuals. The effect of those factors in the Great Recession, particularly as they interact with the housing market, merits further research, as do more refined measures of their effects.

NOTES

1. See Hurd, Michael D., and Susann Rohwedder, "Effects of the Financial Crisis and Great Recession on American Households," NBER Working Paper 16407, September, 2010.

2. I have less confidence in the results based on the full sample rather than the working sample because of the ambiguous labor force status in 2004.

PART II

FAMILY CHANGE

CHAPTER SEVEN

Marriage Timing, Motherhood Timing, and Women's Well-Being in Retirement

Amalia R. Miller

FAMILY STRUCTURE AND ECONOMIC WELL-BEING

For many women, marriage and motherhood transitions mark the onset of adulthood. The exact timing of these events is determined by a combination of intentional planning and decision-making and random chance. Although young women may have strong preferences about the ideal timing of their family events, based on their desired number of children, family background, and career aspirations, the actual timing of their initial family formation often depends on various factors outside of their control. Some of the "unexpected lifecycle events" that affect the timing of initial marriage and motherhood are biological in nature. For example, the quantitative importance of biological fertility shocks is indicated in recent research (Miller 2011) finding that such shocks affect initial motherhood timing and thereby generate significant differences in women's earnings over their careers. Shocks that shift motherhood timing earlier, such as contraceptive failure, tend to lower women's career prospects, while those that lead to motherhood delay, such as miscarriage or a longer time to achieve pregnancy, tend to improve them. In addition to those biological factors, shocks of a more economic nature, relating to employment and housing market conditions, or marriage market conditions that affect search costs and the pool of

I am grateful to Robert Willis for a thoughtful discussion. I also thank Carmit Segal for helpful suggestions. Sarah Bana provided excellent research assistance.

available mates, can also cause meaningful variation in the actual timing of family formation.

Similarly, random shocks affect divorce, widowhood, remarriage and coresidence with children (family events that are studied in the following chapters). That unexpected and uncontrollable events shape our material well-being is a fact that holds true in employment, health, and family spheres. It is a thread that runs through the three sections of this book.

This chapter explores the lifecycle effects of changes in the timing of initial family formation. One motivation for the focus on marriage and motherhood is to understand the economic implications of the dramatic changes in family formation over the past half-century. This chapter first documents the key trends underlying the increasing delays in family formation since the baby boom, and then investigates the links between the timing of initial family formation and women's economic well-being over the lifecycle. In theory, shocks that affect family formation timing may have economic effects that range from large to small, brief to persistent. Delayed marriage and childbearing have previously been shown to increase women's wages and income in the short run (Miller 2011; Loughran and Zissimopoulos 2009). This chapter presents new evidence of a *lasting* association between delayed initial family formation and higher earnings over decades, as well as greater asset accumulation well into retirement age. These results indicate that small shocks to demographic outcomes early in life—shifting fertility a year earlier or later, for example—can have substantial and irreversible economic effects. This echoes the finding in Chapter 3 by Till von Wachter, Jae Song, and Joyce Manchester that workers who are displaced by mass layoffs accumulate substantially lower work experience over future decades.

The separate impacts of motherhood and marriage delay on income (own and spousal) and wealth (assets, debt, and net wealth) are explored in a multivariate regression framework using data on women born between 1922 and 1954. This approach, by focusing the empirical analysis on variation in timing and outcomes *within* cohorts of women, makes it possible to account for macroeconomic fluctuations and major social and economic changes that affected the economic status of all women during the period. Delays in both marriage and motherhood are each associated with improved economic status, but the effects for motherhood delay are substantially larger. The median change in maternal age at first birth (A1B) between 1960 and 2006 was about five years. The estimates imply that this five-year delay in motherhood increased wealth by $62,000 (in current 2010 dollars) for women in their fifties, by $41,000 for women in their sixties, and by $59,000 for women in their seventies. These values represent increases of 15 percent to 27 percent in the average wealth of women in those age groups.

The results suggest cause for optimism about the financial well-being of future cohorts of older American women. Women born in the 1940s, at the forefront of the transition to delayed family formation, are currently reaching retirement age. In contrast to the previous cohorts of women, who participated in the baby boom and started families earlier and earlier, these cohorts of retiring women started families later and later. These women also experienced more divorce and remarriage than prior cohorts together with increases in life expectancy, which made them more likely to have the means of providing support to their adult children.

The chapters in this section highlight the importance of family structure as a determinant of economic well-being for adults. The results suggest that historic changes in the timing and incidence of family transitions (both formation and dissolution) over the past half-century have already affected the financial well-being of American adults and will continue to affect their well-being at older ages.

ECONOMICS OF FAMILY FORMATION

By focusing on the impact of family formation on lifecycle economic outcomes, this chapter relates to a growing literature in economics on the causes and consequences of motherhood and marriage decisions. Although changes in social norms and preferences likely played a central role in changing family formation decisions, several recent studies have attempted to identify root economic explanations. For example, the development of home appliances in the 1940s and 1950s lowered the cost of household production and may have increased demand for children (Greenwood, Seshadri, and Yorukoglu 2005; Bailey and Collins 2011). In the same vein, improvements in contraceptive technology in the form of the birth control pill lowered the costs of averting birth as it diffused to young unmarried women in the 1960s and 1970s (Goldin and Katz 2002; Bailey 2006). Changes in the labor market may have also affected demand for children: the lowering of legal and institutional barriers to women's labor market participation likely increased the opportunity cost of child-rearing (Blau and Kahn 2000), and increasing male wage inequality may have increased the value to women of taking more time to search for a mate (Loughran and Zissimopoulos 2009).

The short-term economic impacts of marriage and motherhood on women have been studied extensively, and several researchers have explored the timing dimension directly. The early literature on motherhood timing focused on teenage childbearing and found mixed evidence of its impact on maternal schooling, wages, and welfare participation (e.g., Geronimus and Korenman 1992; Hotz, Mullin, and Sanders 1997; Klepinger, Lundberg, and Plotnick 1999). Early motherhood was associated with adverse outcomes (low education, low wages, greater welfare dependency), but much of the relationship could be explained by preexisting risk factors.

The shift to delaying motherhood, however, was not entirely the result of a decline in teen motherhood, as described later in this chapter. Rather, much of the action came from women delaying births from their early to late twenties, from their twenties to thirties, and even from their thirties to forties. Miller (2011) estimated the impact of motherhood delay for women in their twenties and thirties. That study found a career benefit of 9 percent higher earnings per year of delayed motherhood in data from the 1979 National Longitudinal Survey of Youth. The results are similar in standard regression models that treat motherhood timing as conditionally random and in instrumental variables models that exploit biological fertility shocks (miscarriage, failed contraception, and time to conception from first attempt) to estimate causal effects.[1] This average effect hides important heterogeneity: the benefits of delay were largest for women with college degrees and those working in professional, managerial, and technical occupations. This implies two things. First, the limited benefit to women from avoiding teenage motherhood need not carry over to delays at later ages. Second, as women's educational attainment increases (and even surpasses men's attainment; Goldin, Katz, and Kuziemko 2006), the average financial benefit from motherhood delay should only increase. Loughran and Zissimopoulos

(2009) find that both motherhood *and* marriage are associated with lower wages, suggesting that delaying either act of family formation may increase retirement wealth.

Although previous economic research has largely focused on the effects of family timing within a decade or two of formation, there are reasons to expect lasting effects later in life. Hofferth (1984) studied cohorts of U.S. women born from 1900 to 1916 in the 1976 Panel Study of Income Dynamics and found that women who delayed motherhood past age 30 were better off financially at retirement age than earlier mothers or than childless women.[2] Because motherhood has been shown to lower women's wages, rather than increase them, this reversal in the motherhood penalty for late mothers suggests some positive selection into late motherhood (where late mothers have higher labor market ability or ambition) or negative selection into childlessness.

Bailey, Hershbein, and Miller (2012) use more recent cohorts in the National Longitudinal Survey of Young Women (NLS-YW) and exploit within-state cross-cohort variation to document the effects of early legal access to oral contraceptives (the Pill) on women's career investments and outcomes. A key result of that analysis is that women with early access to the Pill had lower wages in their early twenties as they invested in human capital. This led to steeper wage profiles and higher wages later in life. The total impact of that investment on career earnings is thus proportionately lower than a simple wage comparison at older ages would imply. Hence, in assessing the impact of delayed family formation in this chapter, it will be important to consider both earned income and accumulated wealth.

Finally, by considering effects later in the lifecycle, this chapter also relates to the literature on the determinants of economic well-being in retirement. In particular, this research explores how the variation in timing of motherhood and marriage, including differences within cohorts and changes between cohorts, may contribute to the observed and future variation in well-being at retirement. Married couples tend to have greater retirement wealth than do single individuals, and single women have lower wealth than their male counterparts (Schmidt and Sevak 2006). Furthermore, there is evidence that an unstable marital history, including past disruptions and shorter marriage durations, also leads to lower retirement wealth for women (Zissimopoulos, Karney, and Rauer

2008). This suggests that timing of first marriage and motherhood may also be factors in determining wealth and well-being at later ages. Understanding these associations can improve our ability to predict savings behavior of younger women and their economic security at retirement. This may in turn have implications for the design and long-term financing of public income support programs.

HISTORICAL TRENDS IN FAMILY FORMATION AND DISSOLUTION

A clear indicator of the current trend of fertility delay in the United States is the gradual increase in the average age of new mothers (age at first birth, A1B) by about five years from age twenty to age twenty-five over the past fifty years. That trend is depicted in Figure 7.1, using estimates in Hamilton and Cosgrove (2010) for the period from 1960 to 2005.[3]

But the data in that report reveal more than just an increase in average A1B; they also reveal the source of the increase. Between 1960 and 1980, teenage mothers became much less common. Birthrates among girls ages fifteen to nineteen dropped by almost half, and the share of twenty-year-olds with any children dropped by a similar proportion.[4] Between 1980 and 2005, these rates increased and then declined, but these fluctuations were small relative to the earlier drop. First birthrates for older women increased dramatically during the period, starting around 1970. The probability that a previously childless woman in her early thirties would become a mother within a year increased from 6 percent in 1975 to 11 percent in 2005. For women in their late thirties, that probability tripled. It quadrupled for women in their early forties.

During this period of increasing motherhood delay, total birthrates (calculated per 1,000 women ages fifteen to forty-four) declined, but then they were relatively stable starting in the early 1970s. Infant mortality rates (per 1,000 live births) continued to decline through the mid-1990s (shown in Figure 7.1).

A second report, from the National Center of Health Statistics (Mathews and Hamilton 2009), shows that within the United States, the dramatic increase in A1B was not limited to any single geographic area or demographic group: It occurred in every state and for every racial and ethnic group. The report also shows that motherhood delay was not

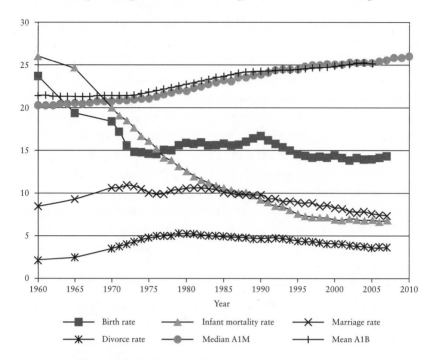

Figure 7.1   Historical trends in family formation and dissolution

NOTES: Birth rate is defined as the number of births per 1,000 women in the population ages 15–44. Infant mortality rate is the number of deaths in the first year of life per 1,000 live births. Marriage and divorce rates are defined per 1,000 adults in the population ages 15–64. Median A1M is the median age (in years) of first-time brides. Mean A1B is the average age (in years) of all new (first-time) mothers.

limited to the United States; it occurred in each of the fourteen industrialized countries studied in the report. In fact, by 2006, women in the United States were still having children earlier than women in any of the comparison countries. The highest reported average maternal ages at first birth were 29.2 in Japan and 29.4 in Switzerland, about four years later than the U.S. average. This suggests that motherhood delay may continue to increase in the United States.

There was a similar five-year delay in average first marriage timing over the same period. This emerges from annual marriage data on the age of first-time brides (A1M) plotted in Figure 7.1 using estimates from the census (2007) for the years 1960 to 2010. The steady increase starting in 1960 ends with median A1M exceeding twenty-six in 2010.[5]

Figure 7.1 shows that marriage rates (per 1,000 adults ages fifteen to sixty-four) increased between 1960 and 1970 and then declined.

Expanding our scope to include the past 150 years makes both the baby boom and the current period appear unusual. For example, Stevenson and Wolfers (2007) report that both 1960 and 2000 were outlier years: 1960 had the highest rates of early marriage (and any marriage through age forty), while 2000 had the lowest rates of marriage for adults at all ages through age sixty (but with the highest marriage rates for those over age seventy, likely due to increased male life expectancy).

Although the secular trends in average ages of new mothers and brides provide a view of delayed family formation over time, a more complete picture of the changes that individual women experienced over their lifecycles emerges by plotting changes across different birth cohorts of women as they aged.

The cross-cohort analysis in Web Appendix Figure A7.2 shows two major changes in family formation timing across generations. First, there was a sharp *increase* in early family formation for women born in the 1920s and 1930s, corresponding to the postwar baby boom from the mid-1940s to the mid-1960s. This was followed by an extended period of increasing shares of women delaying their initial family formation, in a pattern that continued through the most recent data for cohorts born in the 1970s.

Although marriage and motherhood are often thought of as linked events, this linkage was substantially weakened in recent decades. Part of the separation occurred at entry into each of the states: Women who married were more likely to wait before having children, and women who had children were less likely to be married at the time of birth.[6]

The weakening link between marriage and motherhood is evident in the comparison between the cohorts of women born in the 1920s and 1930s and those born in prior decades. Women born in the 1920s and 1930s were far more likely to be young mothers, but they were also more likely to ever be mothers. The share of women who were childless by their early forties dropped in half, from 21.5 percent to 9.8 percent, across about thirty years of birth cohorts from 1910 to 1939. By contrast, the large increase in early marriage for cohorts born in the 1920s and 1930s coincided with an equivalent decrease in later marriage for those cohorts, leading to a decline of only four percentage points over fifty years of birth cohorts in the 1880s and 1930s in the share of women in their forties who were never married. See Web Appendix Figure A7.3.

The weakening link between initial marriage and motherhood also appears for later cohorts. Women born in the 1940s and later were less and less likely to marry and start childbearing by their late twenties. The rate of cross-cohort decline in early motherhood appears to have slowed for cohorts born in the late 1950s. By contrast, the decline in early marriage continued apace through the 1970s.

Although both marriage and motherhood were increasingly delayed, there is an important distinction. The increase in motherhood timing was derived from both a decline in early motherhood and substantial growth in later motherhood (first births after ages thirty, thirty-five, and forty), leading to a total increase in motherhood between the earliest cohorts (born in the 1910s and earlier) and the most recent ones (born after 1950).[7] By contrast, the decline in early marriage continued over fifty birth-year cohorts, and marriage at later ages has not increased to compensate. The share of women who had ever been married by their forties decreased by about 2 percent between women born in the 1930s and those born in the 1940s, and then by another 3 percent between those born in the 1940s and 1950s.

Another factor that loosened the linkage between marriage and motherhood during the period was the rise in divorce (illustrated using period data in Figure 7.1). Divorce rates per population more than doubled between 1960 and 1980. Although later marriages are generally more stable (Heaton 2002), divorce rates per intact marriage initially increased along with delay. First marriages that started in the late 1950s had a 13.2 percent chance of ending in divorce within ten years; that probability more than doubled for marriages that started in the late 1970s (U.S. Census 2011). The increased risk of divorce has been linked to a relaxation of state divorce laws and changing social mores (e.g., Stevenson and Wolfers 2007; Wolfers 2006; Friedberg 1998). As a result, many women who entered motherhood as wives found themselves unexpectedly heading households as single mothers. Although divorce rates appear to have declined for marriages started in the 1980s (Heaton 2002), motherhood remains a more lasting state than marriage.

To summarize, the pattern of delayed family formation over the past fifty years is evident in both marriage and motherhood. However, the growth in later motherhood entry, after ages thirty, thirty-five, and forty, was not matched by a commensurate increase in later first marriage. The decline in motherhood for women in their teens and early twenties was to a large extent a reversion to pre–baby boom behavior, but the increase in fertility for women in their thirties and forties was unprecedented.

FAMILY FORMATION TIMING AND ECONOMIC
WELL-BEING OVER THE LIFECYCLE

Delayed family formation has previously been shown to increase women's earnings from their twenties through their forties (Miller 2011; Loughran and Zissimopoulos 2009). If this were the only financial impact of delay, then the higher wages around the time of motherhood (and over the last decades) would be reflected dollar-for-dollar in greater accumulated wealth later in life (accounting for accrued interest). If, instead, delayed family formation also affected savings rates, the correspondence would be inexact. If later mothers consumed a greater share of their incomes on themselves, or invested a greater share in the quality of their children's lives, their higher lifecycle incomes would only marginally improve their economic status at retirement age. Conversely, if they spent less on their children or saved more for retirement (possibly because they expected less support from their children or preferred to transfer wealth to them), then their wealth at retirement age would increase by more than their incomes.

Because of these considerations, the analysis in this chapter explores income and wealth effects separately over the lifecycle. The analysis also considers the main outside source of income that affects a woman's wealth at retirement—the income of her spouse or partner. The effects of motherhood and marriage delays on spousal income are theoretically unclear. On the one hand, later first marriages may be more stable and early childbearing could disrupt a household, which would lead to positive associations between delay and spouse income. On the other hand, delayed childbearing may increase a woman's financial independence and her propensity for divorce. The net effect for each type of delay is estimated directly.

Empirical Framework

This chapter aims to measure the relationship between a woman's timing of initial family formation and her economic well-being as she ages. Family formation is measured separately by variables for A1M and A1B. Economic well-being is captured by variables for income and wealth at different ages. The empirical approach is to estimate a regression model that relates the economic outcomes to family timing:

$$Y_{it} = \alpha + \beta_{A1B}A1B_i + \beta_{NoB}NoBirth_i + \beta_{UnB}UnknownA1B_i$$
$$+\gamma_{A1M}A1M_i + \gamma_{NoM}NoMarriage_i + \delta_{YoB} + \delta_{Race} + \varepsilon_{it}.$$

Y_{it} is the outcome for individual i measured at time t. The main outcome measures are: Own Annual Income (from wages and salary); Spouse or Partner Annual Income (also from wages and salary); Total Assets; and Net Wealth (Total Assets minus Total Debts). In order to capture the lifecycle effects, the model is estimated separately using observations of women from different age groups.[8]

The fertility variables are $A1B_i$ for age at first birth (in years); $NoBirth_i$, an indicator for a woman with no reported children; and $UnknownA1B_i$, an indicator for unknown A1B for a woman who reports having at least one child. The marriage variables are $A1M_i$ for age at first marriage (in years) and $NoMarriage_i$ to indicate a woman who is never married. The main regression model also includes a set of control variables for each birth year cohort. This accounts for cross-cohort differences and exposure to economic conditions (stemming from the business cycle, for example). The model also contains indicators for the woman's race being African American or other non-white.

Data Description

The data sources for this analysis are the long panel surveys collected by the Bureau of Labor Statistics as part of the National Longitudinal Studies (NLS). In particular, we study: 1) the original cohorts of women born between 1922 and 1937 who were surveyed as part of the NLS-Mature Women (MW) cohort starting in 1967; and 2) the women born between 1942 and 1954 who were surveyed as part of the NLS-Young Women (YW) cohort starting in 1968. The mature women were reinterviewed twenty times and the young women were reinterviewed twenty-one times until 2003, when both studies were discontinued.

Annual values for own earnings were reported between 1967 and 2003 for the NLS-MW and between 1968 and 2003 for the NLS-YW.[9] Spouse or partner earnings were reported in the NLS-MW through 2003 and in the NLS-YW through 1991. The variable for total assets was constructed by summing several questions about the value of various types of assets owned by the respondent: bank accounts, bonds, investment accounts, mutual funds, life insurance (settlement value and surrender value), business and farm assets, real estate (including a primary home and additional property), and vehicles. Total debt was computed by summing various liabilities: personal debts, home mortgages, and other real estate debt, debt on business and farm property and on vehicles. Net wealth was computed as the difference between total assets and total debts in the year for which the information was available.[10] All dollar values are converted to real (inflation-adjusted) terms using 2010 as the base year.

These women are nationally representative for their cohorts.[11] Average age at first birth (A1B), among women with known A1B values, was 22.2 years, which is slightly older than the average age at first marriage (A1M) of 21.6 years. Nearly 80 percent of women in the sample appear to have been married by the time of their first birth. About 10 percent of the women were never married and 11 percent reported having no children. The great bulk of the women were white (70 percent) or black (28 percent). Women's own wages grew from their twenties through their mid-fifties, when they reached a peak of almost $15,000 per year, and then started to decline. Spouse wages peaked earlier, when the women were in their late thirties, but at a higher value of $32,000.

Young women in the sample started with net wealth under $1,000 in their late teens (not reported) and around $5,000 in their early twenties. They accumulated wealth through their mid-fifties, when average net wealth was over $280,000. In their sixties and seventies, the women consumed more than they earned, and their assets declined by about one quarter by their late seventies. Zero values of income and wealth were included in these averages and as observations in the regressions. However, missing values due to no interview or refusal were excluded.

Main Estimation Results

The results of the regression analysis are presented graphically in Figures 7.2–7.4.[12] The central finding is a strong positive relationship between motherhood delay and economic well-being throughout the lifecycle and a weaker positive relationship between marriage delay and economic well-being in retirement.

The main coefficient estimates for the impact of one additional year of motherhood delay or marriage delay on own income are depicted as curves in Figure 7.2. Although not shown in the figure, the

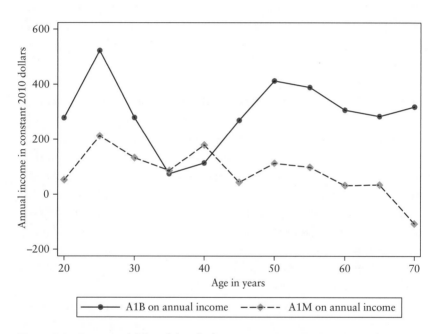

Figure 7.2   Impact of delayed family formation on own income over the lifecycle

NOTES: Figure plots coefficient estimates from separate regressions at different ages of own wage income on linear measures of A1B (age at first birth) and A1M (age at first marriage), as well as indicators for having no children and having never married by the end of the sample period and indicators for race and exact birth year cohort (corresponding to the regression model in Web Appendix Table A7.2, column 4, but with five-year age groups). Each coefficient represents the estimated effect of a single year of delay in either marriage or motherhood on own annual wages for women in the specified age group. The age groups are: 20–24 (indicated by 20), 25–29, 30–34, 35–39, 40–44, 45–49, 50–54, 55–59, 60–64, 65–69, and 70–74. Sample is all women in the NLS-MW or NLS-YW with nonmissing outcome data for that age group.

regression model also includes controls for birth year and race as well as indicators for never marrying, remaining childless, and having children but not reporting the age at first birth. For most years, the curve for motherhood delay (A1B) lies above that for marriage delay (A1M), although there seems to be a temporary reversal for women in their early forties.

Motherhood delay is associated with statistically significant increases in women's own income for all age groups. The magnitude of the relationship puts the effect of a single year's delay at about $290 of additional income, or 3 percent of average income across women and over the lifecycle. This implies that a five-year increase (on par with the observed increase in A1B between 1960 and 2006) would increase wage income by as much as 14 percent.[13] The estimated effects of A1B are larger, more significant, and more robust than those for A1M.

Figure 7.3 shows the estimates for the effects of delayed family formation on spouse income. Although the proportionate impact on own wages may be larger, the absolute size of the coefficients tends to be larger for spouse income than for own income for women ages thirty to seventy. As with own income, motherhood delay is more important than marriage delay. The effects on spouse income may be caused by changes in marital outcomes, for example, if later mothers match with higher income men or have more stable marriages, or by changes in male labor market outcomes, if early fatherhood (possibly leading to a "shotgun" marriage) lowers male mobility and wage growth. The effects of delay on wealth will incorporate changes in both sources of income as well as any changes in consumption.

Turning to the results for wealth, the curves in Figure 7.4 separately plot the progression of coefficient estimates for the impact of A1B and A1M on net wealth over the lifecycle. The results for total assets are extremely similar because changes in total liabilities are relatively small. The regression models are the same as in Figures 7.2 and 7.3, but with a different outcome—accumulated wealth (a stock) instead of annual income (a flow). It is clear that motherhood delay has a substantial positive association with wealth throughout the lifecycle, and especially after age forty. Marriage delay provides negligible benefits in terms of wealth accumulation for women under fifty; there is a small but statistically significant negative association for women in their twenties and a larger but

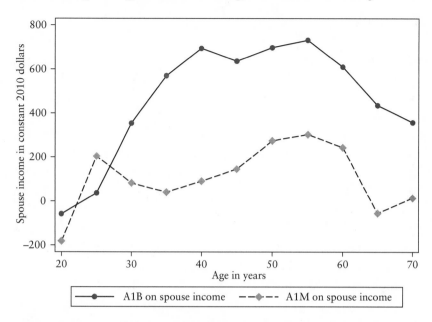

Figure 7.3 Impact of delayed family formation on spouse income over the lifecycle

NOTES: Figure plots coefficient estimates from separate regressions at different ages of spouse income on linear measures of A1B (age at first birth) and A1M (age at first marriage), as well as indicators for having no children and having never married by the end of the sample period and indicators for race and exact birth year cohort (corresponding to the regression model in Web Appendix Table A7.2, column 4, but with five-year age groups). Each coefficient represents the estimated effect of a single year of delay in either marriage or motherhood on spouse annual wages for women in the specified age group. The age groups are: 20–24 (indicated by 20), 25–29, 30–34, 35–39, 40–44, 45–49, 50–54, 55–59, 60–64, 65–69, and 70–74. Sample is all women in the NLS-MW or NLS-YW with nonmissing outcome data for that age group.

statistically insignificant negative association for women in their forties. After age fifty, there are positive and significant associations between wealth and marriage delay, but these are substantially smaller than the comparable associations with motherhood delay. Motherhood delay is associated with greater wealth for women of all ages. The estimated impact increases over time for women in their twenties through their fifties, then declines for women in their sixties. For a woman in her fifties, the estimated wealth improvement from a year of motherhood delay ranges from $12,000 to $20,000, and is statistically significant at the 1 percent level.[14]

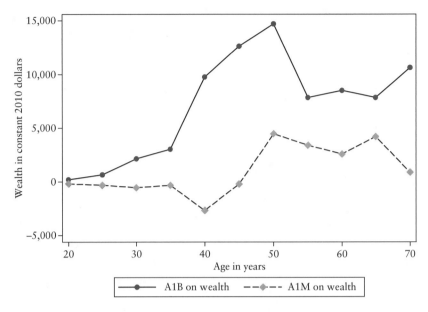

Figure 7.4   Impact of delayed family formation on wealth over the lifecycle

NOTES: Figure plots coefficient estimates from separate regressions at different ages of family wealth (total assets minus liabilities) on linear measures of A1B (age at first birth) and A1M (age at first marriage), as well as indicators for having no children and having never married by the end of the sample period and indicators for race and exact birth year cohort (corresponding to the regression model in Web Appendix Table A7.3, column 4, but with five-year age groups). Each coefficient represents the estimated effect of a single year of delay in either marriage or motherhood on net wealth for women in the specified age group. The age groups are: 20–24 (indicated by 20), 25–29, 30–34, 35–39, 40–44, 45–49, 50–54, 55–59, 60–64, 65–69, and 70–74. Sample is all women in the NLS-MW or NLS-YW with nonmissing outcome data for that age group.

Role of Education

The estimation results shown in Figures 7.2–7.4 indicate that fertility timing is a more important factor than marriage timing in determining women's economic well-being over the lifecycle. This is not surprising given the greater time demands of motherhood compared with marriage (especially in the early years), and may reflect the greater drop in female labor force participation following childbirth as opposed to marriage. Motherhood marks a more permanent transition for women than marriage does, and that may pose greater limits on their mobility and career progress.

Among the reasons why family formation timing affects economic outcomes, a primary candidate is that delaying family formation provides young women with more time to invest in their skills and labor market productivity. This section explores the role of education, through years of completed schooling, as a productivity-enhancing investment. The analysis is based on repeating the estimation of models in the previous section with an added control for schooling. Because schooling is not exogenous (or randomly assigned to women), this approach will not accurately measure its impact on economic outcomes. However, by comparing how the estimates for A1B and A1M change with the addition of this covariate, we can learn about its role as a channel for the main effects of family delay.

The results indicate that education is an important channel. Across all age groups and economic outcomes, adding the control for education to the regression model reduces the estimated financial benefit associated with delayed marriage or motherhood.[15] The only significant positive estimate for marriage delay is an increase of about $90 in annual income for women in their twenties. Controlling for education also increases the size of the negative wealth effects from late marriage for women in their twenties and thirties, but the differences are not present for women at older ages. The effects of motherhood delay, by contrast, remain positive and significant for women's earnings (in their twenties and fifties through seventies) and for their wealth (at all ages but their sixties). In every case, the size of the estimated benefit declines substantially with the additional control, which suggests that increased education itself is an important mechanism by which motherhood delay improves women's economic status. This finding also suggests that women who are able to complete their schooling, in spite of challenges associated with unexpectedly early motherhood, for example, may be able to partially recover from the adverse economic impact of the fertility shock. The residual importance of motherhood timing indicates, however, that education is not the only channel but, instead, that other human capital investments, job mobility, and possibly differential treatment of mothers by employers, also contribute to the financial premium for motherhood delay.

CONCLUSIONS

This chapter documents an increase in motherhood and marriage delay over the past half-century and uncovers a strong and stable relationship between family formation timing and women's economic well-being over the lifecycle. In particular, delayed motherhood is associated with higher own and spousal income as well as greater wealth. In contrast, marriage delay is associated with lower wealth for women in their twenties and thirties and with modest increases in income that are only significant at younger ages. These results illustrate the lasting importance of family formation decisions and random fertility shocks that occur early in the lifecycle on women's economic well-being. The effects of motherhood timing especially are substantial and significant for decades after the age at first birth and well into retirement years.

These findings can have important implications for forecasting the economic well-being of future cohorts of women, born after 1950, as they age into their retirement years. Together with the decline in total fertility rates, the trend of increasing fertility delay following the baby boom is a major contributor to population aging. As the population of older Americans increases in size and proportion, their economic well-being becomes increasingly important for public policy. To the extent that women who will reach retirement ages in the next decades are from cohorts who have already delayed motherhood, there are reasons to expect them to have greater financial security at older ages. It is also important to note that the wealth they accumulate may be even larger than what one would predict from those women's income improvements alone (for example, from the narrowing of the gender wage gap in the 1980s and 1990s; Blau and Kahn 2000). Motherhood delay had larger effects on wealth than on income, implying that delay is also associated with an increase in savings rates. Women who delay motherhood earn more and consume more, but their consumption does not increase proportionately, leaving them with greater accumulated wealth at older ages. This suggests some reason for optimism among policymakers and the public about the overall financial well-being of these cohorts in retirement.

Some caveats are in order. The results from earlier cohorts may not generalize to produce reliable predictions for the well-being of later cohorts. Recent economic circumstances, such as the Great Recession, may have disproportionately affected women who delayed motherhood because they had more investment wealth at risk, and may be not be comparable to other fluctuations in the business cycle.

Another limitation of the analysis is that the relationships are conditional correlations. The data are observational and estimation is based on regression models that fit parameters to the data. Hence, the estimates may not capture the structural parameters of interest, the true impact of delay. The basic model includes only a limited set of controls, for the reason that many other "controls" are themselves endogenous outcomes that may be affected by motherhood and marriage timing. To the extent that the omitted variables are correlated by timing but not affected by it, however, and to the extent that they affect the primary outcomes, it is possible that the estimates in this chapter overstate the impact of delay (or understate it if the omitted wage and wealth factors are negatively correlated with delay).

A third limitation is related to the focus of this volume on economic measures of well-being, in this chapter taking the form of own and spousal income and family assets and wealth. These measures omit other forms of material support from transfers (cash or in-kind, including time and assistance) from family members as well as excluded sources of income and assets from pensions, Social Security payments, investment returns, and business or farm income. There are also nonpecuniary aspects of a woman's well-being in retirement, such as the well-being of her own children. The association in Miller (2009) between motherhood delay and higher test scores for first-born children suggests that delayed family formation may entail nonpecuniary benefits as well. If children born to older mothers also have higher incomes, they may be less dependent on transfers from their parents and more able to support them financially, although they will tend to be younger and may not be established in their careers when their mothers retire. However, to the extent that women value living more years in the presence of their grandchildren (and great-grandchildren), there may be nonpecuniary costs of delay as well. There may also be long-term health implications of delayed childbearing, though the current literature provides mixed evidence. While early motherhood and high parity have been linked to worse physical and emotional health outcomes later in life (e.g., Mirowsky 2005), there is also evidence that motherhood delay (past age thirty-five) can have negative consequences for mothers (Alonzo 2002) and for children's health (Royer 2004).

Notwithstanding these caveats, the results of this chapter suggest an important role for changes in fertility timing across cohorts of U.S. women to understanding changes in retirement. The direct role of delayed fertility in population aging is well understood. Motherhood delay leads to relatively smaller young generations, even if individual women have the same number of children in their lifetimes.

The indirect effects of delayed family formation on the retirement picture have been relatively unexamined. Here, the picture is more favorable. The cross-sectional evidence in this chapter from the NLS-YW and NLS-WM suggests that the women who delay motherhood by five years earn on average 24 percent more in their twenties, 8 percent more in their thirties, 7 percent more in their forties, and 15 percent more in their fifties. They reach their sixties with on average 22 percent greater accumulated wealth than earlier mothers. This suggests that future cohorts of retiring women may have improved economic well-being and be less likely to depend on public assistance for financial support.

NOTES

1. The similarity suggests that selection into late motherhood is neutral, on average, after controlling for the woman's education, race, and intelligence test score. Data on the fertility shocks are not available for the earlier NLS samples so the analysis in this chapter is limited to standard regression models. Hence, to the extent that there are systematic factors, omitted from the models, that affect both family formation timing and economic outcomes, the associations reported in this chapter should not be interpreted as the pure causal impacts of family timing.

2. Although not reported in the tables or figures, the regression analysis in this chapter finds that childless women outearn women who become mothers at age thirties until their mid-fifties, after which point the later mothers earn more. Later mothers have greater assets, debt, and net wealth than childless women at all ages.

3. The average A1B value in the figure is calculated by averaging across first births to women ages fifteen to forty-four in Hamilton and Cosgrove and estimating additional births to women ages ten to fourteen assuming a first birth probability of 1 in 1,000. The estimate of a five-year increase is consistent with maternal ages reported in Mathews and Hamilton (2009) and in Goodwin, McGill, and Chandra (2009).

4. The trends in birth rates by age described in this paragraph are plotted in Web Appendix Figure A7.1.

5. Although not shown in the figure, prior to 1960, median A1M had actually declined slightly, from 21.5 in 1940 to 20.1 in the mid-1950s. This pattern is also reflected in Vital Statistics reports on ages of brides at the time of their first marriages for the years 1951 to 1990 (Annual Vital Statistics Report 1960; Annual Vital Statistics Report 1972; Monthly Vital Statistics Report 1983; Monthly Vital Statistics Report 1995). Women's median A1M decreased from 21.4 in 1950 to a low of 19.8 in 1961, from which point it increased gradually and steadily (nearly every year-to-year change is an increase) to 24 in 1990.

6. The share of births to unmarried women went from 27 percent in 1990 to 40 percent in 2006 (National Center for Health Statistics 2010; table 86).

7. This is shown in the period analysis in Web Appendix Figure A7.1. It is also evident in the cross-cohort analysis in Web Appendix Figure A7.2, where the share of first births after age thirty-four is depicted by the vertical distance between the top line (for ages forty to forty-four) and the third line (for ages thirty to thirty-four). This share narrowed between 1910 and 1934 birth cohorts from 8.5 percent to almost 2.2 percent and then increased across cohorts to 10 percent for women born in 1960 and 11.5 percent for those born in 1964. The share of women with any children by ages forty to forty-four did decline after the baby boom cohort, in the two decades of birth cohorts after 1939, from 91.6 percent to 83.7 percent, only to increase slightly to 84.9 percent for those born in 1964. However, that share of women born in 1960 with children by ages forty to forty-four was actually 5 percent higher than the share for cohorts born in 1910 and 4 percent higher than the share for those born in 1900.

8. The main results are shown in figures for five-year age groups ranging from twenty to seventy-four. Additional estimates are reported in Web Appendix Tables A7.2 and A7.3. Those results use ten-year age groups for the range from 20 to 79.

9. Own income is reported for the years 1967–1971, 1974, 1976, 1979, 1981, 1984, 1986, 1988, 1992, 1995, 1997, 1999, 2001 and 2003 for the NLS-MW and for the years 1968–1973, 1975, 1977, 1978, 1980, 1982, 1983, 1985, 1987, 1988, 1991, 1993, 1995, 1997, 1999, 2001 and 2003 for the NLS-YW.

10. Wealth information is used for the years 1967, 1972, 1977, 1982, 1987, 1989, 1995, 1997, 1999, 2001 and 2003 for the NLS-MW and for the years 1968–1973, 1978, 1983, 1988, 1993, 1995, 1997, 1999, 2001 and 2003 for the NLS-YW.

11. Summary statistics are reported for the key independent and dependent variables in the Web Appendix. The main fertility and marriage variables are shown in Web Appendix Table A7.1A. Web Appendix Table A7.1B shows average income (own and spouse) and net wealth values over the lifecycle.

12. Additional results are in Web Appendix Tables A7.2 and A7.3.

13. These values are smaller than those in Miller (2011) for women born between 1957 and 1965, possibly because the impact of delay on women's careers has grown over time. See Web Appendix Tables A7.2 and A7.3 for the full set of coefficient estimates and standard errors for all models.

14. The apparent increase in the point estimates in Web Appendix Table A7.3 between women in their sixties and seventies is not simply due to the latter being averaged over a smaller sample of women, drawn from the earliest birth cohorts, who remained in the survey past their sixties. When the regression in column 5 was repeated for women in their sixties who were also present in the data in their seventies, the point estimate was $4,226 (significant at the 5 percent level), which lies between the point estimates for women in their sixties ($3,024) and seventies ($7,525).

15. The point estimates and standard errors for the models with education are reported in column 5 of Web Appendix Tables A7.2 and A7.3.

REFERENCES

Alonzo, Angelo A. (2002). "Long-Term Health Consequences of Delayed Childbirth: NHANES III." Women's Health Issues 121:37–45.

Bailey, Martha (2006). "More Power to the Pill: The Impact of Contraceptive Freedom on Women's Life Cycle Labor Supply." *Quarterly Journal of Economics* 121(1): 289–320.

Bailey, Martha, and William J. Collins (2011). "Did Improvements in Household Technology Cause the Baby Boom? Evidence from Electrification, Appliance Diffusion, and the Amish." *American Economic Journal: Macroeconomics* 3(2): 189–217.

Bailey, Martha, Brad Hershbein, and Amalia R. Miller (2012). "The Opt-In Revolution? Contraception and the Gender Gap in Wages." *American Economic Journal: Applied Economics* 4(3): 225–54.

Blau, Francine, and Lawrence Kahn (2000). "Gender Differences in Pay," *Journal of Economic Perspectives* 14(4): 75–99.

Friedberg, Leora (1998). "Did Unilateral Divorce Raise Divorce Rates? Evidence from Panel Data." *American Economic Review* 88(3): 608–27.

Geronimus, A., and S. Korenman (1992). "The Socioeconomic Consequences of Teen Childbearing Reconsidered." *Quarterly Journal of Economics* 107(4): 1187–1214.

Goldin, Claudia, and Lawrence Katz (2002). "The Power of the Pill: Oral Contraceptives and Women's Career and Marriage Decisions." *Journal of Political Economy* 110(4): 730–70.

Goldin, Claudia, Lawrence Katz, and Ilyana Kuziemko (2006). "The Homecoming of American College Women: The Reversal of the College Gender Gap." *Journal of Economic Perspectives* 20(4): 133–56.

Goodwin, Paula, Brittany McGill, and Anjani Chandra (2009). "Who Marries and When? Age at First Marriage in the United States: 2002." NCHS Data Brief No. 19. Hyattsville, MD: National Center for Health Statistics.

Greenwood, Jeremy, Ananth Seshadri, and Mehmet Yorukoglu (2005). "Engines of Liberation." *Review of Economic Studies* 72(1): 109–33.

Hamilton B. E., and C. M. Cosgrove. "Central Birth Rates, by Live-Birth Order, Current Age, and Race of Women in Each Cohort from 1911 Through 1991: United States, 1960–2005. Table 1." Hyattsville, MD: National Center for Health Statistics. Available from: http://www.cdc.gov/nchs/nvss/cohort_fertility_tables.htm. Released: June 30, 2010. (Accessed April 20, 2011).

Heaton, Tim B. (2002). "Factors Contributing to Increasing Marital Stability in the United States." *Journal of Family Issues* 23(3): 392–409.

Heuser, R. L. "Fertility Tables for Birth Cohorts by Color: United States, 1917–73." Rockville, MD: U.S. Department of Health, Education, and Welfare, National Center for Health Statistics, 1976. Available from: http://www.cdc.gov/nchs/data/misc/fertiltbacc.pdf. (Accessed April 20, 2011).

Hofferth, Sandra (1984). "Long-Term Economic Consequences for Women of Delayed Childbearing and Reduced Family Size." *Demography* 21:141–55.

Hotz, Joseph, Charles Mullin, and Seth Sanders (1997). "Bounding Causal Effects Using Data from a Contaminated Natural Experiment: Analysing the Effects of Teenage Childbearing." *Review of Economic Studies* 64: 575–603.

Klepinger, Daniel, Shelly Lundberg, and Robert Plotnick (1999). "How Does Adolescent Fertility Affect the Human Capital and Wages of Young Women?" *Journal of Human Resources* 34: 421–48.

Loughran, David S., and Julie M. Zissimopoulos (2009). "Why Wait?: The Effect of Marriage and Childbearing on the Wages of Men and Women." *Journal of Human Resources* 44: 326–49.

Mathews, T. J., and Brady E. Hamilton (2009). "Delayed Childbearing: More Women Are Having Their First Child Later in Life." NCHS Data Brief No. 21. Hyattsville, MD: National Center for Health Statistics.

Miller, Amalia R. (2009). "Motherhood Delay and the Human Capital of the Next Generation." *American Economic Review* 99(2): 154–58.

Miller, Amalia R. (2011). "The Effects of Motherhood Delay on Career Path." *Journal of Population Economics* 24(3): 1071–1100.

Mirowsky, John (2005). "Age at First Birth, Health, and Mortality." *Journal of Health and Social Behavior* 46(1): 32–50.

Royer, Heather (2004). "What All Women (and Some Men) Want to Know: Does Maternal Age Affect Infant Health?" University of California, Berkeley, Center for Labor Economics Working Paper # 68. http://emlab.berkeley.edu/users/cle/wp/wp68.pdf.

Ruggles, Steven J., Trent Alexander, Katie Genadek, Ronald Goeken, Matthew B. Schroeder, and Matthew Sobek. Integrated Public Use Microdata Series: Version 5.0 [Machine-readable database]. Minneapolis: University of Minnesota, 2010.

Schmidt, Lucie, and Purvi Sevak (2006). "Gender, Marriage, and Asset Accumulation in the United States." *Feminist Economics* 12(1–2): 139–66.

Stevenson, Betsey, and Justin Wolfers (2007). "Marriage and Divorce: Changes and Their Driving Forces." *Journal of Economic Perspectives* 21(2): 27–52.

U.S. Census Bureau (2011). "Number, Timing and Duration of Marriages and Divorces: 2004." Available from: www.census.gov/compendia/statab/2011/tables/11s0128.xls. (Accessed April 20, 2011).

National Center for Health Statistics (2010). "National Vital Statistics Reports (NVSR), Births: Final Data for 2007." Vol. 58, No. 24.

Wolfers, Justin (2006). "Did Unilateral Divorce Laws Raise Divorce Rates? A Reconciliation and New Results." *American Economic Review* 96(5): 1802–20.

Zissimopoulos, Julie, Benjamin Karney, and Amy Rauer (2008). "Marital Histories and Economic Well-Being." Santa Monica, CA: RAND Corporation, RAND Working Paper WR-645. http://www.rand.org/pubs/working_papers/WR645.

CHAPTER EIGHT

Divorce, Women's Earnings, and Retirement over the Life Course

Kenneth A. Couch, Christopher R. Tamborini,
Gayle L. Reznik, and John W. R. Phillips

INTRODUCTION

Unanticipated changes in family composition can have long-lasting consequences for individuals. Among the most frequent family status changes over the life course is divorce. While divorce rates have fallen somewhat from their peak in the 1970s and early 1980s, divorce remains a high probability lifecycle event (Stevenson and Wolfers 2007, table 1; see also, Cherlin 1992; Goldstein and Kenney 2001). Information presented in Chapter 7 of this volume by Amalia Miller shows that divorce is the third most common lifecycle event related to family structure, following marriage and childbirth.

Changes in marital status and family structure have important implications for the economic well-being of women. A large body of literature has linked divorce with a decline in women's income and wealth in the United States (Holden and Smock 1991; Smock, Manning, and Gupta 1999; Zissimopoulos 2009); in Canada (Finnie 1993); and in Europe (Aassve et al. 2007; Burkhauser et al. 1991; Dewilde and Uunk 2008). This decline likely puts financial pressure on women to increase their labor supply to raise their incomes. Although some studies have examined the labor market consequences of marital dissolution for women (e.g.,

Kenneth Couch was an IPA (Intergovernmental Personnel Act) visiting scholar at the U.S. Social Security Administration while working on this chapter. The views expressed here are those of the authors and do not represent the views of the Social Security Administration or any agency in the federal government.

Johnson and Skinner 1988), the relationship is not well investigated. Moreover, because of short follow-up periods and infrequent use of longitudinal data, previous research has not documented the long-term economic trajectories of divorced women. Most studies also do not account for heterogeneity across marital groups and potential selectivity into divorce. Thus, whether the relationship between marital dissolution and women's economic circumstances reflects selective characteristics of women who divorce relative to women who stay married is difficult to determine.

Beyond women's labor supply, divorce may also affect women's retirement outcomes, such as their entitlement to Social Security retirement benefits, and their propensity to claim benefits based on a spouse's earnings records or their own. We are unaware of prior research that directly links a change in family structure through the mechanism of increased labor supply and earnings to the type and level of retirement benefits.

To address these issues, this chapter examines the long-term effects of marital dissolution on women's earnings and retirement. Using a longitudinal approach and a fixed-effects model, we consider three main questions. First, what is the effect of divorce on women's earnings? Second, do these changes persist over the lifecycle? Third, what is the effect on the timing, type, and level of benefit as women enter into the Social Security retirement program?

We use restricted data that link U.S. respondents in the 2004 Survey of Income and Program Participation (SIPP) to their longitudinal earnings and benefit records from the Social Security Administration (SSA). The SIPP data contain retrospective marital, fertility, and educational histories, which allow us to look back in time and select a sample of married women who subsequently divorce within an observational window and compare them to similar married women who never divorce. The matched longitudinal administrative data, which cover a 40-year period spanning the years from 1968 to 2008, then make it possible to assess these women's earnings trajectories and actual Social Security benefits.

In our analysis, we track a cohort of women in their first marriages in the early to mid-1970s. Using fixed-effects models to control for unobserved differences across groups, we compare continuously married women to those who experienced a marital dissolution between 1971 and 1976. To shed light on the role of subsequent marital events, we also compare divorced women who never remarried and those who did.

Our findings show that marital dissolutions in the early and mid-1970s led to substantial increases in women's earnings over their life course. Marital dissolution also had strong effects on women's own Social Security benefit. These results hold when controlling for important time varying characteristics such as age, education, and number of children. The observed earnings increases associated with divorce are more sustained over the life course than previously recognized in the literature. Particularly large and persistent effects are found among divorced women who never remarry. We also find evidence that marital dissolution increases the chances that women delay their entry into the Social Security program. Higher earnings over the lifecycle lead to larger Social Security benefits based on one's own eligibility and a reduced chance of claiming benefits through a spouse's eligibility. Accordingly, we find that relative to continuously married women, those who divorced also had higher average initial Social Security benefits that were more likely to be determined by their own earnings history. Finally, by using fixed-effects estimators to control for cross-group heterogeneity, this study makes a methodological contribution to the study of the long-run financial impacts of changes in family composition.

The chapter is organized as follows. The next section situates this study within the related literature. A discussion of the data and estimation strategy follows. The results section presents estimates of the long-term effects of marital dissolution on a cohort of women's earnings, Social Security retirement benefit, and various retirement outcomes. The final section summarizes our results and provides discussion points.

BACKGROUND AND SIGNIFICANCE

The focus of this chapter is whether life events, such as divorce, trigger changes in women's labor supply and retirement outcomes over the lifecycle. A central reason it is interesting to examine the long-term financial implications of divorce is the association between marital status and family well-being. Both economic and sociological literatures suggest numerous economic benefits from marriage, including greater income and wealth, particularly late in life (Lupton and Smith 2003; Waite and Gallagher 2000; Wilmoth and Koso 2002; Zagorsky 2005; Zissimopoulos, Karney, and Rauer 2008). A prominent mechanism underlying this correlation is economies of scale, which permit more rapid accumulation of assets due to the sharing of incomes and costs (Becker 1981).

Marital status also influences work patterns. Labor decisions, such as whether and how many hours to work, involve a complex calculation of trade-offs that correlate with family variables. Among married women, spouses' wages tend a have a negative effect on labor supply, although less so in more recent years (Blau and Kahn 2007). The presence of children, particularly younger ones, tends to reduce women's employment and earnings (Gangl and Ziefle 2009). Further, marriage expands the dimensions of expected caregiving for women to relatives of their spouse, further complicating their labor supply decisions (Couch, Daly, and Wolf 1999).

Insofar as marriage alters individual decision-making regarding labor supply, then there should be an observable change when a marriage dissolves. Consistent with this, a large multidisciplinary literature has examined the consequences of marital dissolution for women's economic status (Aassve et al. 2007; Burkhauser et al. 1991; Smock 1993). Research has documented immediate and sharp economic losses in family income and wealth, particularly for women (Smock, Manning, and Gupta 1999; Zagorsky 2005; Zissimopoulos 2009). While evidence suggests somewhat mitigated losses among more recently divorced women due to increases in work attachment and educational attainment in successive cohorts (McKeever and Wolfinger 2001), studies nonetheless continue to find substantive economic decline following a divorce (Gadalla 2009; Smock 1993).

Women experience economic loss after a marital dissolution for varied reasons. Prominent explanations include the loss of the husband's labor income and economies of scale. Lower human capital investments prior to a marital disruption for women relative to men are also relevant (Bradbury and Katz 2002; Hoffman and Duncan 1988; Holden and Smock 1991). Furthermore, alimony and child-support payments, two common sources of non-labor income for divorced women, rarely offset the decline in family income (Duncan and Hoffman 1985; Teachman and Paasch 1994).

An important question that has not received adequate research attention is the earnings consequences of divorce. A large strand of the empirical literature has focused on women's employment and earnings as a determinant of divorce (for review, see Burstein 2007 or Sayer and Bianchi 2000) rather than a consequence of it. Yet marital dissolution is likely to put financial pressure on women to increase their earnings by expanding labor supply. This correspondingly raises the opportunity costs for home production, particularly for women not already working full-time. Women can improve their economic status after a marital dissolution (without remarrying) by entering the labor market, working longer hours, or finding higher paid employment.

A handful of researchers have empirically assessed the labor supply consequences of divorce, but only over a short observation period. Johnson and Skinner (1986) use Panel Study of Income Dynamics (PSID) data to examine changes in the labor supply of American women experiencing a marital disruption between 1973 and 1977. They find that women, particularly those with little work experience, respond to higher divorce probabilities by increasing working hours (see also, Johnson and Skinner 1988). In another study, Haurin (1989) uses longitudinal data covering a four-year period and finds a positive labor response among women to unanticipated changes in household income, including divorce events. Mueller (2005), however, finds little change in the work hours of Canadian women who divorce. Less research has been devoted to women's earnings after divorce. In a recent paper, Tamborini, Iams, and Reznik (2012), utilizing SIPP marital history data matched to longitudinal W-2 tax records, document significant average earnings gains in the years immediately following a marital disruption among U.S. women in the labor force. While useful, such analyses offer only clues about the longer-term consequences of divorce.

Divorce also has implications for women's retirement (Holden and Kuo 1996; Tamborini and Whitman 2010; Tamborini, Iams, and Whitman 2009). One mechanism is its impact on an individual's Social Security benefit, which is based on one's own earnings history or that of a spouse. If 50 percent of a spouse's benefit is greater than one's own benefit, an individual is eligible to receive the higher amount. Divorced individuals need to have been married for ten years to be eligible for a spousal benefit. The details of benefit receipt will be explored in more depth later in the chapter, but the essential point is that if women increase their career earnings to make up for the economic loss following a marital dissolution, this will increase their own future Social Security benefit, making it less likely they would receive a spousal benefit. Similarly, divorces that occur prior to ten years of marriage preclude the possibility of a spousal benefit, thus influencing the type of benefit received.

The impact of divorce on private savings is unclear. Increased employment and/or earnings might lead to greater contributions to private retirement savings vehicles (Munnell and Zhivan 2006). However, deterioration in economic status after divorce may lead women to dip into—or interrupt—retirement savings, increasing the probability that they would enter retirement with fewer resources. In this chapter, we examine women's Social Security benefits conditioning on their marital histories to shed light on the extent to which divorce affects retirement resources. Zissimopoulos, in Chapter 9 of this volume, uses the Health and Retirement Study (HRS) to examine a wider range of factors that influence retirement and its relationship to family structure.

Examining the economic consequences of marital dissolution also necessitates consideration of socioeconomic and demographic variables (Tamborini, Iams, and Reznik 2012). Human capital plays a large role in female labor force outcomes (Blau and Kahn 2007). The lower the level of educational attainment the more difficult it will be, on average, to generate higher market wages or to find employment after a marital dissolution. Children may also influence female labor market behavior. After divorce women tend to be the primary caretakers of children (Kreider 2008, table 9; Smock 1994). Because children increase the consumption needs of a household, mothers may face increased financial pressure to increase their own earnings after a divorce. However, because children tend to reduce women's labor supply during marriage (Bianchi 2000; Gangl and Ziefle 2009), mothers may find it harder to find employment or higher wages after a marital dissolution.

In addition, remarriage may act as a potential buffer against the decline in economic status associated with divorce (Duncan and Hoffman 1985). Insofar as remarriage improves divorced women's economic well-being, it could lower the financial impact of the divorce. Analyzing cross-national longitudinal data in the European context, Dewilde and Uunk (2008) find a positive association between remarriage and women's postdissolution well-being (see also, Jansen, Mortelmans, and Snoeckx 2009). Using HRS data from 1992 to 2006, Zissimopoulos (2009) provides evidence that remarriage at older ages tends to enhance women's wealth.

In this study, an important consideration is whether the long-term earnings and retirement benefit implications of divorce vary between divorced women who subsequently remarry and those who do not. This is a salient distinction because remarriage is quite common, particularly among earlier birth cohorts. For example, among ever-divorced persons born between 1940 and 1945, 70.5 percent had remarried by age 45 (Stevenson and Wolfers 2007).

In sum, the financial consequences of divorce for women over the life course are not well examined. Most existing studies use cross-sectional or panel data that cover short observation periods. The typical follow-up window is one to three years after a separation or divorce. Prior research also typically has not controlled for possible heterogeneity between married and divorced women. Thus, whether observed differences in labor market outcomes reflect differences in married women who divorced and those who stayed married, or a structural impact of divorce is difficult to determine. Moreover, any changes in labor market behavior by divorced women would be expected to influence the timing, type, and level of their Social Security benefit.

DATA AND METHOD

Data Source

We draw data from wave 2 of the 2004 SIPP panel matched to SSA's longitudinal earnings and benefit records. The SIPP is a nationally representative household panel survey of the civilian noninstitutionalized U.S. population administered by the Census Bureau. Wave 2 topical modules contain retrospective marital, fertility, and educational histories, which allow us to date important life events. Specifically, a marital history file includes the date of marriage, separation, and divorce for up to three marriages. The fertility histories provide the reported year of birth for the first and last child among women. Detailed educational histories contain the years in which respondents' high school and college degrees were obtained.

Based on agreements between SSA and the Census Bureau, SIPP respondents are matched to their SSA earnings and benefit records.[1] Specifically, we use SSA's Summary Earnings Record (SER) and the Master Beneficiary Record (MBR) to extract information on respondents' annual Social Security earnings and monthly benefits over a forty-year period from 1968 through 2008. Olsen and Hudson (2009) provide detailed information about SSA's earnings files, and McNabb et al. (2009) discuss the matching method.

Not all of the SIPP respondents are matched with the administrative data. The match rate for our final sample is high, at around 80 percent. Sensitivity analyses revealed strong similarities between the matched and full SIPP samples in terms of age, birth cohort, current marital status, educational level, and race/ethnicity. Nevertheless, to account for unequal probabilities of being matched to administrative records, we adjust the SIPP person weights for nonmatches by treating them as nonresponses (Carlson and Williams 2001). Using the results of a logistic regression to predict a match across a range of characteristics, we multiply the inverse of the match probability given the characteristics by SIPP wave 2 person weights.[2] This modified weight is used to correct all of our estimates for possible bias due to unsuccessful matching across the SIPP and SSA records.

Estimation Approach

To estimate the long-term effects of a marital dissolution on women's earnings we use a longitudinal fixed-effects estimator, adopting a strategy commonly used to examine the impact of discrete events such as job displacement on subsequent labor market behavior (Couch, Jolly, and Placzek 2009; Couch and Placzek 2010; Couch, Jolly, and Placzek 2011). We use an estimator that equalizes the earnings paths of those divorced relative to a comparison group prior to the time of separation so that subsequent changes in labor market behavior can reasonably be inferred to relate to the event being studied rather than cross-group differences. By using fixed-effects models, we can account for unobserved heterogeneity across the two groups and the potential selection bias of divorce. Such a strategy represents a contribution in itself to the literature, which has heretofore not employed fixed-effects techniques to deal with these issues.

More formally, the fixed-effects (ϕ_j) are for group j attributes. The groups are defined by the focus of the analysis (e.g., the continuously married versus those who separate and divorce). A standard estimator examining earnings (Y) that employs panel data with repeated observations over time (t) for each individual (i) can be written as:

$$y_{ijt} = \beta X_{ijt} + \sum\nolimits_{t=-3}^{T} D_{ijt} \gamma_t + \phi_j + \varepsilon_{it}.$$

Observable characteristics, such as the level of education for each person in each year, are subsumed in the matrix X. The parameters included in β relate the observed characteristics to the earnings outcome. The variables included in D_{ijt} indicate whether a person was either in the continuously married portion of the sample or in one of the other groups. The summation simply indicates that a variable is needed each period to track which members of the sample examined belong to different subgroups. The indexing extends from three years before the event being studied to the length of the time period being examined (T) minus those initial three years. The parameter, γ_t, measures the impact of being in the sample coded with the value one (usually having had a separation leading to divorce) relative to those coded with having the value zero (always those who are continuously married throughout the sample); ε_{it} is an error term that is distributed randomly across individuals in time periods.[3]

Sample Selection

The initial step in our sample construction involves dating marital transition events of marriage, separation, and divorce. We identified all women who faced the risk of a marital dissolution from 1971 to 1976 by selecting women in their first marriage of at least three years in duration by 1970. The next step was to identify the divorced group, which consists of women who reported a marital separation between the years of 1971 and 1976 (time t) that ended in divorce. Conceptually, this identifies all women in their first marriage who are at risk of divorce as well as those who experience a separation leading to divorce.

To provide a baseline to analyze the earnings consequences of marital dissolution, the "comparison group" consists of women who remained continuously married (in their first marriage) up to 2004. Women in the divorced or "treatment" group are also at risk of remarriage after their divorce. We consider only marital dissolutions from the early and mid-1970s instead of from more recent decades to allow for a follow-up period that captures women's career earnings as well as their entry into retirement. The total sample contains information on 88,014 unweighted person-years covering the interval from 1968 to 2008. There are 2,471 persons in the sample, 1,873 continuously married and 598 divorced.

To balance the age distribution of the treatment and control groups, we require women in the study sample to be between the ages of twenty-two and thirty-six in 1971. This cohort spans fifteen years and is centered on the age of twenty-nine in 1971. Because the matched longitudinal data extends through 2008, those who were age twenty-nine in 1971 will be sixty-six in 2008, past their full retirement age.[4] Thus, one way of viewing the cohort examined in this chapter is that it allows us to track a group of women who on average would be eligible for their full Social Security retirement benefit in the last year of the matched administrative data. Those who are older than age twenty-nine in 1971 would reach eligibility in earlier years of the person-year sample.

One implication of our sample construction is that the analysis does not incorporate later-life marital dissolutions (past age forty-one), which are less frequent and may have different properties than those that occur at younger ages. The analysis also excludes married women who experienced a change in marital status outside the interval 1971–1976. We do not consider the effects of divorce from remarriages because they likely reflect different properties than first marriages. This implicitly subsumes those effects within those we attribute to the first divorce.

Analysis of Earnings

Our estimation strategy uses fixed-effects models to examine earnings as the dependent variable for the sample of divorced and continuously married women. We estimate two models. The first model is parsimonious and includes age, age-squared, and year controls along with a set of dichotomous independent variables measuring the marital dissolution relative to the timing of the event. The second model adds educational attainment and total children to test whether the observed relationships hold when controlling for important socioeconomic variables that may vary over time. Importantly, among the divorced group, separate estimates are also made for those who subsequently remarried and those who never did. This allows us to directly observe whether increased labor supply following divorce is more pronounced among those who never remarry.

Following previous work, we flag the marital dissolution as the year of separation from a marriage ending in divorce.[5] Focusing on the year of separation, rather than year of legal divorce, allows us to capture any anticipatory run-up of earnings prior to the marriage disruption. To control for women's predissolution earnings, our time window covers three years prior to the dissolution event $(t - 3)$, the earliest being 1968.

Dependent Variable. The central dependent variable used for the fixed-effects model is annual Social Security–covered earnings. Our measure of earnings reflects all wages and salaries, bonuses, and self-employment income covered by Social Security in a given year. A key advantage of these data is historical earnings information.[6] Administrative earnings are also less subject to measurement error than respondent reports in surveys.

Two limitations of our earnings measure are noteworthy. First, Social Security earnings do not capture individuals in the U.S. population in noncovered employment. The rate of coverage in the U.S. labor force has changed over time. In 1970, about 90 percent of the paid labor force was in Social Security–covered employment, compared to about 96 percent in 2000. In our earnings data, workers in noncovered employment in a given year would have a zero for their earnings in that year. Noncovered earnings also would not count toward a person's Social Security benefit. Individuals in the public sector are particularly problematic, especially federal civilian employees hired before 1984 and certain state and local government workers. In 1980, for example, 96 percent of private-sector workers were in employment covered by Social Security, compared to 62 percent of public-sector employees (Nelson 1985). Our earnings estimates, while still capturing the vast majority of workers, even in the 1970s and early 1980s, should be seen as applicable to individuals in Social Security–covered employment. A second complication is that earnings are capped at the Social Security taxable maximum.[7] Truncation of earnings does not introduce substantive bias into our estimates because it affects a small share of women in our sample and indirectly serves to minimize the impact of outliers.

Sensitivity analysis replicating the fixed-effects model of earnings using women's matched W-2 records after 1982 (which include covered and noncovered earnings that are not capped) shows similar results to those reported here. Because we examine women's earnings starting in 1968, we use Social Security earnings throughout the analysis for consistency. All earnings are expressed in 2008 dollars using the Consumer Price Index (CPI-W).

Independent Variables. The main independent variables measure the impact of divorce on women's earnings over the life course. Specifically, a series of dichotomous variables measure the timing of the marital dissolution for each person-year. For example, the year before the separation $(t - 1)$ is measured by the dummy variable D_{-1} and the year after $(t + 1)$ is captured by the variable D_1. We date the year of the separation as period zero and generally refer to preceding years as *pre* and those that occur afterwards as *post*. A series of these dummy variables capture the persistent effects of the marital dissolution (e.g., $t + 10$, $t + 20$). This longitudinal framework is similar to that found in the study of other discrete lifecycle events and can be seen in Chapter 2 by Farber, Chapter 4 by Stevens and Moulton on job loss, and Chapter 13 by Meyer and Mok on disability, in this volume.[8]

The base model, in addition to the aforementioned set of dummy variables measuring the timing of the marital dissolution, includes age, age-squared, and calendar year dummy variables representing the year earnings are observed. The second model adds time-varying measures of educational attainment, total number of children (under eighteen), and total children squared. Education level in a given person-year is measured using binary indicators for high school and bachelor's degrees for that year. The total number of children is measured by another set of indicators relative to the person-year.[9] We include a quadratic term to control for a potential reduction in the negative effect of children on women's earnings.

In the Web Appendix accompanying this volume, Table A8.1 contains descriptive information for the selected marital groups. Those data are drawn from 1970, a year in which all women in our study sample were married; that is, one year prior to when they were at risk of marital dissolution. Before we employed the fixed-effects estimation techniques, the earnings level among the subset of women who eventually divorced was modestly higher than for the continuously married group. The average number of children was modestly larger in the continuously married group. The overall divorced group and the married group had a similar proportion of high school degree holders in 1970, but those who divorced were a bit less likely to hold a college degree. The race/ethnic distribution between the divorced and married groups was similar; however, we observed a modestly higher proportion of black women among the subset of divorced women who never remarried over the span of the study.

Analysis of Retirement Outcomes

In addition to the multivariate fixed-effects models, we tabulate women's Social Security benefit claiming age, type (own, spousal, etc.), and amount across the marital groups. We focus on a subset of women from our main sample who reached age sixty-six by 2008 and who claimed their initial retirement benefit at age sixty-two or older. These women were between the ages of twenty-nine and thirty-seven in 1971. The sample excludes women who ever received a Social Security disability benefit. We provide t-tests for differences across the marital groups to uncover important differences in outcomes.

Three retirement outcomes are examined. The first indicates the distribution of claiming ages: (a) sixty-two, (b) sixty-three to sixty-four, and (c) sixty-five or older. Generally speaking, the longer an individual postpones claiming his or her Social Security benefit, the higher it will be. Thus, when benefits are claimed at age sixty-two, Social Security's early eligibility retirement age (EEA), or at any time before the person's full retirement age, they are subject to a permanent and actuarially fair reduction.[10] The full retirement age was set at age sixty-five; however, the Social Security Amendments of 1983 set in motion a gradual increase in the full retirement age in two-month intervals beginning with the 1938 birth cohort, until it reaches persons born in 1960 or later, at which time the full retirement age will be sixty-seven.[11]

The second and third outcomes of interest are benefit types and benefit amounts upon entry into the Social Security program. At retirement age, women can be entitled to benefits in three different ways depending on their earnings history relative to that of their spouse (or former spouse): (a) a retired-worker benefit, (b) a spouse/widow only benefit, or (c) a dually entitled benefit. Retired-worker benefits are based entirely on a person's own earnings history, determined by his or her Primary Insurance Amount (PIA). The PIA is the amount the Social Security Administration calculates an individual will receive based on that individual's work history. Divorced persons may also qualify for a spouse or widow benefit provided that their marriage lasted at least ten years. Spouse and divorced-spouse benefits are up to 50 percent of the spouse's (or former spouse's) worker benefit. Widow benefits reflect up to 100 percent of the deceased spouse's benefit. An individual entitled to his or her own retired-worker benefit and to a benefit on the earnings record of a spouse (or former spouse) that yields a larger benefit payment is referred to as a dually entitled beneficiary. Should a woman's retired-worker benefit be higher than the spouse or widow benefit, she would receive the retired-worker benefit and not be considered to be dually entitled.

RESULTS

Earnings Trajectories of Divorced Women

Figure 8.1 presents estimates of the long-term effect of divorce on the inflation-adjusted Social Security earnings of a cohort of women (ages twenty-two to thirty-six in 1971) experiencing a marital dissolution between 1971 and 1976 relative to a comparison group of continuously married women. For this analysis, we observe the years 1968 through 1994 in order to include the prime working ages of our sample (the oldest women are fifty-nine in 1994). The points plotted in each line are the parameter estimates associated with the three *pre* and twenty-two *post* variables along with that from the year of the marital separation. These parameter estimates are taken from the parsimonious fixed-effects model that controls for age, age-squared, and year effects (along with the year of the separation numbered at zero). To examine the impact of subsequent marital events following a divorce, the figure also contains similar parameter estimates of the differences in earnings for divorced women who remarry and those who do not relative to a continuously married comparison group.

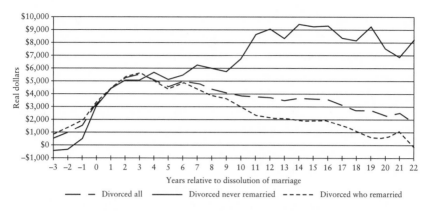

Figure 8.1 Fixed-effects estimates of annual Social Security earnings for divorced women by remarriage status, baseline continuously married women

Several findings stand out. First, in the second and third years preceding the marital dissolution, the earnings gap between the married and divorced groups is not statistically significant, although a modest anticipatory increase can be observed.[12] The lack of statistical significance between the married and divorced groups prior to the separation is important in establishing the inference that subsequent changes in behavior are due to the divorce rather than prior cross-group differences. Second, in the year following marital dissolution, we find a statistically significant increase ($P = .000$) in earnings of $4,361 for divorced women relative to the baseline. Third, the increase in the average earnings of women who divorced was substantively and statistically greater than for continuously married women in each subsequent year after the dissolution, up to two decades after the event. Overall, the results show a strong association between marital dissolution and the path of women's earnings over the life course.

The results also highlight distinctive differences by remarriage status. Notably, the positive effects of marital dissolution are greater in size, have stronger patterns of statistical significance, and are more durable over time for divorced women who never remarry relative to those who do. As Figure 8.1 depicts, the trajectories of the different divorce subsamples begin to differentiate around five years after the event. From that point onward, the earnings trajectory of divorced women who do not remarry steadily increases up to the last observed year. By contrast, the positive effect of marital dissolution on earnings for divorced women who remarried remains statistically significant up to ten years after the event (rather than twenty-two years), at which point their earnings seem to approach their predissolution levels.

We also calculated a second set of fixed-effects estimates for the earnings impact of divorce to see whether the relationships found in the main model presented in Figure 8.1 would hold when we controlled for time-varying measures of educational level and the number of children. Web Appendix Table A8.2 reports the coefficients for all of the covariates. In short, adding the time-varying education and total children variables does not change the systematic earnings differences shown in Figure 8.1 between women who divorced and women who stayed married, in size or significance. Also, the distinct earnings trajectories by remarriage observed in the main model hold in model 2. In terms of the covariates, education and total children have, not surprisingly, statistically significant effects on women's earnings. Obtaining a bachelor's degree increased women's earnings, on average, by \$6,193 ($P = .000$); whereas, each child reduced women's earnings by \$3,427 ($P = .000$), but only up to a certain point, shown by the positive and significant coefficient for total children squared. Age and age-squared have the expected effects.

Social Security Claiming Age, Benefit Type, and Amount

Table 8.1 presents estimates of various retirement-related outcomes among women who reached age sixty-six by 2008 (women ages twenty-nine through thirty-seven in 1971), claimed initial benefits at age sixty-two or older, and never received Social Security disability benefits. Comparing the continuously married and divorced groups reveals substantial (and statistically significant) differences in the claiming age distributions. In essence, women who divorced had a higher propensity to delay claiming Social Security. Approximately 28 percent of divorced women claimed their initial benefit at or after age sixty-five, whereas only 15 percent of the continuously married women did so. By contrast, continuously married women had the highest proportion claiming at Social Security's early retirement age of sixty-two (66 percent). Divorced women tend to retire later than the continuously married, and these group differences expand when we exclude divorced women who remarried.

Table 8.1 also demonstrates sharp differences in initial benefit type by marital experience. The share of divorced women drawing retired-worker-only benefits determined solely by their own earnings history is significantly higher (60 percent) than the share among those who are continuously married (43 percent). By remarriage status, the differences appear greater, with divorced women who never remarried registering a 20-percentage-point higher proportion of retired-worker benefits than continuously married women. Conversely, continuously married women had more than double the proportion drawing spouse- or widow-only benefits, based entirely on the earnings history of their husbands.

Results also reveal statistically significant differences in the initial monthly benefit amount by marital experience. Women who divorced had an average initial benefit of $875, whereas the average benefit

TABLE 8.1

Estimates of retirement outcomes: Retirement-age women with a Social Security benefit by 2008, by marital group

		DIVORCED COHORT		
	Married	*All*	*Never remarried*	*Remarried*
PERCENTAGE WHO . . .				
Claimed at 62	66.2	52.2*	44.5**	55.6
Claimed at 63 or 64	18.8	20.0	21.2	19.5
Claimed at 65 or older	15.1	27.8**	34.3**	25.0
Total	100	100	100	100
TYPE OF BENEFIT AT INITIAL CLAIMING (%)				
Retired worker only	42.9	59.6*	63.3**	57.9
Dually entitled	33.4	29.8	23.3	32.8
Spouse or widow only	23.7	10.5*	13.3**	9.3**
Total	100	100	100	100
Mean initial benefit	$756	$875**	$911*	$858*
N =	929	148	45	103

N O T E S : Authors used Survey of Income and Program Participation person weights adjusted for nonmatches. Sample excludes women who had ever qualified for Social Security disability benefits, women who had drawn their initial benefit before age 62, and women who had not reached age 66 by 2008.

Estimates with superscripts differ significantly from continuously married: *p < .05 level, **p < .01 (two-tailed t-test for comparing proportions of two subsamples). Standard errors account for SIPP's complex survey design.

amount for their married counterparts was $756. This difference is driven, in part, by the distribution of benefit types. Higher proportions of divorced women in our sample received retired-worker benefits, which tend to yield larger benefits than spouse-only benefits. Divorced women who never remarried had the highest monthly benefit of $911. In addition, when we looked at the benefit levels of retired-worker beneficiaries by marital experience, divorced women who never remarried had the highest monthly benefit of the marital groups ($1,097; results not shown in table).

It is important to note that retirement-age married women likely reside in the same household as their husbands, who would probably also have a Social Security benefit. We investigated the benefit level of the husbands of the continuously married women using linkages between the SIPP data and the Master Beneficiary Record of the Social Security Administration and found that their average initial benefit was $1,302. Thus, among the continuously-married-women group, the combined average initial benefit was $2,231, a figure significantly higher than that for divorced women who do not remarry. The family incomes of retired married women living with their spouses will be much higher than for divorced women residing alone.

Similarly, divorced women who remarry are also more likely to have partners who receive their own Social Security benefit. We again investigated this possibility for the women in our sample and found that the average benefit amount among their spouses was $1,210. When combined with their own average benefit of $858, the total benefit ($2,068) for the married households exceeds the average among those never remarried ($991) by a large margin.

CONCLUSIONS

The goal of this chapter was to shed light on the long-term financial consequences of marital dissolution for women. Using the SSA's longitudinal earnings and benefit records matched to a nationally representative sample of U.S. women in the 2004 SIPP, we compared the earnings trajectories of women who experienced a marital dissolution between 1971 and 1976 to similar married women who did not divorce. Fixed-effects models allowed us to account for different characteristics of those who divorced during this time and to control for several important time-varying characteristics such as education and children.

Our findings suggest that marital dissolution results in increases in women's career earnings trajectories over the life course. We consistently found substantial and significant positive effects of marital dissolution on women's earnings, even when controlling for children and education. These effects were more sustained over the life course than previously recognized, lasting more than two decades after the event.

Another key finding is that subsequent marital events moderate the earnings implications of divorce from a first marriage. The earnings gains associated with divorce were larger and longer-lasting among divorced women who never remarried relative to those who did. This is consistent with the notion that remarriage reduces women's labor supply. The pattern also suggests that estimates of the earnings consequences of marital dissolution that include women who eventually remarry may underestimate the long-run earnings response to divorce itself.

A final result relates to the relationship between divorce and women's Social Security retirement benefits. Our analysis shows that the women who experienced a marital dissolution in the 1970s were less dependent on their spouses for their Social Security benefits upon retirement entry than the control group. Divorced women not only relied more on their own earnings history than women who stayed married, but also claimed their initial retirement benefit later in the life course and had higher average benefit amounts. Overall, divorced women delay retirement and receive larger initial benefits. An important caveat is that both married and remarried women typically reside in the same household as their spouse. Consequently, their total household Social Security benefit, as we discussed, would be significantly greater than that of divorced women living alone.

One policy implication of our results, therefore, is that trends in marriage behavior that affect long-term earnings patterns can influence whether women will receive initial Social Security benefits as a worker or as a spouse or widow. We find that a greater proportion of divorced women initially claimed benefits as a retired worker, a benefit based solely off their own earnings records. This could possibly be due to having relatively higher lifetime Social Security earnings than their ex-spouse or not meeting the ten-year marriage duration requirement for divorced spouse or widow benefits. Changes to the marriage duration requirement, for example, would be expected to have an impact on the distribution of these benefit types and, thus, consequences for women's retirement income.

Another observation that can be drawn from the study is that marriage and remarriage reduce the pressure the average individual faces economically, holding other factors constant. During working life, marriage comes with additional pressures and expectations, but also with additional resources and supports. This is reflected in the lower earnings trajectories of continuously married and remarried women in this study that are reflective of both additional demands and resources. Divorce reduces the level of resources available to meet existing burdens and places pressure for additional earnings on women, as reflected in the sharp increases in their earnings paths observed in this study. However, it is well known that the households of divorced women nonetheless suffer from a reduced standard of living. Thus, although the sharply higher earnings paths of divorced women contribute to greater Social Security benefits, compared to married households, they remain at a large disadvantage economically. Beyond potential changes that might be made in benefit formulas to narrow this gap across divorced and nondivorced women, it is important for individuals to realize that their own choices can have large and lasting effects on their own economic well-being: Forming durable and lasting relationships is an important ingredient in the recipe for personal economic well-being.

These results should be interpreted in the context of several important limitations. First, they may not be generalizable to more recent divorces. Increases in women's educational attainment, employment, and earnings may reduce differences between the economic trajectories of continuously married and divorced women. Second, the results refer to women who survived to 2004. Some women who experienced a marital dissolution in the 1970s or who never divorced died before 2004. Our analysis does not observe such individuals. Third, as previously noted, our measure of earnings does not include noncovered employment or amounts above the taxable maximum. However, this approach should not produce substantial distortions in our estimations of the average effects of divorce. Despite these limitations, documenting the patterns presented in this chapter is a necessary first step in advancing our understanding of the effects of a family composition change on an individual's life course.

NOTES

1. To protect respondent confidentiality, potentially identifying information is removed after the data are linked. All users of the data must be approved by SSA and the Census Bureau, and the data must be used for approved research projects only and analyzed at a secured site.

2. Specifically, we estimated a logistic regression on the likelihood of an administrative match for SIPP wave 2 female respondents (over age eighteen) across a range of characteristics, including age, age-squared, education, number of children, race/ethnicity, family income, and marital history. We used the regression results to calculate the match probability as a function of the characteristics.

3. The estimation equation also includes a set of dummy variables denoting the year of each observation.

4. The full retirement age is the age at which a person may first become entitled to unreduced retirement benefits. The full retirement age for women who turned age twenty-nine in 1971 is 65 and 10 months.

5. While we follow the literature in establishing the timing of divorce beginning with separation, altering this scheme to begin with the date of divorce would likely result in larger estimates of earnings increases during the separation period prior to divorce. This is because in the current analysis, as will be seen, we find sizeable and significant increases in earnings around the time of separation for those who ultimately divorce.

6. Prior to 1982, SSA's administrative records only contain information on earnings from work covered by the Social Security program.

7. The level of a worker's earnings subject to this cap, and the share of workers with earnings above it, has changed over time. In 1975, for example, around 15 percent of covered workers had earnings over the maximum. Since 1983, the proportion of covered workers in the population with earnings above the maximum has fluctuated around 6 percent (SSA 2010).

8. As previously mentioned, examples from the job displacement literature can be found in Couch, Jolly, and Placzek (2009); Couch and Placzek (2010); and Couch, Jolly, and Placzek (2011).

9. SIPP reports the total number of children, but only the dates of birth for the oldest and youngest child. For women with more than two children, we assume that the birth dates of additional children are evenly distributed between the birth years of the oldest and youngest child. The independent variable that measures the number of children under age eighteen in a given year is based on this assumption.

10. Widow(er)s may receive benefits at age sixty.

11. For a chart of incremental changes in the full retirement age (FRA) by birth year, see www.socialsecurity.gov/retire2/agereduction.htm.

12. We followed the prior literature in dating marital dissolution from the point of separation. However, if we had dated it from the time of divorce, the significant increases in earnings at the time of separation would be seen as an anticipatory effect of the divorce.

REFERENCES

Aassve, Arnstein, Gianni Betti, Stefano Mazzuco, and Letizia Mencarini. 2007. "Marital Disruption and Economic Well-Being: A Comparative Analysis." *Journal of the Royal Statistical Society, Series A* 170(3): 781–99.

Becker, Gary S. 1981. *A Treatise on the Family.* Cambridge, MA: Harvard University Press.

Bianchi, Suzanne. 2000. "Maternal Employment and Time with Children: Dramatic Change or Surprising Continuity?" *Demography* 37(4): 401–14.

Blau, Francine D., and Lawrence M. Kahn. 2007. "Changes in the Labor Supply Behavior of Married Women: 1980–2000." *Journal of Labor Economics* 25(3): 393–437.

Bradbury, Katherine, and Jane Katz. 2002. "Women's Labor Market Involvement and Family Income Mobility when Marriages End." *New England Economic Review* Q4: 41–74.

Burstein, Nancy R. 2007. "Economic Influences on Marriage and Divorce." *Journal of Policy Analysis and Management* 26(2): 387–429.

Burkhauser, Richard V., Greg J. Duncan, Richard Hauser, and Roland Berntsen. 1991. "Wife or Frau, Women Do Worse: A Comparison of Women and Men in the United States and Germany After Marital Dissolution." *Demography* 28(3): 353–60.

Carlson, Barbara L., and Stephen Williams. 2001. "A Comparison of Two Methods to Adjust Weights for Non-Response: Propensity Modeling and Weighting Class Adjustments." In *Proceedings of the Annual Meeting of the American Statistical Association.* Alexandria, VA: American Statistical Association.

Cherlin, Andrew J. 1992. *Marriage, Divorce, Remarriage,* rev. ed. Cambridge, MA: Harvard University Press.

Couch, Kenneth A., Mary Daly, and Douglas Wolf. 1999. "Time? Money? Both? The Allocation of Resources to Older Parents." *Demography* 36(2): 219–32.

Couch, Kenneth A., Nicholas Jolly, and Dana Placzek. 2009. "Earnings Losses of Older Displaced Workers: A Detailed Analysis using Administrative Data." *Research on Aging* 21(1): 17–40.

Couch, Kenneth A., Nicholas Jolly, and Dana Placzek. 2011. "Earnings Losses of Displaced Workers and the Business Cycle." *Economics Letters* 111(1): 16–19.

Couch, Kenneth A., and Dana Placzek. 2010. "Earnings Impacts of Job Displacement Revisited." *American Economic Review* 100(1): 572–89.

Dewilde, Caroline, and Wilfred Uunk. 2008. "Remarriage as a Way to Overcome the Financial Consequences of Divorce." *European Sociological Review* 24(3): 393–407.

Duncan, Greg J., and Saul D. Hoffman. 1985. "Economic Consequences of Marital Instability." In *Horizontal Equity, Uncertainty, and Well-Being*, Martin David and Timothy Smeeding (Eds.). University of Chicago Press, 427–67.

Finnie, Ross. 1993. "Women, Men, and the Economic Consequences of Divorce: Evidence from Canadian Longitudinal Data." *Canadian Review of Sociology and Anthropology* 30:205–41.

Gadalla, Tahany M. 2009. "Impact of Marital Dissolution on Men's and Women's Incomes: A Longitudinal Study." *Journal of Divorce and Remarriage* 50:55–65.

Gangl, Markus, and Andrea Ziefle. 2009. "Motherhood, Labor Force Behavior, and Women's Careers: An Empirical Assessment of the Wage Penalty for Motherhood in Britain, Germany, and the United States." *Demography* 46(2): 341–69.

Goldstein, Joshua, and Catherine Kenney. 2001. "Marriage Delayed or Marriage Forgone? New Cohort Forecasts of First Marriage for U.S. Women." *American Sociological Review* 66:506–19.

Haurin, Donald R. 1989. "Women's Labor Market Reactions to Family Disruptions." *The Review of Economics and Statistics* 89:54–61.

Hoffman, Saul, and Greg Duncan. 1988. "What Are the Economic Consequences of Divorce?" *Demography* 25:641–45.

Holden, Karen C., and H. D. Kuo. 1996. "Complex Marital Histories and Economic Well-Being: The Continuing Legacy of Divorce and Widowhood as the HRS Cohort Approaches Retirement." *The Gerontologist* 36(3): 383–90.

Holden, Karen C., and Pamela J. Smock. 1991. "The Economic Costs of Marital Dissolution: Why Do Women Bear a Disproportionate Cost?" *Annual Review of Sociology* 17:51–78.

Jansen, Mieke, Dimitri Mortelmans, and Laurent Snoeckx. 2009. "Repartnering and (Re-) employment: Strategies to Cope with the Economic Consequences of Partnership Dissolution." *Journal of Marriage and the Family* 71:1271–93.

Johnson, William R., and Jonathan Skinner. 1986. "Labor Supply and Marital Separation." *American Economic Review* 76(3): 455–69.

Johnson, William R., and Jonathan Skinner. 1988. "Accounting for Changes in the Labor Supply of Recently Divorced Women." *Journal of Human Resources* 23:417–36.

Kreider, Rose M. 2008. "Living Arrangements of Children: 2004." *Current Population Reports*. Washington, DC: U.S. Census Bureau, 70–114.

Lupton, Joseph P., and James P. Smith. 2003. "Marriage, Assets, and Saving." In S. Grossbard-Shechtman (Ed.) *Marriage and the Economy: Theory and Evidence from Advanced Industrial Societies*. New York: Cambridge University Press.

McKeever, Matthew, and Nicholas H. Wolfinger. 2001. "Reexamining the Economic Costs of Marital Disruption for Women." *Social Science Quarterly* 82(1): 202–17.

McNabb, Jennifer, David Timmons, Jae Song, and Carolyn Puckett. 2009. "Uses of Administrative Data at the Social Security Administration." *Social Security Bulletin* 69(1): 75–84.

Mueller, Richard E. 2005. "The Effect of Marital Dissolution on the Labour Supply of Males and Females: Evidence from Canada." *The Journal of Socio-Economics* 34:787–809.

Munnell, Alicia H., and Natalia Zhivan. 2006. "Earnings and Women's Retirement Security." Center for Retirement Research WP 2006–12, Boston College.

Nelson Jr., William J. 1985. "Employment Covered Under the Social Security Program, 1935–1984." *Social Security Bulletin* 48(4): 33–39.

Olsen, Anya, and Russell Hudson. 2009. "Social Security Administration's Master Earnings File: Background Information." *Social Security Bulletin* 69(3): 29–45.

Sayer, Liana C., and Suzanne M. Bianchi. 2000. "Women's Economic Independence and the Probability of Divorce," *Journal of Family Issues* 21(7): 906–43.

Smock, Pamela J. 1993. "The Economic Costs of Marital Disruption for Young Women over the Past Two Decades." *Demography* 30(3): 353–571.

Smock, Pamela J. 1994. "Gender and the Short-Run Economic Consequences of Marital Disruption." *Social Forces* 73(1): 243–62.

Smock, Pamela J., Wendy Manning, and Sanjiv Gupta. 1999. "The Effect of Marriage and Divorce on Women's Economic Well-Being." *American Sociological Review* 64(6): 794–812.

Social Security Administration [SSA]. 2010. *Annual Statistical Supplement, 2009*. Washington, DC: U.S. Government Printing Office.

Stevenson, Betsey, and Justin Wolfers. 2007. "Marriage and Divorce: Changes and their Driving Forces." *Journal of Economic Perspectives* 21(2): 27–52.

Tamborini, Christopher R., Howard M. Iams, and Kevin Whitman. 2009. "Marital History, Race, and Social Security Spouse and Widow Benefit Eligibility in the United States." *Research on Aging* 31(5): 577–605.

Tamborini, Christopher R., Howard M. Iams, and Gayle L. Reznik. 2012. "Women's Earnings Before and After Marital Dissolution: Evidence from Longitudinal Earnings Records Matched to Survey Data." *Journal of Family and Economic Issues* 33(1): 69–82.

Tamborini, Christopher R., and Kevin Whitman. 2010. "Lowering Social Security's Duration-of-Marriage Requirement: Distributional Effects for Future Female Retirees." *Journal of Women & Aging* 22(3): 184–203.

Teachman, Jay D., and Kathleen M. Paasch. 1994. "Financial Impact of Divorce on Children and Their Families." *The Future of Children* 4(1): 63–83.

Waite, Linda J., and Maggie Gallagher. 2000. *The Case for Marriage: Why Married People are Happier, Healthier, and Better Off Financially.* New York: Doubleday.

Wilmoth, Janet, and Gregor Koso. 2002. "Does Marital History Matter? Marital Status and Wealth Outcomes Among Preretirement Adults." *Journal of Marriage and Family* 64:254–68.

Zagorsky, Jay L. 2005. "Marriage and Divorce's Impact on Wealth." *Journal of Sociology* 41(4): 406–24.

Zissimopoulos, Julie M. 2009. "Gain and Loss: Marriage and Wealth Changes over Time." MRRC Working Paper No. 2009–213. Ann Arbor, MI: University of Michigan Retirement Research Center.

Zissimopoulos, Julie M., Benjamin Karney, and Amy Rauer. 2008. "Marital Histories and Economic Well-Being." MRRC Working Paper 2008–180. Ann Arbor, MI: University of Michigan Retirement Research Center.

CHAPTER NINE

Marriage and Wealth Changes at Older Ages

Julie M. Zissimopoulos

INTRODUCTION

Family composition has changed dramatically over the past twenty-five years. Divorce rates rapidly increased from the late 1960s through the 1980s, and remarriage rates declined (Cherlin 1992). Changes in family or household composition, whether planned or unexpected, have both immediate and long-term economic consequences for individuals. Considerable research has established a correlation between marital and socioeconomic status: in particular, a positive relationship between marriage and the earnings of males (Korenman and Neumark 1991; Lundberg and Rose 2002; Loughran and Zissimopoulos 2009). Much less attention has been paid to the effect of marriage on women's earnings, due to the strong correlation between marriage and childbirth. The work of Loughran and Zissimopoulos (2009), who found that marriage lowers female wages in the year that the marriage takes place and reduces subsequent growth in wages during the years that follow, and research by Miller (2011), who found that delayed marriage and childbearing

The research reported herein was pursuant to a grant from the U.S. Social Security Administration (SSA) funded as part of the Retirement Research Consortium (RRC). The findings and conclusions expressed are solely those of the authors and do not represent the views of SSA, any agency of the federal government or the RRC. I would like to thank Joanna Carroll for her excellent programming assistance and the Schaeffer Center for Health Policy and Economics for its support of this research.

increase women's wages, are the exceptions. New evidence presented in this book shows a lasting effect of marriage and divorce on the earnings of women. Amalia Miller's research in Chapter 7 reveals a lasting association between delayed initial family formation and higher earnings over decades. In Chapter 8, Kenneth Couch and coauthors present new evidence that divorce increases women's labor earnings over a lifetime.

Earnings are undoubtedly a critical measure of well-being. Yet wealth, as distinct from earnings, is an important complementary measure—arguably the most important one for older individuals because it represents the resources that they will have available for consumption during retirement. But despite its importance, far less is understood about the effect of marriage on wealth than about the effect of marriage on earnings. A focus of other early studies had been the relative low level of wealth of widows compared with that of other individuals (Hurd and Wise 1989; Smith 1995; Zick and Holden 2000). A more recent study found that older married couples have higher wealth than unmarried individuals and that wealth increased with the duration of the marriage (Lupton and Smith 2003). Zissimopoulos et al. (2008) confirmed this relationship between marriage, length of marriage, and wealth. They found that, for men, the association was explained by their lifetime earnings; but the same did not apply to women. For women, including Social Security and pension wealth into a measure of household wealth reduced wealth differences between married and unmarried women.

There are many hypotheses on the manner in which marriage affects wealth. An important implication of economic models of savings with no uncertainty (or models of agents maximizing expected utility) and perfect capital markets is that an individual's permanent income determines consumption. This suggests that people consume increases in their permanent income, while they save increases that are temporary. Accordingly, one hypothesis of how a change in marital status would affect wealth is that a permanent loss in income from divorce or widowing would reduce consumption and have no impact on wealth. Yet if a person expects a separation or divorce to be temporary, this may lead him or her to save less in order to avoid a drop in consumption. Indeed, a study by Lupton and Smith (2003) supports this hypothesis, finding that the shorter the time an individual remains unmarried, the more common it is that the individual will spend more than his or her disposable income, as the person attempts to maintain prior levels of consumption. Another study found declines in savings before a divorce took place (Zagorsky 2005).

There are several other hypotheses. Wealth may result from the economies of scale that marriage provides (Waite 1995): Married couples may jointly consume many goods and services (e.g., entertainment, housing) for the same cost as a single person, which may translate into additional wealth or additional consumption. Married couples may save more to finance the consumption of children or to leave them bequests (Hurd, Smith, and Zissimopoulos 2007). Marriage may also produce better health, leading married couples to save more to insure against outliving their resources (Lillard and Weiss 1996). Conversely, because marriage reduces the risk associated with fluctuations in income, it may have the opposite effect, as people feel less need to save as a precaution against income or other shocks (Mincer 1978).

Marriage and wealth are potentially associated in many ways, but identifying the relationship between marriage and wealth in an empirical manner is challenging because individuals are not randomly sorted into marriage. For example, couples in low-income families are more likely to divorce or to be widowed than couples in high-income families. In addition, previous empirical studies have been hindered by a lack of control measures for permanent income. Another obstacle is the use of cross-sectional surveys and short panels ill-suited for distinguishing between selection into marriage or divorce based on characteristics that are also associated with low economic status and may be unobserved (e.g., low ability) and wealth levels that are a direct result of a change in marital status.

In this chapter, we present our study of the relationship between changes in wealth and marital status among individuals over age fifty. For this work we employed eight waves of panel data from the Health and Retirement Study (HRS). This research advances understanding of this topic in several ways. First, it incorporates a rich set of covariates into models of change in wealth, so that the resulting estimates are independent of the effects of current and lifetime earnings, risk of mortality, and other characteristics that vary by marital status. Second, it measures the magnitude of wealth loss and gain associated with divorce, widowing, and remarriage at ages when wealth holdings are often at their peak.

Third, it estimates the change in wealth before and after a change in marital status, so that the change in wealth measured is not the result of individuals entering or leaving the household. This approach also enabled us to factor out other sources of unobserved differences from our estimates of the effect of marital status on wealth.

In the next section we describe the data and how we derived key variables. Following that we present our results for levels and changes in wealth, and for individuals who do and do not change marital status.

DATA

Our research relied on longitudinal data from the HRS, a set of biennial surveys first fielded in 1992 and 1993 by the University of Michigan. Its objective is to monitor economic transitions in work, income, and wealth, and changes in health among Americans over fifty.[1] We used data from annual survey waves from 1992 to 1996, and then from biennial waves to 2006.[2] Our sample included birth cohorts from 1947 and earlier. In addition, we used restricted data on Social Security earnings to compute a measure of lifetime earnings for each individual. We derived variables related to marital history (e.g., all prior marriages, divorces, and widowing) on the basis of the raw HRS files. Most of the other variables that we used in the study are from the RAND HRS Data file, Version I.[3]

Marital Status

We categorized respondents at a given point in time as married, divorced, widowed, partnered, or never married. For some analyses, we used respondents' reports of past marital events to distinguish between married and remarried individuals. Changes over the panel were based on respondents' reports of any changes between waves. We grouped these changes into six categories: (1) separated to divorced, (2) married to divorced, (3) married to widowed, (4) divorced to married, (5) widowed to married, and (6) other single (partnered or never married) to married.

Lifetime Earnings

We calculated lifetime earnings on the basis of historical earnings reported to the Social Security Administration.[4] The administrative records are accurate, less subject to measurement error than self-reported earnings from household surveys, and they cover a long history of earnings. They are, however, limited in two ways: First, the level of earnings is reported only up to the Social Security maximum. This maximum level changed over time, as did the number of individuals whose earnings were above the maximum. Second, individuals employed in a sector not covered by Social Security had no earnings records for the years they were employed in that uncovered sector.[5] We calculated lifetime earnings as the present discounted value (3 percent real interest rate) of real Social Security earnings adjusted to 2006 dollars using the CPI-U-RS (Consumer Price Index Research Series Using Current Methods). We also adjusted earnings of high earners because Social Security earnings are reported only up to a maximum level.

Mortality Risk, Risk Aversion, and Time Rate of Preference

Mortality risk is a respondent's subjective assessment of the probability that he or she will live to age seventy-five and eighty-five on a scale of 0 to 100. We included it in our empirical models as an individual's deviation from what Social Security life tables, based on respondent's sex and age, state as that individual's mortality risk. With regard to risk aversion, our basis for categorizing an individual's level was a series of questions that asked respondents to choose between pairs of jobs. One job would guarantee current family income, while the other would offer the chance to increase income but would carry a risk of losing income. Drawing from responses to these questions, we categorized respondents' level of risk aversion in four groups from low to high. In terms of respondents' time rate of preference, we measured it by their responses to the length of time they use for financial planning. The answers are categorical, ranging from a few months to ten or more years.

Wealth

Our main outcome measures were household wealth and change in wealth. We defined wealth as housing plus nonhousing wealth, and computed it as the sum of wealth from real estate, businesses, IRAs, stocks, bonds, checking accounts, CDs, and housing, less the value of a mortgage, home loans, and other debt. We imputed missing data on wealth.[6] In some of our analyses, we used information about whether a respondent owned a pension and if he or she did, the type of pension owned (e.g., defined benefit, defined contribution, or both). A married couple will need to finance the consumption of at least two people in retirement, thus we expect couples to have more wealth than singles. Zissimopoulos et al. (2008) found married couples have about 2.5 times the mean wealth that singles do and almost 4 times the median wealth that singles have. There is no consensus as to what should be an equivalent amount of wealth for a single person relative to a married person. While we have widely used measures of household income based on equivalence scales, no single accepted measure for wealth exists. Because of economies of scale, we would expect couples to have just under twice as much wealth as singles.

RESULTS

Changes in marital status occur over the lifespan, even at older ages. We present the distribution of current marital status and future changes in marital status over the next fourteen years in Table 9.1. Among the birth cohort 1931–41, 70 percent were either married or remarried in 1992 and remained so over the next fourteen years. Another 15 percent were not married (divorced or widowed) and stayed so over this time period. Fifteen percent of the sample—on average individuals age fifty-five—changed marital status during this period: About 4 percent of the married respondents divorced and 10 percent were widowed. Just over one percent of the individuals who were divorced or widowed remarried at some point in the fourteen years.

The level of wealth this birth cohort held in 1992 varied with marital status in that year. Consistent with prior findings, we find married individuals have more wealth than unmarried individuals. We can gain insight into the relationship between marital status and wealth by examining wealth levels by current marital status combined with future changes in marital status over the next fourteen years. The first three rows in Table 9.1 are groups that, as of 1992, had not experienced a marital disruption. The data in Table 9.1 show that respondents who were married in 1992 and had no changes in marital status over the next fourteen years had higher mean and median wealth than married respondents who would eventually divorce or be widowed. This group of continuously married individuals had, on average, $363,814 in housing

TABLE 9.1

Wealth, lifetime, and current earnings in 1992 by marital status changes from 1992 through 2006

	N	Percentage	MEDIAN Wealth	MEAN Wealth	MEAN LTE	MEAN Earnings	RATIO Wealth/LTE
Married in 1992 & no change	5,472	51.70	$173,457	$363,814	$1,241,020	$57,201	0.293
Married in 1992 & divorced	204	1.93	99,919	278,365	1,026,509	60,821	0.271
Married in 1992 & widowed	760	7.18	121,618	254,362	923,538	37,259	0.275
Remarried in 1992 & no change	1,939	18.32	125,311	281,843	1,346,968	57,668	0.209
Remarried in 1992 & divorced	203	1.92	85,080	232,421	1,215,924	46,496	0.191
Remarried in 1992 & ever widowed	322	3.04	98,271	201,530	1,021,238	35,652	0.197
Divorced in 1992 & no change	962	9.09	33,175	116,572	636,788	24,444	0.183
Divorced in 1992 & ever remarried	106	1.00	105,525	188,366	888,625	42,503	0.212
Widowed in 1992 & no change	583	5.51	47,684	125,835	403,610	14,904	0.312
Widowed in 1992 & ever remarried	34	0.32	129,137	199,769	521,556	26,421	0.383
All	10,585	100	$129,928	$293,975	$1,127,296	$49,511	0.261

SOURCE: Health and Retirement Survey 1992–2006.

NOTES: Sample birth cohort 1931–1941 in 1992 (HRS wave 1). Excludes 47 observations with unknown marital status. Wealth reported in 2006 dollars. LTE is lifetime earnings.

and nonhousing wealth (not including pension wealth). In contrast, married respondents who would eventually divorce had, on average, $278,365 in wealth from these sources, and married respondents who would be widowed, $254,362. Age differences by group were small and are thus unlikely to account for the mean and median differences.

Remarried individuals who stayed married throughout the fourteen years had lower average wealth ($281,843) than married individuals who remained married over the course of the panel. Looking at mean and median wealth, remarried individuals who stayed married had only marginally higher wealth than married individuals who would go on to divorce or be widowed. All individuals who were not married had lower mean wealth than married individuals. However, at the median, the wealth of not-married individuals who remarried over the course of the panel was higher than that of some married individuals. Focusing specifically on the not-married groups, we found that the mean wealth of divorced ($116,572) and widowed ($125,835) individuals who did not remarry was about 60 percent of the mean wealth of not-married individuals who went on to remarry—$188,366 for those who remarried after being divorced, and $199,769 for those who remarried after being widowed.

The differences we saw in levels of wealth at around age fifty-five by current and future marital status may have resulted from several things. The source could have been a loss of wealth due to divorce or widowing; or it may have been observable differences in earnings or preferences for savings, for example. Different marital groups may save at similar rates, for instance, but some groups may have lower levels of income from which to draw savings. In terms of the second possibility, we compared married individuals who stayed married with married individuals who went on to divorce and found this not to have been the case: Lifetime earnings and current earnings were similar between these two groups (Table 9.1). Consequently, differences in earnings over the lifecycle were unlikely to have accounted for the differences in wealth; thus, the results suggest that other differences, for example in terms of preferences for savings or risk, can explain some of wealth difference between married and divorced individuals.

In contrast to individuals who go on to divorce, remarried individuals in 1992 (either after divorce or widowing) who stayed remarried had slightly higher lifetime earnings and the same current earnings as individuals who remained in their original marriage over the course of the panel. Yet the mean wealth of the remarried group was 77 percent of the wealth of individuals who stayed in their original marriage. This finding is consistent with a long-lasting effect of divorce or widowing on wealth levels near retirement.

Changes in Wealth by Marital Status

The magnitude of the change in wealth over time among individuals whose marital status changes will be dominated by the change in household wealth that stems from individuals moving out of the household (e.g., as part of a divorce) or moving into the household (e.g., after a marriage). To study wealth change in the panel, we separately examined individuals who did and did not change their marital status over four waves or six years. For individuals who changed status, we examined levels of wealth and changes in wealth during three phases: (1) the two waves prior to the change in marital status (t–1 and t); (2) the two years over which the change in marital status occurred (t and t+1); and (3) the two years after the change in marital status occurred (t+1 and t+2). In this way, we limited our sample to individuals in four consecutive waves of data and excluded individuals who had more than one marital change between survey waves.[7] We present our results in Table 9.2.[8]

Among married and separated individuals who divorced between waves, their wealth had already been declining in the wave (or waves) before the divorce. Married individuals who were divorced about two years later, at time t+1 in Table 9.2, experienced a $39,918 loss in wealth while married, from time (t–1) to (t)—in other words, a loss of 14 percent of their wealth (at time (t–1) in Table 9.2). Over the two-year period during which a divorce occurred, married individuals lost another $132,779 in wealth, or about 53 percent of their total wealth (time t wealth in Table 9.2). We saw some recovery of wealth after the divorce, with an increase of $22,210, or 19 percent. Wealth loss before the divorce, and then saving after a divorce, led to a change in wealth of $62,128 from before, (t–1) to (t), to after, (t+2) – (t+1), the divorce (see the far-right-hand column of Table 9.2).

The wealth of separated individuals declined by $42,858 over the two years they were separated, (t) – (t–1), and prior to their divorce. This

TABLE 9.2

Wealth change among individuals changing and not changing marital status

Status at t−1 & t	Status at t+1 & t+2	N	Time				BEFORE STATUS CHANGE (IF ANY) Δt	DURING STATUS CHANGE (IF ANY) Δ(t+1)	AFTER STATUS CHANGE (IF ANY) Δ(t+2)	Δ(t+2) − Δt
			t−1	t	t+1	t+2	(t) − (t−1)	(t+1) − (t)	(t+2) − (t+1)	
STATUS CHANGES										
Married	Divorced	95	291,125	251,206	118,428	140,638	−39,918	−132,779	22,210	62,128
Separated	Divorced	60	160,531	117,673	161,568	171,434	−42,858	43,895	9,866	52,724
Married	Widowed	1,518	241,539	240,363	228,761	229,410	−1,176	−11,602	649	1,826
Divorced	Married	67	154,940	190,505	255,293	278,591	35,565	64,789	23,298	−12,267
Widowed	Married	65	288,861	312,180	447,799	508,835	23,318	135,619	61,036	37,718
Single	Married	76	264,758	310,712	384,774	398,305	45,954	74,061	13,531	−32,423
NO STATUS CHANGES										
Married	Married	38,129	334,700	354,144	374,555	399,985	19,444	20,411	25,430	5,986
Divorced	Divorced	3,823	135,639	146,657	152,885	169,882	11,019	6,227	16,997	5,978
Widowed	Widowed	8,276	170,562	174,701	171,482	170,578	4,140	−3,219	−904	−5,044
Single	Single	2,298	169,071	182,858	195,303	212,353	13,786	12,445	17,050	3,264

SOURCE: Health and Retirement Survey 1992–2006.

NOTES: Sample in top panel is individuals changing marital status and in four consecutive waves of data: time 't−1,' 't,' 't+1,' and 't+2.' Wealth in 2006 dollars. Single is never married or partnered. Trimmed top and bottom 2 percent of Δ.

amount constituted 27 percent of their wealth, at time (t–1). Unlike married couples that divorced, the wealth of separated individuals increased both during the wave in which they divorced and the subsequent wave(s) in which their marital status was stated as divorced.

All groups with a change in marital status experienced a positive change in wealth, but only *after* the marital change. In fact, the change in wealth from t+1 to t+2 for married to divorced, divorced to married, and married to married individuals was similar—between $22,000 and $25,000. But this change represents a larger percentage of wealth for individuals who went from married to divorced. In contrast, married individuals who were widowed had a much different experience than those who divorced: They experienced no significant loss of wealth in the years before the widowing occurred. But after the spouse died they experienced a decline in wealth of $11,602 over two years. This amount constituted only about 5 percent of their married (pre-widowed) wealth at time (t).

Divorced individuals who remarried over the fourteen-year period of the panel accumulated more assets while divorced than those who remained divorced. The change (t–1) to (t) was $35,565 for those who remarried, as opposed to $11,019 for those who stayed divorced. Assets entered the household with marriage, with levels of wealth increasing by $64,789 between the wave in which individuals were divorced and the wave in which they were married. After marriage, wealth then settled back to levels and rates similar to those of individuals who remained married. This is again consistent with the finding for individuals who remarry: A divorce earlier in life has long-lasting effects on wealth levels near retirement. In other words, differences are not fully explained by earnings or preferences. Similarly, widowed individuals and other singles (never married and partners) who got married showed substantial increases in wealth during the wave in which they got married. They then experienced a smaller increase in (in level and rate) in the following waves, when they were married.

The bottom panel of Table 9.2 shows that wealth increased over time for all individuals who did not change marital status during the fourteen years between 1992 and 2006. The exception was widows who were substantially older and, accordingly, may have been drawing on their wealth to support consumption. Married and remarried individuals experienced larger changes in wealth than divorced, widowed, or single (never married and partnered) individuals.

In sum, divorce is associated with a loss of wealth and this loss is likely to be long-lasting. The loss begins before the divorce occurs. Any recovery takes the form of increased savings after the divorce. In contrast, becoming widowed is associated with a much smaller loss of wealth. Both remarriage and marriage (for the never before married) are associated with increases in wealth at the time of the remarriage (or marriage). This may be expected, as an individual entering a household is likely to bring wealth along. In the years following the marriage, the household will increase its wealth at lower annual levels.

Empirical Estimates of Change in Wealth

We next empirically examined the two-year change in wealth by marital status among individuals who did not change their marital status over time in a multivariate framework. We controlled for basic demographic differences in sex, race, and age, and included year indicators. and show results in the first column of results in Table 9.3 (Model 1).[9] The second column of results in Table 9.3 (Model 2) shows estimates of the marginal effects of marital status on the change in wealth over two years, again controlling for basic demographics. It also includes other covariates that are likely to vary by marital status: lifetime earnings (which is a measure of permanent income); current earnings; education; number of children; ownership of pension wealth and type of pension; risk of mortality, risk aversion; and financial planning horizon.

The results from Model 1 show that remarried and all categories of not-married individuals accumulated less wealth over two years than did married individuals. By including the additional covariates (Model 2), we can explain all of the difference in the change in wealth between married and remarried individuals: The covariates reduce this difference in Model 1 and Model 2 by $1,192 (27 percent), so that it becomes no longer statistically significant. The additional covariates in Model 2 explain about 50 percent of the difference in the change in wealth between married and either divorced or widowed individuals. That is, the marginal effect is reduced from $-9,792 in Model 1 to $-5,146 in Model 2 for divorced individuals, and from $-15,886 to $-7,922 for widowed individuals. These same covariates explain about 30 percent of

TABLE 9.3
Estimation results for wealth change among individuals not changing marital status

	ALL		MEN		WOMEN	
	(1)	*(2)*	*(3)*	*(4)*	*(5)*	*(6)*
[Married]						
Remarried	−4,432^	−3,240	−4,012	−3,245	−4,806*	−3,054
Divorced	−9,792^	−5,146*	−5,136	−368	−12,397^	−7,390*
Widowed	−15,886^	−7,922^	−8,227	−4,133	−17,948^	−9,172^
Never married	−8,513*	−5,977	−8,128	−7,400	−9,174	−5,740
Partnered	−18,354^	−13,067^	−18,825^	−13,355*	−17,824^	−12,591*
Male	1,464	358				
Black	−12,887	−8,432	−15,232	−10,134	−11,210	−7,252
Other nonwhite	−9,549	−4,218	−9,968	−3,748	−9,087	−4,452
Age, year	yes	yes	yes	yes	yes	yes
Income + controls	no	yes	no	yes	no	yes
Mean dep.	19,949	19,949	21,986	21,986	18,312	18,312
Obs.	71,128	71,128	31,685	31,685	39,443	39,443

SOURCE: Health and Retirement Survey 1992–2006.

NOTES: Sample is individuals not changing marital status in consecutive waves, excluding unknown married (339 observations), birth cohorts 1931–1947. Wealth change trimmed top and bottom 2 percent. Other covariates included are education, number of children, subjective mortality risk, risk aversion, financial planning horizon, current earnings, present discounted value of lifetime earnings, pension ownership and type, birth cohort, and survey year. * indicates significant at the 5 percent level; ^ indicates significant at the 1 percent level. Dep is dependent variable = wealth change.

the difference in the change in wealth between married and either never married or partnered individuals. Overall, measures of socioeconomic status (e.g., lifetime and current earnings, education); pensions; and risk of mortality explain between 30 percent and 50 percent of the difference in wealth between married and not-married individuals.

Models 3 to 6 in Table 9.3 show the effects of marital status on the change in wealth separately for samples of men and women. For men, demographic characteristics (included in Model 3) explain the full range of differences in the change in wealth between married, remarried, and not-married men. The sole exception is partnered men. By including the additional covariates in Model 4, we explain about 30 percent of the difference in the change in wealth between married men and partnered men. For women, the change in wealth is lower for remarried and all not-married women than for married women. Here, never-married women are the one exception. The inclusion of the additional covariates in Model 6 explains all of the difference between married and remarried or never married women, 40 percent of the difference between married and divorced women, 49 percent of the difference between married and widowed women, and 30 percent of the difference between partnered and married women.

Although basic demographics explain all of the differences in the change in wealth by marital status for men (except for partnered men), this is not the case for women. In their case, the inclusion of additional controls for socioeconomic status and other household and individual characteristics explains all of the difference in the change in wealth between those who are married and those who are remarried. These controls also explain between one-third and one-half of the difference between married women and not-married women. Thus, for women, some of the variation in wealth change is left unexplained.

Empirical Models of the Change in the Change in Wealth

Demographic controls, measures of lifetime and current earnings, and other rich measures of characteristics accounted for all of the differences in the change in wealth by marital status among men. (The exception was partnered men.) Among women, they accounted for some of the difference for samples of individuals whose marital status did not change. If any unobserved heterogeneity correlated with marital status were to remain, then the marginal effects of marital status on wealth change would be biased. We consequently eliminated unobserved heterogeneity fixed over time (e.g., caution or foresight with respect to savings), and measured the effect of marital status and changes in income growth using additional controls for age and year by estimating models of the change in wealth change. We estimated the change in wealth for individuals who changed marital status in the waves before and after that marital change, but not in the wave in which the change actually took place $[(t+2) - (t+1)] - [(t) - (t-1)]$. The change, $(t+1) - (t)$, is the wave in which marital status changed and is omitted from the calculation. In this way, the measured change in wealth is not primarily the result of an individual entering or leaving a household.

Our model of the change in wealth change—for a sample of respondents included in four consecutive waves—includes a number of variables: (1) all possible marital statuses (except for married, no change over time); (2) change in the change in income over this same time period; (3) age; (4) sex; and (5) year indicators. We trimmed the top and bottom 2 percent of the dependent variable (the change in wealth change). If there were no change in saving behavior over time, we would expect the change in wealth change to be zero. The change in wealth here is not active savings. It thus reflects increases or decreases in the value of existing assets with or without active savings. The mean dependent variable is $4,188.

The results of this model are shown in Table 9.4. The standard errors around most estimates are large, so we found few statistically significant differences. Consistent with our earlier findings from models of the change in wealth that inputted a sample of individuals who did not change marital status, the effect of marital status on the *change in wealth change* among individuals who remained divorced, widowed, or

TABLE 9.4

Model of the difference in wealth accumulation before (t) – (t–1) and after (t+2) – (t+1) marital status change

Marital status at (t) and (t–1)	Marital status at (t+2) and (t+1)	Marginal effect	Standard error
[Married]	[Married]		
Divorced	Divorced	–912	4,981
Widowed	Widowed	–3,266	4,040
Other single	Other single	–1,963	6,270
Married	Divorced	46,858	29,986
Separated	Divorced	46,828	37,706
Married	Widowed	3,494	7,772
Divorced	Married	–17,606	35,677
Widowed	Married	31,907	36,224
Other single	Married	–40,975	33,526
Age	—	–539	145
Male	—	730	2,641
Income change ((t+2) – (t+1)) – ((t) – (t–1))		0.208	0.011
Intercept		29,660	9,686
Mean dep.		4,188	
Observations		54,407	

SOURCE: Health and Retirement Survey 1992–2006.

NOTES: Sample is individuals in four consecutive waves, excluding unknown married (339 observations), birth 1947 and earlier. Time is a wave of data: time 't–1,' 't,' 't+1,' and 't+2.' Dependent variable, "change in wealth change" excludes wealth changes between the waves in which the marital transition occurs (t and t+1); values in the top and bottom 2 percent are trimmed. Age is measured at time (t). Also included are indicators for four consecutive waves of data 1992–1998, 1994–2000, 1996–2002, and 2000–2006.

single over the four waves is small. Moreover, the effect is not different than for individuals who remained married. For example, the change in wealth change is only $912 less among divorced individuals than among married individuals.

The marginal effects on changes in marital status from married or separated to divorced or widowed are positive. This suggests that a transition to a not-married state leads to higher savings, relative to the change in the savings of married couples. As Table 9.2 shows, the large positive change in wealth change is due, first, to wealth loss that occurs in the waves before the wave in which the divorce occurs and, second, to the recovery of savings once in the divorced state. We did not find that this was due to a change in income because our inclusion of the covariate change in income change did not affect the estimated coefficient.

Divorced individuals who remarried had a change in savings that was less ($–17,606) than that of individuals who remained married. Widowed men and women who remarried had a change in wealth change that was more ($31,907) than individuals who stayed married. In both . cases, the estimates are imprecisely measured and our having included the change in income change and age did not change the magnitude of the differences relative to married couples.

Estimates of the other included covariates show that the change in savings declined slowly with age ($–539). Savings increased with the change in income growth. For example, a $1,000 increase in income growth increased the change in savings by $208.

We emphasize the importance of interpreting these findings cautiously. Our model estimates of the effects of marital status on the change in wealth change were imprecisely measured. Moreover, the estimates for individuals who changed marital status were based on short-term changes in wealth immediately before and after a marital status event; they did not reflect long-term changes in wealth. Finally, throughout this analysis, we measured the change in wealth and not in active savings. In other words, the sources of the change in wealth included capital gains or losses and other transfers into a household through mechanisms such as pension and inheritance. But they did not include transfers into a household through the marital transition itself.

CONCLUSION

As the population of older Americans increases in the coming decades, both in terms of absolute numbers and as a proportion of the total population, their economic well-being takes on added importance. Given the higher divorce rate and higher prevalence of multiple divorces among the early baby boomer cohort, an understanding of how marriage disruptions over the lifecycle impact savings is becoming increasingly important to policymakers and economists seeking to understand the economic security of soon-to-be retired individuals and families.

The goal of the studies in this chapter was to better understand the relationship between marriage and well-being. In particular, we studied wealth and the loss and gain in wealth associated with family or household composition and the changes in those circumstances at older ages. Indeed, loss of income or wealth from a divorce is more difficult to recover from at older ages than it is at younger ages because older individuals have fewer healthy work years remaining to recoup the loss. Moreover, older individuals have more wealth to lose than their younger counterparts. By age fifty-five mean wealth is just under $300,000.

Our research begins to shed light on whether marriage and remarriage protect against poverty in old age and whether divorce at older ages puts economic security in retirement at risk. It addresses how changes in household and family composition affect wealth accumulation independent of the characteristics and earnings of individuals. Indeed, we found that individuals remarried by age fifty-five have lower wealth than married couples at that age despite having similar lifetime earnings and similar wealth accumulation patterns later in life consistent with an interpretation that divorce has a long-lasting effect on wealth.

We also found that men who are not married accumulate less wealth at middle and older ages than married (or remarried) couples, but the difference is accounted for by differences in the lifetime and current earnings and other observable differences (an exception is partnered men). These differences in earnings and characteristics account for only between a third and a half of the difference in the wealth accumulation of married women and women who are divorced, widowed or partnered. They account for all of the difference between couples with a stable marital status and never-married women. Further research is needed to understand the gender differences in wealth accumulation of divorced and widowed men and women near retirement age so policymakers can better address the economic security of a particularly vulnerable group—older, not married women.

Changes in family and household structure change the economic resources of older individuals. Remarriage is protective and associated with wealth gain at the time the marriage takes place and wealth accumulation thereafter. The loss of wealth associated with divorce begins several years before the divorce takes place and results in about 60 percent less wealth after the divorce. One response to changes in family and household composition that diminish wealth is to increase one's savings. Older individuals appear to respond to divorce by increasing their savings. That said, divorce is costly at older ages and the effects for some are long-lasting.

NOTES

1. The first survey, the Health and Retirement Study (HRS) began as a national sample of about 7,600 households (12,654 individuals) with at least one person in the birth cohorts of 1931 through 1941 (about fifty-one to sixty-one years old at the wave 1 interview in 1992). The second, the Assets and Health Dynamics of the Oldest Old (AHEAD), began in 1993 and included 6,052 households (8,222 individuals) with at least one person born in 1923 or earlier (seventy or over in 1993). In 1998, HRS was augmented with baseline interviews from at least one household member from the birth cohorts 1924–30 and 1942–47 and was representative of all birth cohorts born in 1947 or earlier. In 2004, the HRS was again augmented with interviews from the birth cohort 1948–53. We do not use data from this latest birth cohort as the analysis requires four waves of data that is not yet available.

2. For the original HRS respondents from survey wave 1992, we use a total of eight waves of data from 1992 to 2006. For the original AHEAD respondents from 1993, we have seven waves of data. For respondents added in 1998, we have five survey waves from 1998 to 2006.

3. RAND HRS is a longitudinal data set based on the HRS data and developed at RAND with funding from the National Institute on Aging and the Social Security Administration.

4. See Haider and Solon (2000) for a discussion of characteristics of individuals with and without matched Social Security records. We use earnings from 1951 to 1991 for 9,539 HRS respondents. Earnings data for the war babies cohort are available for 1,330 respondents for years 1951 to 1997.

5. In 1996, 92 percent of non-self-employed wage and salary workers were covered by Social Security.

6. Imputation methods are described in RAND HRS Version I.

7. We analyze characteristics of this sample restricted to be in four consecutive waves and find no statistically significant differences in average age, education, number of children, mean and median wealth, or earnings. Although the differences are not statistically significant, the sample in four consecutive waves has slightly higher wealth and earnings.

8. We trim the top and bottom 2 percent of wealth change values.

9. Estimated effects of all model covariates and covariate's mean levels are available upon request.

REFERENCES

Cherlin, A. 1992. *Marriage, Divorce and Remarriage.* Cambridge, MA: Harvard University Press.

Haider, Steven, and Gary Solon. 2000. Non Random Selection in the HRS Social Security Earnings Sample. Working Paper 00–01, RAND Corporation Publications Department.

Hurd, Michael, James P. Smith, and Julie Zissimopoulos. 2007. Inter-Vivos Giving over the Lifecycle, Working Paper 524, RAND Corporation Publications Department.

Hurd, Michael, and David Wise. 1989. The Wealth and Poverty of Widows: Assets Before and After the Husband's Death. In D. A. Wise (Ed.), *The Economics of Aging.* Chicago: University of Chicago Press, 177–200.

Korenman, Sanders, and David Neumark. 1991. Does Marriage Really Make Men More Productive? *The Journal of Human Resources* 26(2): 282–307.

Lillard, Lee, and Yoram Weiss. 1996. Uncertain Health and Survival: Effect on End-of-Life Consumption. *Journal of Business and Economic Statistics* 15(2): 254–68.

Loughran, David, and Julie Zissimopoulos. 2009. Why Wait? The Effect of Marriage and Childbearing on the Wage Growth of Men and Women. *The Journal of Human Resources* 44(2): 326–49.

Lundberg, Shelly, and Elaina Rose. 2002. The Effects of Sons and Daughters on Men's Labor Supply and Wages. *Review of Economics and Statistics* 84(2): 251–68.

Lupton, Joseph, and James Smith. 2003. Marriage, Assets and Savings. In Shoshana Grossbard-Shechtman (Ed.) *Marriage and the Economy: Theory and Evidence from Advanced Industrial Societies.* New York and Cambridge: Cambridge University Press, 129–52.

Miller, Amalia R. 2011. The Effects of Motherhood Delay on Career Path. *Journal of Population Economics* 24(3): 1071–1100.

Mincer, Jacob. 1978. Family Migration Decisions. *The Journal of Political Economy* 86(5): 749–73.

RAND HRS Data, Version I. Produced by the RAND Center for the Study of Aging, with funding from the National Institute on Aging and the Social Security Administration. Santa Monica, CA (December 2009).

Smith, J. P. 1995. Racial and Ethnic Differences in Wealth in the Health and Retirement Study. *Journal of Human Resources* 30:158–83.

Waite, Linda. 1995. Does Marriage Matter? *Demography* 32(4): 483–507.

Zagorsky, Jay. 2005. Marriage and Divorce's Impact on Wealth. *Journal of Sociology* 41(4): 406–24.

Zick, Cathleen, and Karen Holden. 2000. An Assessment of the Wealth Holdings of Recent Widows. *Journal of Gerontology: Social Sciences* 55b(2): S90–97.

Zissimopoulos, J., B. Karney, and A. Rauer. 2008. Marital Histories and Economic Well-Being. MRRC Working Paper 2008–180. Ann Arbor, MI: University of Michigan Retirement Research Center and RAND WR-645, November 2008.

CHAPTER TEN

Family Structure and Financial Well-Being
Evidence from the Great Recession

Juyeon Kim and Linda J. Waite

Resource sharing is one of the most fundamental features of families. Members of immediate families tend to live together, sharing housing, meals, utilities, entertainment, income, and expenses, although perhaps not all of these equally among all members (Burch and Matthews 1987). Over the life course, families form as young adults leave home for school or jobs, find partners, and have children of their own. Families grow with the addition of children, shrink when children grow up and leave home, and shrink again with the death of members. At some stage in their lives, many people live independently of families, alone or with friends; among older adults, nonfamily living tends to follow divorce or the death of a spouse or partner (Wilmoth and Longino 2006; Klinenberg 2012). People may add members to their household in response to their own needs or those of the others. The recession that began in 2006 increased the share of families with members in need.

In approximately 2006 the rapid rise in housing values came to an end and mortgage delinquencies, defaults, and foreclosures rose dramatically. The National Bureau of Economic Research (NBER) later concluded that the United States entered a recession in December 2007 (Temin 2010), and called it the Great Recession. Unemployment rose to

The National Social Life, Health, and Aging Project (NSHAP) is supported by the National Institutes of Health, including the National Institute on Aging, the Office of Women's Health Research, the Office of AIDS Research, and the Office of Behavioral and Social Sciences Research (Grants 5R01AG021487 and R37 AG030481).

more than 10 percent, with many job losers, especially those ages fifty and older, finding reemployment extremely difficult. The labor market for new entrants yielded relatively few jobs. These economic events created, for many families, exactly the types of shocks against which their members expected insurance. The number of persons and families sharing households increased, as families drew on the insurance implicit in coresidence across generations; the Pew Research Center estimates that among adults ages twenty-five to thirty-four about one in five now lives in a multigenerational household, as does the same share of those sixty-five and older (Pew Research Center 2010).

Recent studies indicate, however, that parent-child coresidence or household extension as a resource sharing strategy is more often influenced by the children's needs than by the parent's health or economic needs (Aquilino 1990; Ward, Logan, and Spitze 1992; Choi 2003). The option to live at home with parents is a valuable form of insurance for young adults (Kaplan 2010), especially given the increase in the median age at first marriage and recent high unemployment among young adults. Aquilino (1990), for instance, found that parents are likely to be the homeowners in households shared by parents and children, and that the marital status of children is a strong predictor of parent-children co-residence. In addition, recent statistics show that 37 percent of eighteen-to-twenty-nine-years-olds were either unemployed or out of the labor force (Pew Research Center 2010), suggesting that children's economic hardships may be a motivation for changes in household composition. But to the extent that the new additions to the household bring fewer resources than they require and need to rely on those of the older generation, changes in the living arrangements of older adults in response to economic needs of extended family members may damage the economic well-being of the older adults.

This chapter examines changes in the composition of the households of older adults from the period just before the Great Recession to five years later, when economic conditions remained very difficult. We describe in detail the changes that took place and the consequences for households, focusing especially on changes in household economic resources relative to needs. We use a theoretical framework based on the household production model, over the life span. And we build on conceptual models of cultural differences in intergenerational living arrangements to mitigate the effects of financial strain. We compare the experience of older white adults to those of older black and Hispanic adults.

HOUSEHOLDS AS A SITE OF PRODUCTION

A person's living arrangements, and the people he or she shares a household with, define each other's lives in important ways. Lindau et al. (2003) argue that physical and emotional health is produced most often and most efficiently in intimate dyads, usually consisting of spouses, within a social and cultural context. So those living in other types of families or independent of families may be disadvantaged, with fewer resources with which to maintain a healthy mind and body. Perhaps as a result, older adults living alone face a heightened risk of being lonely. Although having another person in the house seems like an obvious way to avoid feeling lonely, other people do not tend to fill the same needs as a spouse; older single women who live with their children and single older adults who live with others also are more likely to be lonely than those living with their husband or wife (Greenfield and Russell 2011).

People who live together bring various resources to the household, including time, money, labor, attention, and skills. They also make demands on the others in the household for the time, attention, and resources of others. Adults of working age tend to be net producers, bringing more resources than they consume. Older adults and children often have greater needs than they can supply from their own current labor. So the balance between the resources available in a household and the demands made by members depends on the characteristics of household members. Perhaps as a result, adults living with only their spouse and own children tend to show the best physical and emotional health, whereas those living with other relatives or nonrelatives or by themselves are worse off on these dimensions (Waite and Hughes 1999; Hughes and Waite 2002). And clearly the financial well-being of people is better, all else equal, if they live with well-off others who make few demands than if they live with those who have little money but many needs (Citro and Michael 1995).

Families provide resources to their members directly, but they also provide insurance against negative shocks to the group as a whole or to the individuals in it. These shocks include poor health, loss of a job, divorce, or unexpected periods of dependency (Kotlikoff and Spivak 1981; Rosenzweig and Wolpin 1993, 1994; Kaplan 2010). Coresidence is one important mechanism through which families can transfer resources to young members, old members, and others in need (Rosenzweig and Wolpin 1993; Hughes et al. 2007; Kaplan 2010). Some scholars have argued that black and Hispanic families are more likely than whites to use coresidence to alleviate the effects of poverty, especially across the generations, with strong norms supporting extended family households (Angel and Tienda 1982; Angel and Hogan 1992).

Although sharing a household in response to economic need can benefit those involved, it comes with costs. The doubling up of living arrangements with other distal relatives/nonrelatives should be considered simultaneously with their contributions through income, or sharing of domestic work or other nonmonetary contribution, such as care for household members. In particular, if coresidence with other distal members is mainly driven by the economic hardship of those others, it may increase the economic burden on older adults.

We argue that the efficiency with which households incorporate additional members depends on the relationships between them. Members of the nuclear family share close and long-term bonds, with expectations for support and exchange generally quite clear. Expectations for exchanges with more distal relatives are both lower and vaguer, with friends and other nonrelatives expected to give and get less, and with more variation in expectations (Rossi and Rossi 1990). So households can most easily take in, for example, young adult children having a hard time finding a job, and least easily take in a friend, a second cousin, a great nephew, or an acquaintance. The more distant the relationship the more difficulty incorporating new members into the household division of labor, agreeing on sharing of expenses, and sharing common space or household resources such as food or the washing machine. So the more distant the connection with new members, the more social and emotional burden on the older adults involved.

Households can change along two dimensions: size and complexity. A household might get bigger because an additional adult child returns home. This increases size but not complexity, as an adult child has clear role relationships with his or her parents. A household might get more complex if a grandchild or a great nephew moves in. The second change is more disruptive to family functioning than the first, on average, because the relationships are more distant. Therefore, those who moved in may consume already limited resources of older adults with negligible contribution of either monetary or nonmonetary (e.g., support and care) resources. This is especially true if the new members are dependent children.

The normal life course at older ages would suggest that many more households lose members and complexity than gain them, given that ordinarily adult children tend to move out and spouses become more likely to die. However, the Great Recession increased the economic stressors that heighten risk of coresidence. The two trends vie for dominance, affecting families differentially.

RACIAL DIFFERENCES IN HOUSEHOLDS

Previous research suggests that black and Hispanic adults are substantially more likely than whites to live in complex households, and during the past few decades these differentials appear quite consistently. Among older adults, blacks are about as likely as whites to live alone, but both blacks and Hispanics are more likely to form coresidential relationships with grandchildren and nonrelatives (U.S. Census 2000 Summary File 1). In 1989 (March 1990 Current Population Survey), 31.2 percent of black elderly (age sixty-five and over) lived alone and 32.1 percent lived with others, compared to 32.0 percent and 12.7 percent for white counterparts, respectively (Angel and Hogan 1992). By 2000 there was a significant increase in the proportion of elderly blacks living with a spouse (49.4 percent) matched by a precipitous decline in the proportion living with others (20.4 percent) but relative stability in living alone (30.2 percent), while the proportions of white and Hispanic elderly changed little during the same period (Bicket and Mitra 2009).

The two major sources of household dynamics are the normal life-course factors, such as nest-leaving and widowhood, that tend to decrease size and complexity of older households over time, and the economic factors that over the past few years have exerted pressure toward household consolidation. Research on racial and ethnic differences, however, considers another important determinant of household extension: cultural preferences for multigenerational living arrangements (Angel and Tienda

1982; Hofferth 1984; Hogan, Hao, and Parish 1990; Aquilino 1990; Angel and Hogan 1992; Choi 1999; Burr and Mutchler 1999; Kamo 2000; Peek et al. 2004; Gonzales 2007). Although it is not easy to separate economic from cultural factors, previous findings suggest that racial and ethnic groups differ in their preferences for adapting to practical concerns, such as health problems and economic insufficiency, with family extension. For instance, Hogan, Hao, and Parish (1990) found that white mothers tend to help their daughters through financial support, while black mothers more often use informal support through coresidence and child care. Gonzales (2007) found that even after controlling for socioeconomic factors (marital status, education, income), cultural values are strongly associated with household extension; moreover, income is a positive predictor of coresidence for Hispanic households and thus may serve to enable families to act on cultural preferences for living in a multigenerational household.

Although cultural preferences and need to deal with economic constraints affect many minority older adults, there are sizeable differences in living arrangements among blacks, Hispanics, and Asians (Choi 1999; Kamo 2000; Peek et al. 2004). Peek and colleagues (2004) found that the source of household complexity and dynamics among black households is predominantly the movement of grandchildren, while that of white elderly households tends to be the movement of adult children. Choi (1999) directly compared black elderly couples and Hispanic elderly couples and found that Hispanic elderly couples were more likely to head a household containing relatives, while black elderly couples were more likely than Hispanic elderly couples to head households containing grandchildren only (Hughes et al. 2007). Kamo (2000) also found that black elderly are more likely than white elderly to take in children and grandchildren; Hispanics are more likely to coreside with siblings and other relatives; and Asian elderly are more likely to move into their children's households. This suggests that the processes underlying changes in household composition differ for these racial and ethnic groups.

This chapter examines the effect of the recent recession on changes of household composition and the effects of those changes on the economic well-being of the households of older adults. We use data from the National Social Life, Health, and Aging Project (NSHAP), a nationally representative population-based study of community-residing older adults. Wave 1 was fielded between the summer of 2005 and the summer of 2006, just prior to the high point of the U.S. housing bubble. Wave 2 was fielded between the summer of 2010 and the summer of 2011, after the Great Recession had been underway for more than three years, with unemployment still high and housing values continuing to fall. Specifically, the study asks:

1. What changes in the household composition of older adults took place between 2005–06 (wave 1) and 2010–11 (wave 2)?

2. Do families that increase in size see improvements in their economic well-being relative to household needs?

3. Do families that increase in complexity see similar improvements?

4. Are black and Hispanic older adults more likely than whites to increase household size and/or complexity? Are the economic consequences similar to those faced by whites?

DATA AND METHODS

Data

The NSHAP sample was selected from a multistage area probability design screened by the Institute for Social Research (ISR) for the Health and Retirement Study (HRS). The HRS design oversampled by race/ethnicity; NSHAP retained this design and also oversampled by age and gender. The first wave (Wave 1) was fielded from summer 2005 to spring 2006 and 3,005 individuals, ages fifty-seven to eighty-five, were interviewed, achieving a final weighted response rate of 75.5 percent. In wave 2 3,377 respondents and their partners were interviewed. Most of the data for the NSHAP study were collected during a two-hour in-home interview. Following the in-person interview, respondents were given a paper-and-pencil questionnaire to return by mail. The return rate for the leave-behind questionnaire was 84 percent for wave 1.

Living Arrangements

We constructed measures of living arrangements from the answers to questions about the respondent's social networks, which included household membership and detailed information on relationship to the respondent.[1] We followed Waite and Hughes (1999) and Hughes and Waite (2002) in categorizing living arrangements but separated those living with others only and those living with others and children. We used the following categories: (a) spouse or partner only; (b) spouse or partner and own children; (c) spouse or partner and others; (d) spouse or partner, own children, and others; (e) single alone; (f) single with own children; (g) single with others; (h) single with own children and others. The category *single* includes those who were never married, widowed, or divorced. *Others* include distal relatives, such as siblings, parents, and grandchildren, and nonrelatives such as friends. Web Appendix Table A10.2 shows the distribution of respondents across these living arrangements in 2005–06 and 2010–11.

Methods

To estimate changes in households we examined the number of persons in each household, and the detailed relationship of household members to the respondent for the households in which the older adult lived in 2005–06 and 2010–11. We assessed *change* on two dimensions: (1) household size, and (2) household complexity. Households increase in size if there are more people living in the household at the second interview than at the first and decrease in size if there are fewer. Complexity reflects the relationships among the residents. We follow Rossi and Rossi (1990) in assessing the closeness of relationships between kin of various degrees of relatedness, with relationships with nonrelatives having the fewest socially recognized expectations for exchange. Households with more types of relationships are more complex than those with fewer, so households consisting of one or two parents and own children do not increase complexity by adding another child, but they do add complexity if that child brings a grandchild with him or her. Households in which a person loses a spouse or partner and then lives alone are less complex than they were before, as are households from which the adult children move out, leaving only the couple. By separating size from more relational and qualitative aspects of household structure, we can compare the effects of these changes on the economic well-being of older adults. Specifically, we defined changes in household complexity as follows:

- For *spouse only* living arrangements, changes to *spouse, children, spouse, others,* and *spouse, children, others* are defined as an increase in complexity.

- For *single alone* living arrangements, changes to *single, children, single, others*; *single, children, others*; and any type of living arrangements with a spouse, are defined as an increase in complexity.
- For *spouse only* living arrangements, changes to *single, children, single, others*, and *single, children, others* are defined as an increase in complexity.
- For *spouse only* living arrangements, changes to *single alone* are defined as a decrease in complexity.

We use descriptive statistics to report the changes in number and percentage and conduct significant tests to examine whether the changes are notable.

For the analysis of the effect of change, especially doubling up of households, we first present descriptive statistics of living arrangements and economic well-being for 2005–06 and 2010–2011. We use the income-to-needs ratio, which adjusts the income available to the household by the number of people dependent on that income and their ages, at the two interviews to assess changes in economic well-being. NSHAP household income is assessed through a global question on household income followed by an unfolding bracket methodology.[2] Missing values from income and assets are imputed using the interval-censoring method of multiple imputations via the Stata 11.2 ice command (Royston 2005). Income is transformed on the log scale so that income and assets are imputed under a log-normal distribution. Ten data sets were imputed, using information from the bracketing questions (interval-censored variable), age, gender, race and ethnicity, and education level. We followed the definitions from the Current Population Survey (CPS)[3] for the calculation of household income-to-needs ratio and income-poverty. Our descriptive analysis compares changes in household composition, income relative to needs, and poverty status. This comparison enables us to determine the extent to which doubling up of families, which often leads to an increase in complexity of households, may be a strategy to counter economic hardship; our measure of economic well-being is a proxy for financial resources available in a doubled-up household in which the members are sharing these resources.

We then conducted multivariate regression to examine the sociodemographic factors associated with living in a doubled-up household and to assess whether some groups are more vulnerable to changes between

2005–06 and 2010–11, the period during which the recession began. We added age, gender, race and ethnicity, education level, and self-rated physical health to examine whether some sociodemographic groups are more vulnerable to changes in household size and composition during the recent economic downturn.

RESULTS

When interpreting changes in living arrangements, we consider changes in both household size and complexity. On one hand, some older adults may have not changed their types of living arrangements (e.g., married couple living with children) but they may have increased their household size, if, for example, adult children moved back home. On the other hand, some older adults maintained the same household size but increased or decreased complexity, for example, if a newly widowed person moved in with a child. Table 10.2 and Web Appendix Table A10.2 capture these differences. Table 10.1 presents sociodemographic characteristics of the NSHAP respondents, their household characteristics, and economic well-being (measured by income-below-needs).

General Characteristics of Households, Composition,
and Economic Well-Being

Table 10.1 presents the sociodemographic and household characteristics of respondents in 2005–06 and 2010–11. On average, the population of older adults did not experience large changes in household size or complexity (see also Table 10.2 and Web Appendix Table A10.2) between these two waves; however, we see differences by race and ethnicity. Overall, average household size is relatively constant. The households of white older adults contain the fewest members, averaging 2.01 people in 2005–06 and 1.94 people in 2010–11. Hispanics have the largest households, with 2.52 people in 2005–06 and 2.59 in 2010–11, on average. For Hispanics, larger households may be due to the persistence of higher fertility and to norms that favor large families (Angel and Tienda 1982; Choi 2003), as well as economic challenges or immigrant status (PEW Research Center 2010).

Between 2005–06 and 2010–11 inflation-adjusted median household income decreased from $47,654 to $43,220, a 9.3 percent

TABLE 10.1
Sociodemographic characteristics and changes in household characteristics[a]

	TOTAL		WHITE		BLACK		HISPANIC, NONBLACK	
	2005[b]	2010	2005[b]	2010	2005[b]	2010	2005[b]	2010
Age	—	72.1	—	72.3	—	71.6	—	70.9
		(7.3)		(6.9)		(8.7)		(8.2)
Female (%)	—	52.2	—	52.2	—	56.5	—	50.0
Attend college (%)	—	54.4	—	57.7	—	40.2	—	34.0
		(0.5)		(0.46)		(0.64)		(0.57)
Household size (average)	2.07	2.01	2.01	1.94	2.22	2.16	2.52	2.59
Household income (median)	$42,681	$43,220	$46,018	$47,586	$26,930	$30,662	$26,583	$23,238
Household income in 2010 dollars (median)	$47,654	$43,220	$51,380	$47,586	$30,068	$30,662	$30,221	$23,238
Income relative to needs (median)	3.36	3.31	3.63	3.6	2.14	2.11	1.87	1.46
Proportion below poverty (%)	8.9	8.8	5.9	5.9	23.5	18.8	22.0	27.9
Observations	2,210	2,210	1,599	1,599	377	377	234	234

NOTE: Standard error in parentheses.

[a]Survey-adjusted and weighted to account for the probability of selection, with poststratification adjustments for nonresponse.

[b]Analytic sample includes only those respondents available in Wave 2 (n = 2,210).

reduction; median income-relative-needs also declined.[4] However, the Great Recession may have affected black and Hispanic older adults differently than it did whites. White older adults in NSHAP showed a 7.4 percent reduction in median household income, while blacks saw an increase of 2.0 percent. Hispanic older adults were most negatively affected by the Great Recession, showing 23.1 percent reduction in their household income. In addition, the proportion of households below poverty among Hispanic older adults increased substantially (from 22 percent in 2005–06 to 27.9 percent in 2010–11).

Changes in Household Composition

Has household composition changed between 2005–06 and 2010–2011? Some types of living arrangements are more vulnerable to changes that stem from life-course, social, and economic factors. Loss of a spouse is one major life-course event that shifts household composition. Widowed older adults may combine households with an adult child, move in with friends or relatives, or live alone. Another factor is economic hardship faced by the older adult or by other family members. Table 10.2 presents changes of living arrangements between 2005–06 and 2010–11.[5]

Table 10.2 shows whether those in each living arrangement in 2005–06 changed by 2010–11 and, if so, whether they have moved toward either increasing or decreasing complexity by adding to or reducing the number of other distal relatives (e.g., siblings, in-laws, grandchildren) or friends. Because our sample consists of older adults, we expect living arrangements to be fairly stable. However, older adults in complex living arrangements, perhaps with their children or other distal relatives or friends in their household, may face more instability in household composition as their children and others move out or move in. Overall, 68.0 percent of older adults stayed in the same type of living arrangements, 18.6 percent experienced a decrease, and 13.4 percent had an increase in household complexity. Married older couples and single older adults living alone are the two groups with the highest stability: 78.6 percent of single older adults living alone and 78.2 percent of married couples in 2005–06 had neither increased nor decreased their household complexity by 2010–11. Households that contained distal relatives or friends were more apt to change, especially toward decreasing complexity: 68.6 percent of *single, others* and 69 percent of *spouse, others* shifted

TABLE 10.2

Changes in complexity of living arrangements between 2005–06 and 2010–11 (N = 2,210)

	No change	Decreased	Increased	Total
Single, live alone	78.6	0	21.5	100
(unweighted N)	435	0	127	562
Single, child(ren)	46.2	34.6	19.3	100
(unweighted N)	42	34	14	90
Single, others	22.6	68.6	8.8	100
(unweighted N)	22	45	7	74
Single, child(ren), others	50.1	41.7	8.2	100
(unweighted N)	23	21	2	46
Spouse, only	78.2	10.8	11.1	100
(unweighted N)	867	122	128	1,117
Spouse, child(ren)	31.4	57.0	11.6	100
(unweighted N)	65	109	31	205
Spouse, others	14.9	69.0	16.1	100
(unweighted N)	12	38	10	60
Spouse, child(ren), others	25.9	74.1	0	100
(unweighted N)	13	43	0	56
Total	68.1	18.6	13.4	100
	1,479	412	319	2,210

toward reducing complexity of household composition. This is consistent with our argument that other distal relatives and friends are less likely to share the family history, knowledge, and empathy that facilitate household function (e.g., sharing domestic tasks) and are more likely to cause strain in the relationships between household members, thus increasing the chances that the household will split up (Kim 2011). Quite a large proportion of older adults in some types of living arrangements experienced an increase in household complexity. This was the case for those in the categories *single, living alone* (21.5 percent), *single, children* (19.3 percent), *spouse, children* (11.6 percent), and *spouse, others* (16.1 percent). Single older adults who lived alone may have moved in with their siblings or friends to share expenses; single older adults who already lived with their children increased household complexity by adding extra persons, probably grandchildren. These changes in economic well-being are discussed later.

Changes in Economic Well-Being

How does household composition relate to the economic well-being of older adults? More important, how do changes in household composition relate to changes in economic well-being? *Change* could indicate both changes in quantity (i.e., size) and quality (i.e., complexity, composition).

As we have seen, some types of living arrangements are more likely than others to show dramatic changes in size or complexity between 2005–06 and 2010–11. How are these related to changes in the economic well-being of the household and its members? Table 10.3 shows the association of changes in complexity with changes in average income relative to needs. Table 10.3 shows that the two-thirds of older adults who saw no change in household complexity showed a decline in average income-needs (–0.16); the 18.6 percent of people whose households decreased in complexity saw their average income-to-needs ratio increase by 0.24. Those whose household increased in complexity, who constituted 13.4 percent of older adults, showed declines of 0.97 in their income relative to their needs. That is, income relative to needs fell both for older adults whose households remained the same type and for those whose households increased in complexity, with large declines in economic well-being when household relationships were complicated. Only people whose household declined in complexity experienced increases in economic well-being as measured by the income-to-needs ratio. A notable point here is that increasing complexity of relationships among household members greatly reduces the average income-relative-to-needs ratio, indicating that the economic well-being of older adults declined quite substantially. Changes in type of living arrangement, such as moving into more complex households, significantly decreased income relative to needs of whites and blacks, compared to those who had no such changes (for whites, complexity reduced income relative to needs by 1.01; for blacks, complexity reduced by 0.77) .

The results from Table 10.4 show that some changes in household complexity had significant effects on log household income in 2010–11. The reference group is older adults who did not experience change in household complexity between 2005–06 and 2010–11, among the single in any type of household and the married in complex households. We index separately those who continued to live with a spouse in both survey years.[6] We also index separately the married in 2005–06 who were unmarried in 2010–11 in any type of household. Compared to those who did not change household composition (excluding those who continued to live with a spouse), older adults who either moved into or moved

TABLE 10.3

Changes in complexity of living arrangements and average changes in income relative to needs by race
(N = 2,210[a])

Complexity	TOTAL			WHITE				BLACK				HISPANIC		
	%	n	Δ	%[b]	n	Δ		%[b]	n	Δ		%[b]	n	Δ
No change	68.1	1,479	−0.16	70.5	1,138	−0.23		54.7	206	0.48[c]		57.7	135	0.02
Decreased	18.6	412	0.24	17.8	275	0.34		24.9	93	0.04		19.5	44	−0.47
Increased	13.4	319	−0.97[d]	11.7	186	−1.01[d]		20.4	78	−0.77[d]		22.8	55	−0.99[d]
Total	100	2,210	−0.19	100	1,599	−0.22		100	377	0.12		100	234	−0.30

[a]Asians and other race and ethnicity groups (n = 51) are excluded.
[b]Survey-adjusted and weighted to account for the probability of selection, with poststratification adjustments for nonresponse.
[c]Differs significantly from white.
[d]Differs significantly from "No change."

TABLE 10.4
Multivariate regression on log income in 2010–11 (N = 2,190[a])

	COMPLEXITY MODEL		SIZE MODEL	
	Model 1	*Model 2*	*Model 1*	*Model 2*
REFERENCE: NO CHANGES IN LIVING ARRANGEMENT[b]				
Decreased (complexity/size)	0.04	0.11†	0.03	0.09
	(0.06)	(0.05)	(0.06)	(0.06)
Increased (complexity/size)	−0.02	0.01	−0.03	0.00
	(0.04)	(0.05)	(0.04)	(0.05)
Married → single[c]	−0.09	−0.11†	−0.08	−0.11
	(0.06)	(0.06)	(0.06)	(0.06)
Married → married[d]	0.22***	0.23***	0.22***	0.22***
	(0.03)	(0.03)	(0.03)	(0.03)
Black	−0.08	0.00	−0.08	0.01
	(0.05)	(0.07)	(0.05)	(0.07)
Hispanic, nonblack	−0.29***	−0.19†	−0.29***	−0.18†
	(0.08)	(0.10)	(0.08)	(0.10)
Decreased (complexity/size)				
× Black		−0.23†		−0.24†
		(0.13)		(0.14)
× Hispanic		−0.42*		−0.36*
		(0.17)		(0.17)
Increased (complexity/size)				
× Black		−0.16†		−0.15
		(0.09)		(0.09)
× Hispanic		−0.12		−0.17
		(0.13)		(0.12)
Age	−0.01***	−0.01***	−0.01***	−0.01***
	(0.00)	(0.00)	(0.00)	(0.00)
Female	−0.09**	−0.09**	−0.09**	−0.09**
	(0.03)	(0.03)	(0.03)	(0.03)
Attend college	0.32***	0.32***	0.32***	0.32***
	(0.04)	(0.04)	(0.04)	(0.04)
Log household income in 2005–06	0.39***	0.39***	0.39***	0.39***
	(0.03)	(0.03)	(0.03)	(0.03)
Self-rated physical health in 2005–06	0.09***	0.09***	0.09***	0.09***
	(0.02)	(0.02)	(0.02)	(0.02)
Health declined from 2005 to 2010	−0.09*	−0.09*	−0.09*	−0.09*
	(0.04)	(0.04)	(0.04)	(0.04)
Household size in 2005–06	0.02	0.03	0.02	0.03
	(0.02)	(0.02)	(0.03)	(0.03)
Constant	6.74***	6.71***	6.74***	6.71***
	(0.39)	(0.38)	(0.39)	(0.38)
F test	97.2***	81.2***	94.3***	85.9***
df	(13, 38)	(17, 34)	(13, 38)	(17, 34)

NOTE: Standard error in parentheses.

[a]Survey-adjusted and weighted to account for the probability of selection, with poststratification adjustments for nonresponse; 20 cases were missing in the self-rated physical health, but we found no significant differences in predicting log income in 2010.

[b]No changes in household composition, except older adults continue to live with a spouse.

[c]Includes single living alone and single living with children and/or others.

[d]Includes living with a spouse only, and living with a spouse, children and/or others.

*p < .05, **p < 0.01, ***p < 0.001, †p < .1.

out of complex households between 2005–06 and 2010–11 showed no significant difference in household income in the later year (Model 1). Consistent with previous research on the positive effect of marriage on financial well-being (Waite and Gallagher 2000), older adults who continued to live with a spouse had 24.6 percent (=(exp(0.22)–1)*100)[7] more household income in 2010–11 than those who continued to live in any other type of household. Note that Hispanic older adults saw a 25.2 percent (=(1–exp(-0.29))*100) reduction in income compared to white older adults with the same household structure and changes in structure.

Racial Differences

What are the sociodemographic characteristics of those who face changes in living arrangements? Supplementary analysis (Web Appendix Table A10.1) suggests that living arrangements of black older adults are more unstable than those of whites or Hispanics, with black households more likely to increase or decrease in both size and complexity. Hispanic older adults are more likely than whites to increase household size and complexity.

How do racial and ethnic differences and changes in living arrangements (Table 10.1 and Web Appendix Table A10.2) relate to economic well-being? Table 10.3 presents changes in complexity of living arrangements and changes in income relative to needs separately for white, black, and Hispanic older adults. White older adults are the least likely to change their living arrangements, compared to black and Hispanic older adults, and more likely to decrease than increase the complexity of their households. Black older adults are the most likely to show household dynamics; almost half (45.3 percent for complexity; 48.8 percent for size) of black older adults saw a change in either the complexity or size of their households. Interestingly, black older adults who maintained stable household structures increased their income relative to their needs.

Hispanic older adults, like blacks, show a great deal of change in living arrangements over the five-year period we observed. A large proportion of Hispanic older adults saw either increases or decreases in household complexity (42.3 percent) or size (43.0 percent). For Hispanic older adults, however, a decrease in the complexity of the household does not seem to be associated with improvement in economic well-being.

Twenty percent of Hispanics saw a decline in the complexity of their household, but their income relative to needs decreased as well (−0.47). The recent PEW report points to the very substantial vulnerability of Hispanics generally to declines in economic well-being as a result of macroeconomic forces. A sizeable share of Hispanics are immigrants, often undocumented, concentrated in industries and occupations badly affected by the recession, and disproportionate participants in the housing bubble (PEW Research Center 2011).

Model 2 in Table 10.4 estimated interactions among race and changes in household type. Model 2 showed that those whose households decreased in complexity saw a 11.6 percent increase in income by 2010–11. However, the advantage of moving into less complex households does not appear for black and Hispanic older adults. Blacks who experienced a decrease in complexity of their household saw a drop of 20.5 percent (=[1−exp(−0.23)]*100) in household income compared to older white adults who experienced no changes in household type. Hispanics whose households decreased in complexity experienced a substantial decline in income by 2010–11 (34.3 percent (=[1−exp(−0.42)]*100)).

SUMMARY AND DISCUSSION

Households are a site of resource production and distribution (Becker 1991; Waite and Gallagher 2000). Yet, the efficiency with which households and families produce economic and health outcomes depends, in part, on the nature of the relationship among members. Resource exchanges, such as money and support, among members of the nuclear family tend to be taken for granted, based on long-term relationships and clearly defined role expectations; transactions with distal relatives and friends, however, tend to be less efficient due to higher instability in relationships and less clear expectations for returns (Rossi and Rossi 1990). Consistent with previous research, we found that those living with a spouse only or with their spouses and own children enjoy the best economic well-being.

Households, however, are sometimes dynamic, with changes depending on two major driving forces: the older adults' position in the life course and the economic fortunes of their members. Chapter 9 in this volume examines changes in wealth that accompany divorce and remarriage at older ages, both of which have a substantial impact on assets. The normal life course would suggest that most households at older ages reduce their size and complexity as adult children tend to move out and spouses become more likely to die. Our results show that 32 percent of older adults saw either an increase or a decrease in household complexity between 2005 and 2010 (Table 10.2). Among those who changed (731 out of 2,210), about 42.7 percent (312 out of 731) of those who lived with their spouses (and children or others) became single, either living alone or living with their own children or others, reflecting the influence of normal life-course factors such as nest-leaving and widowhood. Economic factors over the past few years have exerted pressure toward household consolidation. It seems, however, that the recent recession was more likely to influence the economic well-being of older adults through the movement of children, grandchildren, other distal relatives, and friends into and out of their households. As many recent reports indicate (PEW 2010; Aquilino 1990; Kaplan 2010), high unemployment among the younger generation seems to propel intergenerational coresidency. This means that older adults are sharing their limited resources with other members who moved in but brought little income to contribute. Thus, changes in living arrangements of older adults tended to induce changes in their economic well-being. We found that, in simple comparisons, decreases in size and complexity of households are associated with an increase in economic well-being, while increases in size or complexity are strongly associated with declines (Table 10.3). Moreover, decreases in complexity, but not increases, still had effects on household income in 2010–11 even after controlling for demographic characteristics and health status (Table 10.4, Model 2).

Consistent with previous studies on racial differences in living arrangements, we found that black and Hispanic older adults are more likely than whites to live either alone or in a complex household. As mentioned above, older adults living with other distal relatives face quite a different impact on their overall well-being to those living with nuclear family members; living with other distal relatives seems to lead to more instability of household composition. We see this quite clearly among black and Hispanic older adults. Compared to white older adults, blacks are significantly more likely to both increase and decrease the size and complexity of their households while Hispanics are more likely to increase only (Web Appendix Table A10.1).

Supplementary analysis not shown here indicates that the proportion of Hispanic older adults living with other relatives, such as siblings, extended kin, in-laws, or friends, increased between the two survey years (17.5 percent in 2005–06 to 22 percent in 2010–11).[8] The effects of changes, however, are quite different for these two groups. Hispanics experienced a larger decrease in their income relative to needs and a larger increase in the proportion living in poverty level compared to blacks.

The Great Recession reduced household wealth, increased the share of families with members under financial stress, and seems to have had a stronger effect on the households of older members of minorities. Hispanic families with older adults were especially hard hit. Strongly held values of family solidarity have been suggested as the motivation for the sizeable share of Hispanic older adults who took in others during the economic downturn. Our results clearly show that the help provided to relatives and others through coresidence came at a substantial cost to the older adults who opened their homes to those in need; the household income in families that took others in fell dramatically when adjusted for the number of people who shared it (Table 10.3). Other research suggests (Pew 2011) that Hispanics were especially hard hit because of their disproportionate participation in the housing bubble; those who lost their homes in the collapse of housing values apparently made claims for help with housing on their families. This suggests that policies to aid homeowners who owe more than their homes are worth could help both the new homeowners in the younger generation and their parents, grandparents and other family members, who would take them in absent such help. And our results suggest that policies to aid those affected by the downturn should be sensitive to cultural differences in values about how hardship should be shared in families.

NOTES

1. These include: Spouse; Ex-spouse; Romantic/Sexual partner; Parent; Parent in-law; Child; Step-child; Brothers or sisters; Other relative of yours;

Other in-law; Friend; Neighbor; Co-worker or boss; Minister, priest, or other clergy; Psychiatrist, psychologist, counselor, or therapist; Caseworker/Social worker; Housekeeper/Home health care provider/Other (*Specify*).

2. The unfolding bracket questions were assessed through a method that is similar to HRS: for example, "Would you say the income of your household in [current year minus1] was more than $50,000 or less than $50,000?"

3. For the definition of income-to-needs ratio, see http://www.census.gov/population/www/cps/cpsdef.html.

4. $1 in 2005 has the same buying power as $1.12 in 2010 (http://data.bls.gov/cgi-bin/cpicalc.pl).

5. It should be noted that change in household size with no change in composition is not considered as increase or decrease in complexity in Table 10.2. Changes in household size by living arrangements are available from the authors.

6. Previous studies have found consistently that those who live with a spouse only enjoy the greatest financial well-being (Waite and Gallagher 2000) of any marital status or household type, with the stably married especially advantaged (Zissimopoulos, Chapter 9, this volume). The large number of stable married couples dominates any category including Others, leading us to create a separate category for them.

In supplementary analysis we took those who continue to live with a spouse in both survey waves as the reference group and controlled following five groups: those who had a spouse in wave 1 but became single living alone; those who experienced no change in household composition between both years except those who continue to be married; those who had a spouse in wave 1 but moved to a more complex household (either married or single); and those who saw either increased or decreased complexity. In this way, we tried to capture the differences between the normal life-course factors (widowed) and economic factors (had a spouse in wave 1 but moved into complex household). However, taking the continuously married as the reference group was still less effective in showing dynamic changes of financial resources by changes in household composition than other types. It is because those who continued to be married showed the best financial well-being; therefore, even if other types of households made changes in their household composition, their financial status has a negative association compared to the continued to be married group.

7. Those who continue to live with a spouse only showed significantly higher (28.9 percent) income; those who continue to live with a spouse but moved into complex household showed 3.9 percent higher but are not statistically different.

8. The proportion living with others among white older adults has increased slightly (7.2 percent to 8.7 percent) and blacks remained the same at around 21 percent.

REFERENCES

Angel, Jacqueline L., and Dennis P. Hogan. 1992. "The Demography of Minority Aging Populations." *Journal of Family History* 17:95–115.

Angel, Ronald, and Marta Tienda. 1982. "Determinants of Extended Household Structure: Cultural Pattern or Economic Need?" *The American Journal of Sociology* 87:1360–83.

Aquilino, William S. 1990. "The Likelihood of Parent Adult Child Coresidence: Effects of Family Structure and Parental Characteristics." *Journal of Marriage and the Family* 52:405–19.

Becker, Gary S. 1991. *A Treatise on the Family*. Cambridge, MA: Harvard University Press.

Bicket, Mark C., and Aparna Mitra. 2009. "Demographics and Living Arrangements of the Minority Elderly in the United States." *Applied Economics Letters* 16:1053–57.

Burch, Thomas K., and Beverly J. Matthews. 1987. "Household Formation in Developed Societies." *Population and Development Review* 13(3): 495–511.

Burr, Jeffrey A., and Jan E. Mutchler. 1999. "Race and Ethnic Variation in Norms of Filial Responsibility Among Older Persons." *Journal of Marriage and the Family* 61:674–87.

Choi, Namkee G. 1999. "Living Arrangements and Household Compositions of Elderly Couples and Singles: A Comparison of Hispanics and Blacks." *Journal of Gerontological Social Work* 31:41–61.

———. 2003. "Coresidence Between Unmarried Aging Parents and Their Adult Children: Who Moved in with Whom and Why?" *Research on Aging* 25:384–404.

Citro, Constance Forbes, and Robert T. Michael. 1995. *Measuring Poverty: A New Approach*. Washington, DC: National Academies Press.

Gonzales, Alicia M. 2007. "Determinants of Parent-Child Coresidence Among Older Mexican Parents: The Salience of Cultural Values." *Sociological Perspectives* 50:561–77.

Greenfield, E. A., and D. Russell. 2011. "Identifying Living Arrangements that Heighten Risk for Loneliness in Later Life: Evidence From the US National Social Life, Health, and Aging Project." *Journal of Applied Gerontology* 30:524–34.

Hofferth, Sandra L. 1984. "Kin Networks, Race, and Family Structure." *Journal of Marriage and the Family* 46:791–806.

Hogan, Dennis P., Lin-Xing Hao, and William L. Parish. 1990. "Race, Kin Networks, and Assistance to Mother-Headed Families." *Social Forces* 68:797–812.

Hughes, Mary E., and Linda J. Waite. 2002. "Health in Household Context: Living Arrangements and Health in Late Middle Age." *Journal of Health and Social Behavior* 43:1–21.

Hughes, M. E., L. J. Waite, T. A. LaPierre, and Y. Luo. 2007. "All in the Family: The Impact of Caring for Grandchildren on Grandparents' Health." *The Journals of Gerontology Series B: Psychological Sciences and Social Sciences* 62:S108–19.

Kamo, Yoshinori. 2000. "Racial and Ethnic Differences in Extended Family Households." *Sociological Perspectives* 43:211–29.

Kaplan, Greg. 2010. "Moving Back Home: Insurance Against Labor Market Risk." *Federal Reserve Bank of Minneapolis Research Department Staff Report* 449.

Klinenberg, Eric. 2012. *Going Solo: The Extraordinary Rise and Surprising Appeal of Living Alone.* New York: The Penguin Press.

Kim, Juyeon. 2011. "Social Contexts and Health in Late Life: Living Arrangements, Social Networks, Resources and Health." Ph.D. diss., Department of Sociology, University of Chicago.

Kotlikoff, Laurence J., and Avia Spivak. 1981. "The Family as an Incomplete Annuities Market." *Journal of Political Economy* 89:372–91.

Lindau, Stacy Tessler, Edward O. Lauman, Wendy Levinson, and Linda J. Waite. 2003. "Synthesis of Scientific Disciplines in Pursuit of Health: The Interactive Biopsychosocial Model." *Perspectives in Biology and Medicine* 46 (3 Supp):S74–86.

Peek, Chuck W., Tanya Koropeckyj-Cox, Barbara A. Zsembik, and Raymond T. Coward. 2004. "Race Comparisons of the Household Dynamics of Older Adults." *Research on Aging* 26:179–201.

Pew Research Center. 2010. "The Return of the Multi-Generational Family Household." *Pew Research Center's Social & Demographic Trends Project*.

———. 2011. "Wealth Gaps Rise to Record Highs Between Whites, Blacks, Hispanics." *Pew Research Center's Social & Demographic Trends Project*.

Rosenzweig, Mark R., and Kenneth I. Wolpin. 1993. "Intergenerational Support and the Life-Cycle Incomes of Young Men and Their Parents: Human Capital Investments, Coresidence, and Intergenerational Financial Transfers." *Journal of Labor Economics* 11(1): 84–112.

———. 1994. "Parental and Public Transfers to Young-Women and Their Children." *American Economic Review* 84:1195–1212.

Rossi, Alice S., and Peter H. Rossi. 1990. *Of Human Bonding: Parent-Child Relations across the Life Course.* New York: A. de Gruyter.

Royston, Patrick. 2005. "Multiple Imputation of Missing Values: Updates." *The Stata Journal* 5:1–14.

Temin, Peter. 2010. "The Great Recession and the Great Depression." *NBER Working Paper Series*. Working Paper 15645 (http://www.nber.org/papers/w15645).

Waite, Linda J., and Maggie Gallagher. 2000. *Case for Marriage: Why Married People Are Happier, Healthier and Better off Financially.* Westminster, MD: Broadway Books.

Waite, Linda J., and Mary E. Hughes. 1999. "At Risk on the Cusp of Old Age: Living Arrangements and Functional Status among Black, White and Hispanic Adults." *Journals of Gerontology Series B-Psychological Sciences and Social Sciences* 54:S136–44.

Ward, Russell, John Logan, and Glenna Spitze. 1992. "The Influence of Parent and Child Needs on Co-residence in Middle and Later Life." *Journal of Marriage and the Family* 54:209–21.

Wilmoth, Janet M., and Charles F. Longino. 2006. "Demographic Trends That Will Shape US Policy in the Twenty-First Century." *Research on Aging* 28:269–88.

CHAPTER ELEVEN

Family Structure Change

A Discussion

Robert J. Willis

The chapters in this section address the broad questions studied in this volume about the causes and consequences of economic insecurity through the lens of family economics. Family economics is a relatively recent addition to the fields that make up the discipline of economics. The term *family economics* was coined by T. W. Schultz in *Economics of the Family: Marriage, Children and Human Capital* (Schultz 1974).[1] Family economics itself emerged as part of the creation of modern labor economics during the 1960s, drawing especially on theories of human capital (Becker 1964), female labor supply (Mincer 1962), time allocation and household production (Mincer 1963; Becker 1965), and fertility (Becker 1960).

Before the emergence of the field, most economists viewed the study of demographic and family behavior as outside the domain of economic theory despite the role that Malthus played in the history of economics. Demography was an empirical field primarily conducted by sociologists who were instrumental in creating rich bodies of data that linked family structure and behavior ranging from the U.S. Census to smaller surveys focusing on fertility and contraception. By the late 1950s, "The Hundred Years' War of Survey Sampling" (Kish 2003) had ended (more or less) with probability sampling victorious and, therefore, with social scientists able to make valid statements about populations using sample surveys. The ability of family economists and other social scientists to test their theories owes much to the creation of cross-sectional and longitudinal surveys that were built on these principles and have become a vital part of the nation's scientific capital.

Amalia Miller's chapter on the link between the timing of marriage and motherhood, women's lifecycle earnings path, and women's well-being at retirement builds beautifully on the theoretical and empirical foundations of family economics and survey sampling described in the two preceding paragraphs. In the Schultz volume, Mincer and Polachek (1974) presented the pioneering paper about implications of women's decisions about their allocation of time between home and market for lifecycle earnings that plays a central role in Miller's conceptual framework.[2] In addition, her empirical work relies on longitudinal data from the National Longitudinal Studies (NLS) of two cohorts of women born between 1922 and 1954 that began to be collected in the late 1960s, at the same time that the Panel Study of Income Dynamics (PSID) began.

Miller is able for the first time to study the lifetime impact of marriage and childbearing on earnings because these long NLS panels follow cohorts of women through their entire labor market careers. Although her regression estimates cannot be interpreted causally, her main findings are consistent with the predictions of the Mincer-Polachek model and many subsequent theoretical models of the role of investment in human capital in determining lifecycle patterns of female labor force participation, wage rates, and earnings. In particular, Miller finds that the timing of the first birth has a more important impact on earnings than the timing of marriage. This is consistent with the idea that bearing and rearing children raises the value of a woman's non-market time, causing her to reduce labor supply and, when she does work, to choose jobs that involve a lesser degree of investment in labor market skills that might atrophy if she follows an interrupted career. A useful extension to Miller's chapter would be to separate out the effect on total earnings of wage rates and hours of work. This would help illuminate the theoretically important distinction between the effects of children on the value of non-market time, which should be greatest when children are young, and the effects of investment in labor market skills, which should cumulate over the entire career, especially as women choose occupations in which investment in skills has a substantial payoff.

The dramatic change in the timing of marriage and first birth for post-baby-boom cohorts of women that Miller documents is likely both a cause and a consequence of the growing opportunities for women in the labor market. While Ben-Porath (1967) could present a simple and elegant model of the optimal accumulation over the lifecycle for men who were assumed to work full time in the labor market once they left school, tractable theories of how women should optimally balance careers and motherhood have proved to be beyond the reach of economics. After much experimentation and social learning across a number of cohorts, it appears that women have concluded that it is best to focus their efforts on school and careers first and that they should become mothers only after their career is established. They also appear to have found—with the aid of modern contraceptives—that careers can be combined with sex, and that they can search for a long-term partner, with cohabiting unions preceding, and sometimes permanently substituting, for marriage.

The focus of Miller's chapter and, indeed, the focus of much of the related literature is on the effects of the timing of parenthood on women. I have a hunch that the impact of the delay of marriage and parenthood on men has been profound, not always salutary, and certainly understudied, making it a fertile ground of inquiry parallel to that of Miller's research on women. In the period before and during the baby boom, it was pretty clear that American men continued to follow the so called Western model of marriage, in which marriage was delayed until the man was capable of supporting a family and, once married, maintained the responsibility of breadwinner for the rest of his life. While this role was undoubtedly deeply satisfying in many ways, there was always the lure of alternative, less responsible and more autonomous lifestyles. The cynic H. L. Mencken may have had such alternatives in mind when he wrote, "Men have a much better time of it than women. For one thing, they marry later; for another thing, they die earlier."[3] With respect to the ready availability of sexual unions without the responsibilities imposed by marriage, I showed that under certain conditions there may be an equilibrium in which low-productivity women bear children out of wedlock by fathers who provide little or no economic support (Willis 1999). The stagnation during the past two decades of male educational attainment and wage rates and the growth of nonmarital childbearing is consistent with a hypothesis that delayed childbearing (driven by and contributing to the quest for female independence) has undermined the incentive for a man to endure the hard work of building his human capital in favor of exploring the fun to be had as a young man on his own.

The Social Security system was created in an era of low divorce rates and families composed of male breadwinners and female homemakers. In addition to the delay of marriage and increase of cohabitation that I just discussed, the growth of marital instability created by the rise of divorce, especially during the divorce revolution that saw the divorce rate double in a decade beginning in the late 60s, raises questions about the adequacy of the design of the Social Security system in the twenty-first century. In their chapter, Couch, Tamborini, Reznik, and Phillips (hereafter, CTRP) begin to address these questions by exploiting a marvelous new body of data based on a linkage of survey data containing detailed retrospective marriage and divorce histories from the Survey of Program Participation (SIPP) and administrative data from Social Security earnings histories linked to the SIPP participants and their spouses.

CTRP use these data to study the long-term impact of divorce on the earnings of women from the time of divorce until they reach eligibility for Social Security benefits. They claim, correctly I believe, that this is the first empirical study of the long-term effects of divorce on earnings and benefits. They study the next twenty-two years of earnings of a group of women ages twenty-two to thirty-six who were in their first year of marriage of at least three years duration in 1970. They use a group fixed effects econometric model to study the impact of divorce on lifecycle earnings by comparing the earning paths of a "treatment group" of women who divorced between 1971 and 1976 with a "comparison group" of women who remained continuously married. An innovative feature of their model adjusts for earnings in several years before 1971, in order to eliminate differences in sample composition or anticipation of divorce that might influence the initial 1970 earnings of the treatment and comparison groups.

Predicted differences in earnings between the treatment and comparison groups during the twenty-two years following divorce are presented in Figure 8.1. The authors argue that the predicted differences (at least approximately) may be interpreted as the causal impact of divorce on earnings. I think what they mean is that the predicted differences answer the counterfactual question, "What would happen to a woman's expected lifecycle earnings path if she were to divorce?"

It is plausible that the middle curve in the figure ("all divorce") provides an answer to the causal question under the assumptions that

(a) current earnings capacities of the initial group of women have been adequately controlled by adjustment for predivorce earnings, and (b) that the women know no more about their preferences, expectations, talents, or market opportunities than the authors do. The authors make a good argument for (a) but say nothing about (b). While, of course, assumption (b) is completely implausible, for the moment let us assume that it is true. In this case, the middle curve is an estimate of the average treatment effect of divorce on the earnings path of the divorcees. It shows that the average divorcee's earnings grow rapidly during the first three or four years following divorce and then fall back toward the level of earnings of continuously married women but remain significantly above that level more than two decades after the divorce.

By construction, the "divorced all" curve is the weighted average of the other two curves in the figure, one corresponding to the women in the pool of divorcees who never remarry and the other to women who will remarry at some time where the weights are given by the fraction of women in each group. Under assumptions (a) and (b) above, there will be some women who, by chance, will never remarry. The *divorced never remarried* curve shows that, in that eventuality, these women will experience substantial growth in earnings, presumably because they work longer hours and experience higher wage growth from more on-the-job training than their remarried counterparts. The *divorced who remarried* curve suggests that by the end of the twenty-two-year observation period, the earnings of remarried women are approximately equal to the earnings of women who were continuously married, but their lifetime earnings are considerably higher. Taken together, the three curves illustrate the wide range of outcomes that could await a woman who divorces.

The interpretation of this figure becomes more complex if we assume that assumption (b) is false. To illustrate the issues, consider a simple special case in which the baseline pool of women consists of two types who differ in their preferences, talents, and expectations should they become divorcees. Type 1 comprises women who prefer to remarry, have children, and follow careers with modest wage growth that allow them a comfortable mix between work and family. Type 2 women savor their independence, preferring to remain single and devote their efforts to careers involving long work hours and a high rate of investment in human capital. In this case, the middle curve in Figure 8.1 still represents the average treatment effect, but the upper and lower curves largely reflect sorting through self-selection by the two types rather than depicting the potential variation in lifetime earnings outcomes that a given woman might experience if she divorces.

The implications of unobserved heterogeneity become more interesting when we consider the historical context of the women in the CTRP sample who were in their first year of marriage of at least three years duration by 1970, near the start of the divorce revolution. Among the changes then underway under the banner of women's liberation (among other banners) were campaigns against perceived labor market discrimination against women. If expected returns to investments in labor market careers for women shifted up during this period, it seems likely that they would have a larger destabilizing effect on the marriages of Type 2 women than they would on Type 1 women who prefer a more traditional lifestyle. Put differently, the divorce risk faced by Type 1 women may be primarily a function of the idiosyncratic risk of having a bad match, whereas the divorce risk for Type 2 women depends on opportunities outside marriage, which were changing rapidly at that time. To the extent that this is the case, the curves in Figure 8.1 reflect the causal impact of female earnings on divorce as well as the impact of divorce on female earnings.

As subsequent cohorts of girls incorporated the improved prospects for high investment labor market careers for women into their expectations, the heterogeneity model suggests that Type 1 women would choose to delay marriage and childbearing. Cohabiting unions would facilitate the search for a long-term partner and provide a more or less satisfying substitute for the emotional and sexual aspects of marriage. One consequence of this increase in age at marriage would be a decrease in divorce rates among educated women (see Rotz 2011).

CTRP use their model of female earnings to analyze its implications for Social Security claiming age, benefit type, and amount. This line of research will be very important in considering the implications for beneficiaries of reforms to the Social Security system that are likely to be discussed in the near future. It should be noted that the divorce revolution also marked the beginning of the decoupling of marriage and fertility for a rapidly growing part of the U.S. population. In 1970, fewer than 10 percent of births were to unmarried women; by 2007, this fraction had risen to nearly 40 percent of births (Ventura 2009). And, as of 2001, about half of nonmarital births took place within cohabiting unions (Child Trends). Reform of the Social Security system should recognize the implications of the profound changes in marriage and sex roles that have taken place since its founding.

One's marriage history also influences the wealth that one has available to supplement Social Security and pensions at retirement. The chapter by Julie Zissimopoulos uses longitudinal data from the Health and Retirement Study (HRS) to study the association between changes in marital status and the levels and changes in wealth between the HRS baseline in 1992 and its 2006 wave. Her results confirm my prior belief that divorce is a wealth-destroying activity and that people who are married and remain so have both the highest initial levels of wealth and gain the most.

Useful extensions to this intuitive descriptive analysis might focus more closely on what aspects of the relationship between marital status and wealth are most critical for policy or for understanding the impact of divorce on economic behavior. For example, the implications of divorce may differ importantly for men and women in terms of how wealth is divided, who has custody of minor children, what happens to the education of children, the likelihood of remarriage, what resources the individual has available for retirement, and so on. Nonetheless, the issues raised in this essay are of great importance in pointing toward a better understanding of the implications of changing family structure on older Americans, and I look forward to more work in this area.

The sociologists Juyeon Kim and Linda Waite follow in the tradition of their forebears who pioneered the collection of demographic information by presenting research based on an innovative new body of data, the National Social Life, Health, and Aging Project (NSHAP), that Waite and her research team have designed and for which they generated funding to collect. In Chapter 10, they use the NSHAP data on older individuals who were fifty-seven and older when they were first surveyed in 2006 to examine the important question of the degree to which the economic downturn that began in 2007 led to children or other relatives "doubling up" when these respondents were surveyed again five years later in 2010.

While they utilize sociological concepts in their analysis, their reasoning also often invokes theoretical ideas drawn from family economics. In particular, Kim and Waite suggest that there may be a trade-off between the gains from scale economies of living together and the stress induced by living with grown children or other distal relatives. In a classic paper, Michael, Fuchs, and Scott (1980) show that the secular increase in the propensity of young adults and elderly widows to live alone can be explained by the growth in income, suggesting that the demand for privacy is a superior good that increasingly outweighs the scale economies, household collective goods, and the division of labor that increased household size might bring. When times are tough and income is low, Kim and Waite argue, the process may be reversed as family members who had previously lived separately double up. Studying changes in family structure in times of adversity provides indirect evidence about the value of the family as a form of insurance to its members.

A strength of NSHAP is that it collects detailed information about the relationships among people within the household in each wave. This enables Kim and Waite to distinguish "noncomplex" changes, such as marriage, widowing or teenage children leaving the household, from "complex" changes in which adult children or other relatives or persons enter or leave. They argue persuasively that it is the complex changes that impose the greatest economic and psychological costs on household members and find supporting evidence on the economic front indicating that increased complexity is associated with a decrease in household income adjusted for needs. Because NSHAP also collects extensive data on emotional well-being, another interesting inquiry would be an exploration of the psychological cost of complexity.

There are some limitations in the use of the NSHAP to assess the effect of the Great Recession on family structure. Its two waves provide only a single before-and-after observation of changes over five years. Thus, it is not possible to distinguish "normal" changes in household composition that might have occurred in periods prior to the recession from those that were induced by the downturn. In addition, the restriction of the sample to older households limits one's ability to generalize about its effects to other age groups.

Fortunately, recent research that examines the doubling-up phenomenon with other data sources tends to support the theoretical expectations and empirical results of Kim and Waite. Using Census data, Mykyta and Macartney (2011) find that younger adults and those who were not in the labor force were more likely to be doubled up in 2010 than in 2008. In general, doubled-up householders and adults were more disadvantaged and experienced a larger increase in poverty rates during the recession than their counterparts. Using data from the Survey of Income and Program Participation, Wiemers (2011) finds that individuals who become unemployed are much more likely to move in with others and less likely to have others move in with them. While these patterns are most likely among young adults, it also appears that middle-aged adults use coresidence as a way to weather spells of unemployment. As the economy improves, the unbundling of these complex households may provide an increase in new household formation that will be crucial to stimulating the depressed housing market.

NOTES

1. These papers were also published in two special issues of the *Journal of Political Economy* in March/April 1973 and March/April 1974. The citations are to the *JPE* publications.

2. Miller's framework also incorporates other ideas from the Schultz volume such as the female time-intensity of bearing and rearing children (Willis 1973), the choice between market and home provision of childcare (Heckman 1974), the trade-off between the quantity and quality of children (Becker and Lewis 1973; Willis 1973), and marriage market matching (Becker 1973, 1974).

3. http://quotationsbook.com/quote/26246.

REFERENCES

Becker, Gary S. (1960). "An Economic Analysis of Fertility." In *Demographic and Economic Change in Developed Countries*. Princeton, NJ: Princeton University Press.

Becker, Gary S. (1964). *Human Capital: A Theoretical and Empirical Analysis, with Special Reference to Education*, 2nd Edition. New York: Columbia University Press for the National Bureau of Economic Research.

Becker, Gary S. (1965). "A Theory of the Allocation of Time." *Economic Journal* 75 (299): 493–517.

Becker, Gary S. (1973). "A Theory of Marriage, Part I." *Journal of Political Economy* 81(4): 813–46.

Becker, Gary S. (1974). "A Theory of Marriage, Part II." *Journal of Political Economy* 82(2): S11–26.

Becker, Gary S., and H. Gregg Lewis (1973). "On the Interaction between the Quantity and Quality of Children." *Journal of Political Economy* 82(4): S279–88.

Ben-Porath, Y. (1967). "The Production of Human Capital and the Life Cycle of Earnings." *Journal of Political Economy* 75(4): 352–65.

Heckman, James J. (1974). "Effects of Child-Care Programs on Women's Work Effort." *Journal of Political Economy* 82(2): S136–63.

Kish, Leslie (2003). "The Hundred Years' Wars of Survey Sampling." In Graham Kalton and Steven Heeringa (Eds.), *Leslie Kish, Selected Papers*. New York: Wiley, 5–20.

Michael, Robert T., Victor R. Fuchs, and Sharon R. Scott (1980). "Changes in the Propensity to Live Alone: 1950–1976." *Demography* 17(1): 39–56.

Mincer, Jacob (1962). "Labor Force Participation of Married Women." In H. Greg Lewis (Ed.), *Aspects of Labor Economics*. Cambridge, MA: National Bureau of Economic Research.

Mincer, Jacob (1963). "Market Prices, Opportunity Costs and Income Effects." In *Measurement in Economics*. Stanford, CA: Stanford University Press.

Mincer, Jacob, and Solomon Polachek (1974). "Family Investment in Human Capital: Earnings of Women." *Journal of Political Economy* 82(2): S76–108.

Mykyta, Laryssa, and Suzanne Macartney (2011). "The Effects of Recession on Household Composition: 'Doubling Up' and Economic Well-Being." U.S. Census Bureau SEHSD Working Paper Number 2011–4.

Rotz, Dana (2011). "Why Have Divorce Rates Fallen? The Role of Women's Age at Marriage." Harvard University, unpublished paper.

Schultz, Theodore W. (1974). *Economics of the Family: Marriage, Children and Human Capital*. Chicago: University of Chicago Press for the National Bureau of Economic Research.

Ventura, Stephanie J. (2009). "Changing Patterns of Nonmarital Childbearing in the United States." NCHS Data Brief No. 18, May.

Wiemers, Emily E. (2011). "The Effect of Unemployment on Household Composition and Doubling Up." University of Michigan, National Poverty Center Working Paper Series, #11–12, April.

Willis, Robert J. (1973). "A New Approach to the Economic Theory of Fertility Behavior." *Journal of Political Economy* 81(2): S14–64.

Willis, Robert J. (1999). "A Theory of Out-of-Wedlock Childbearing." *Journal of Political Economy* 107(S6): S33–64.

CHAPTER TWELVE

Measuring the Population with Disabilities for Policy Analysis

Richard V. Burkhauser, Andrew J. Houtenville, and Jennifer R. Tennant

Researchers and policymakers creating evidence-based public policy for vulnerable populations must monitor their employment, economic well-being, and public program use. For them to do so, data must be available to identify the targeted populations. The first two sections of this book focus on lifecycle events—job loss and family formation events (divorce, birth of a child)—that can have significant negative effects on outcomes. The chapters in those sections use such data to provide empirical evidence of the consequences of these events on subsequent employment and income as well as the role public policy plays in ameliorating negative outcomes. It is relatively straightforward to both conceptualize and operationally capture job loss or family formation events in large data sets. So while the best policies for reducing the negative consequences of job loss, divorce, or the birth of a child are still in contention, there is general agreement on the prevalence of such events as well as their consequences on future employment and economic well-being.

The chapters in this section focus on events that begin with a health shock and that under certain circumstances result in activity limitations

---

This chapter was written in part with funding from a project of the Rehabilitation Research and Training Center on Disability Statistics and Demographics at Hunter College, which is funded by the National Institute on Disability and Rehabilitation Research (NIDRR, Federal Award #H133B080012); the contents of this chapter do not necessarily represent the policy of NIDRR and readers should not assume endorsement by the federal government (Edgar, 75.620 (b)).

that can also have significant negative effects on employment, economic well-being, and program participation. The conceptualization of disability, let alone the question of how operationally to capture the population with a disability in nationally representative data sets that can be used to monitor these outcomes, has been and remains challenging.

The authors of the next three chapters will use large data sets to provide empirical evidence of the employment, income, or program participation of people with disabilities as well as the role public policy plays in these outcomes. Here, we provide an introduction to an overarching criticism and a defense of the use of such data for these purposes. We first discuss why it has been so difficult to both conceptualize and operationally define the working-age population with disabilities. We then illustrate some of the challenges by focusing on both the controversy surrounding the use of the work-activity limitation question in the Current Population Survey Annual Social and Economic Supplement (CPS-ASES) to capture this population and the attempt to do so more accurately by using a new six-question sequence (not including a work-activity limitation question) in the American Community Survey (ACS) and in the Current Population Survey Basic Monthly Survey (CPS-BMS).

We replicate the work-activity limitation-based finding in the CPS-ASES that the relative employment of the working-age population with disabilities (i.e., relative to their counterparts without disabilities) has been falling continuously since 1989 and compare these findings with those in later years that were found by using both the ACS and CPS-BMS. We conclude that neither the new six-question sequence now being used by the BLS nor the single work-activity limitation question in the CPS-ASES fully capture the working-age population with disabilities. Our results show that in addition to capturing incomplete populations, these measures capture substantially different populations with respect to public program use, employment, and income. The work-activity limitation question does a better job of capturing those with disabilities on public programs, but may understate the employment rates and income among those with disabilities. The ACS and CPS-BMS six-question sequences understate public program use and likely overstate employment and income among those with disabilities.

CONCEPTUALIZING AND OPERATIONALLY
DEVELOPING DISABILITY DEFINITIONS

An antecedent to any empirically based policy analysis of the economic conditions of a given population is its conceptualization and its operational definition via a set of questions capable of capturing a random sample of that population in a data set. Age, sex, and, to a lesser degree, race are relatively easy to define conceptually and operationally and have proven to be relatively noncontroversial ways of identifying specific subpopulations. This has not been the case for disability. What distinguishes disability from age, sex, and race is that these latter three population definitions are largely immutable to the social and physical environment. That is, while the consequences of being old, female, or African American are certainly affected by the social and physical environment, one's calendar age, sex, and race are much less so.

The definition of disability is more complex. Efforts to implement simple health-based conceptualizations of disability as meeting some objective medical standards have been abandoned, in part, because they are not sensitive to the importance of societal factors. Disability is now conceptualized as an interaction between a person's health condition and the social and physical environment (Weathers 2009; World Health Organization 2001).

As Burkhauser and Houtenville (2010) state, there is no universal agreement on the most appropriate definition of disability. However, the two most widely used are the World Health Organization's (WHO 2001) International Classification of Functioning, Disability and Health (ICF) and the conceptual model of disability created by Saad Nagi (1965, 1969, and 1991). Both conceptual models recognize disability as a dynamic process that involves the interaction of a person's health condition and personal characteristics with the physical and social environments. The emergence of the ICF as a systematic and comprehensive way of conceptualizing the population with disabilities has resulted in an international effort to use these classifications to better capture the population with disabilities in government-sponsored data sets (Swanson, Carrothers, and Mulhorn 2003). We focus on that conceptual framework below.

In the ICF framework, a *health condition* is a prerequisite for a disability. Examples of health conditions are listed in the International Classification of Diseases, Tenth Edition (ICD-10), and they encompass diseases, injuries, health disorders, and other health-related conditions. An *impairment* is defined as a significant deviation or loss in body function or structure resulting from a health condition. For example, paralysis of a limb or vision deterioration may be classified as impairments. An *activity limitation* is defined as the difficulty an individual may have in executing activities. For example, a person who experiences difficulty dressing, bathing, or performing other activities of daily living because of a health condition may be classified as having an activity limitation. A *participation restriction* is defined as an issue that an individual may experience in a life situation. For example, a working-age person with a health condition may have difficulty participating in employment as a result of the physical environment (e.g., lack of reasonable accommodations) or the social environment (e.g., discrimination).

In the ICF framework, the term *disability* describes the health-condition-based presence of an impairment, activity limitation, or participation restriction. While these concepts overlap, it is possible that one of them can occur without the others. For instance, it is possible that a person may have a health-based participation restriction without an activity limitation or impairment. For example, a person diagnosed as being HIV positive may not have an evident impairment or activity limitation but may not be able to find employment because of discrimination resulting from his or her health condition alone. Similarly, a person with a history of mental illness, but who no longer has a loss of capacity or an activity limitation, may also be unable to find employment for the same reason.

Because the CPS and ACS are both broad surveys designed to capture a wide array of socioeconomic outcomes for people living in very diverse American dwellings, the problem is how to operationally capture, in a few questions, a random sample of this complex conceptualization of the population with disabilities. One way to describe how this has been done in the CPS and ACS is to imagine three concentric circles (e.g., a target), with the outermost circle representing people with disabilities—as defined above using ICF concepts—the middle circle representing those with work-activity limitations, and the innermost circle representing people currently receiving Social Security Disability Income (SSDI) or Supplemental Security Income-Disabled Adults (SSI) benefits, or both, based on their severe work limitations.

Specifically, the outermost circle contains all the people who identify themselves (or are identified by a survey respondent who is a proxy) as having health-condition-based impairments, activity limitations, or participation restrictions—the ICF conceptualization of disability. We will argue that this is the conceptualization of disability the new six-question sequences in the ACS and the CPS-BMS are attempting to operationally achieve.

The middle circle depicts people with work-activity limitations. The one question regarding disability in the CPS-ASEC focuses on a single activity limitation: a health-condition-based work-activity limitation. Thus one would expect that the population captured by this single work-activity limitation question would be a subset of the broader ICF-defined population captured by the six-question disability sequence in the ACS or CPS-BMS surveys because some people with impairments or other activity limitations are not limited with respect to work. But everyone with a work-activity limitation will be captured by the more broadly conceptualized six-question sequence.

The innermost circle contains recipients of SSDI and/or SSI benefits who, because entry into these programs is restricted to those with work-activity limitations based on severe health conditions, would be a subset of those with work-activity limitations.

This representation of concentric circles for these three populations recognizes that even some people with severe work-activity limitations will not be contained in the SSDI/SSI population and that some people with severe impairments or other activity limitations will not be contained in the work-activity limitation population. And, of course, many people with less severe impairments and other activity limitations will neither be in the SSDI/SSI population nor in the work-activity limitation population. Viewing the broad ICF conceptualization of the population with disabilities in this way is consistent with the view that the social environment will play a role in which one of these concentric circles people with disabilities find themselves. In the next section, we discuss the details of the questions the CPS and ACS use to capture their populations with disabilities.

DATA

Current Population Survey

The CPS is a joint effort of the Bureau of Labor Statistics and the Census Bureau, and is the primary source of monthly labor force statistics in the United States. The multifaceted CPS includes the CPS-BMS, which is fielded every month, and supplements like the CPS-ASEC, which is fielded every March. The CPS uses a rotation system for its interviews.[1]

The CPS-ASEC began asking a work-activity limitation question in 1981 that has become the primary way that researchers capture levels and long-term trends in the prevalence of disability and the social success indicators of the working-age population with disabilities. See the appendix at the end of the chapter for the specific language of this question. But as Hale (2001) correctly points out, this single question was included to facilitate the identification of individuals receiving disability-related sources of income rather than to fully capture the working-age population with disabilities.

Beginning in June 2008, a new sequence of six questions taken from the ACS was included in the CPS-BMS for this purpose. (For a history of the development of these questions, see Miller and DeMaio, 2006, and Brault, Stern, and Raglin, 2007.) The specific wording for these questions is also found in the appendix. The questions were informed by the broad ICF conceptualization of disability and inquire about physical, mental, or emotional conditions that cause serious difficulties with daily activities including vision; hearing; remembering/concentrating/making decisions; walking or climbing stairs; dressing or bathing; and going out of the house for errands.

This six-question sequence was asked of all CPS respondents scheduled to be asked questions in June 2008. Since then, all CPS respondents are asked these six questions in their first and fifth months in the sample (CPS, 2009b). Importantly, while the six-question sequence in the CPS-BMS does not include a work-activity limitation question, all CPS respondents continue to be asked this question in March, when the CPS-ASEC is conducted together with the CPS-BMS. This results in the work-activity limitation question being asked together with the six-question sequence to the 25 percent of CPS-ASEC respondents for whom March is their first or fifth month in the sample. For the other 75 percent of CPS-ASEC respondents, the six-question sequence is asked in a different CPS month.

We will take advantage of this monthly linkage in CPS data to compare a sample of CPS respondents in 2009 and 2010 who answered both the six-question sequence and the work-activity limitation question to measure the prevalence of disability using these two alternative population definitions as well as a disability definition that is based on a positive answer to any of the seven questions. Finally, we will discuss how well these alternative operational uses of the ICF conceptualization of the population with disabilities are able to capture the innermost circle of that conceptualization—the population receiving SSDI or SSI-Disabled Adult benefits.

American Community Survey

The ACS is an annual survey that began in 2000. The Census Bureau designed it to replace the decennial census long form. Substantial testing occurred between 2000 and 2004, which makes it difficult to compare results across years, so we begin our analysis in 2005. The specific wording for the six-question sequence in the 2005–07 ACS is found in the appendix. The questions include the work-activity limitation question as well as questions on physical, cognitive, and activity limitations discussed above, except that the sensory question combines vision and hearing. In 2008, the vision and hearing questions were separated and the work-activity limitation question was dropped from the sequence. (See Miller and De Maio, 2006; Brault, Stern, and Raglin, 2007; and Burkhauser, Houtenville, and Tennant, 2012, for a discussion of the evidence used in making this decision.) It is this revised ACS six-question sequence, without a work-activity limitation question, that is now used in both the ACS and CPS-BMS. We will compare the ACS data between 2005 and 2007 containing the work-activity limitation question with the CPS-ASEC data to show how the addition of these five impairment or other activities limitation questions affects the size of the working-age population with disabilities and its employment. However, because the new six-question disability sequence in the ACS dropped the work-activity limitation, we are not able to do so as completely for later ACS years.

The CPS-BMS and the decennial census long form (now the ACS) have long included demographic information on age, sex, and race, but their current six-question sequence based on ICF concepts to capture the population with disabilities has only been asked since 2008. As we proceed, it is important to recognize that the purposes for using this six-question sequence are consistent with those discussed in the first sentence of this chapter—monitoring the employment, public program use, and economic well-being of vulnerable populations. These public policy objectives are spelled out in the Census 2000 documentation stating that the disability sequence should be designed to capture a population consistent with legislative and programmatic needs, including, among other things, *generating data relevant to the Social Security disability programs* (U.S. Census 2000).

Because the CPS contains precise program participation information on SSDI and SSI benefit receipt, we will be able to show how successfully the work-activity limitation question, the six-question disability sequence, and the seven-question disability sequence in the CPS are able to capture the innermost circle of the ICF-based population with disabilities, a task of relevance to Social Security disability program policy.

In the next section, we will discuss the disagreement surrounding the use of the single work-activity limitation question in the CPS-ASEC to capture a working-age population with disabilities from 1981 through 2007 in the absence of a data set containing a broader ICF-based set of questions.

DISAGREEMENT OVER THE USE OF THE WORK-ACTIVITY
LIMITATION QUESTION

In the absence of a broader set of questions, the CPS-ASEC work-activity limitation question has been used extensively in the economics literature to capture the working-age population with disabilities: its employment, public program use, and economic well-being; how these outcomes compare to those of populations without disabilities; and the role public policy has played in these differences. See Bound and Burkhauser (1999) for an early review of the economic literature on disability. Also see, more recently, Acemoglu and Angrist (2001); Burkhauser et al. (2002);

Stapleton and Burkhauser (2003); Hotchkiss (2004); Houtenville et al. (2009); and Burkhauser and Daly (2011).

In Figure 12.1 we focus on the working-age population ages twenty-five to sixty-one to capture those whose employment is not sensitive to changes around entry into the labor market or exit from the labor market and to report the prevalence of work-activity limitation-based disability over time.[2] To capture business-cycle conditions, we denote official recession years (as defined by the National Bureau of Economic Research) with grey vertical lines. Using our work-activity limitation-based measure of disability we show that over the period from 1981 to 2010, the prevalence of disability has hovered at around 8 percent with no discernible upward or downward trend. With the exception of the most recent recession, disability prevalence rates do not appear to be very sensitive to business cycles.

The long-run trend found in Figure 12.2 is much more controversial. It reports the employment rate of those with disabilities relative to those without disabilities over time, again using the CPS-ASEC work-activity limitation-based measure of disability. During the 1980s, the relative employment of those with disabilities rose following the major recession

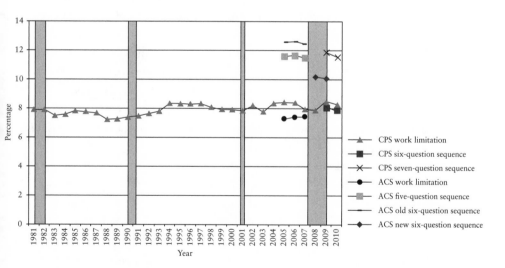

Figure 12.1   Disability prevalence, by disability type, civilian noninstitutionalized population, 25–61

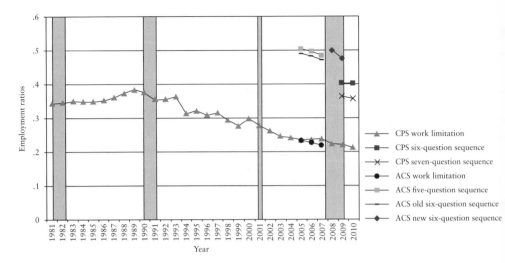

Figure 12.2   Disability/no disability employment rate ratios, by disability type, civilian noninstitutionalized population, 25–61

of 1981–82 and reached a peak of just over 38 percent in 1989, the peak of the 1980s business cycle. But this ratio began to fall as the economy moved into the recession of the early 1990s. Instead of increasing as the recession ended as it had during the previous decade, the relative employment of working-age people with disabilities continued to decline over the major growth years of the 1990s, and has continued to do so ever since. By 2010 the employment of working-age people with disabilities was only 21 percent that of their counterparts without disabilities.

These very grim findings with respect to the relative employment of working-age people with disabilities have been found consistently by those using the CPS-ASEC work-activity limitation question. (See Stapleton and Burkhauser, 2003, for a review of this literature.) The use of this question has been severely criticized. Recalling the concentric circles discussed above, those reporting a work-activity limitation are only a subsample of the broader population with disabilities. It should be the case that the prevalence of disability is far larger using this broader conceptualization of disability. And the work-activity limitation-based population should also be less likely to work than the population captured in this broader definition—since by definition one must report a work-activity limitation to be included in this subpopulation. Thus, using this subpopulation to make inferences about the employment rate of the broader ICF-based population, which also includes people with impairments or other activity limitations but who do not report a work-activity limitation, is likely to understate these rates. Even holding the severity of an impairment constant, however, it is probable that those reporting a work-activity limitation are more likely to not be working, since those who are not working will be more likely to report that their impairment or other activity limitations also affect their ability to work—or, conversely, those who are currently working are less likely to report a work limitation. (See Kirchner, 1996, and Hale, 2001, for examples of this type of criticism.) Furthermore, Hale (2001) correctly argues that the CPS-ASEC work-activity limitation question was never intended to capture a random sample of this broader population with disabilities.

Burkhauser et al. (2002), using data from the National Health Interview Survey (NHIS), which contained questions on a person's impairments as well as a question (in a different part of the survey) on that person's work-activity limitations, demonstrate that those reporting the same severe impairments were much less likely to report being employed if they also reported having a work-activity limitation. For example, only 69 percent of all those men and women ages twenty-five to sixty-one who reported being blind in both eyes also reported having a work-activity limitation—a subset of this impaired population—but in this subset only 20 percent were employed. In contrast, among the 31 percent of those ages twenty-five to sixty-one who were blind in both eyes but reported no work-activity limitation, 81 percent were employed (Burkhauser et al. 2002, table 1, p. 545).

Therefore, not only would a sample of people with work-activity limitations understate the prevalence of people with impairments in the broader population, but it would also exaggerate the percentage of that broader impairment-based population with disabilities who were not working. That is, people with impairments who *also* report a work-activity limitation are a subset of people with impairments. In addition, those with work-activity limitations are more likely to not be working, both because their impairments are likely to be more severe and perhaps because those with impairments who are not working may be more likely to say they have a work-activity limitation for other reasons.

Burkhauser et al. (2002) also show, however, that despite the fact that the work-activity limitation-based population with disabilities understates the prevalence of the impairment-based population with disabilities as well as its employment rate, the trends in these two disability populations between 1983 and 1996 (the last year that such detailed information on impairments and work limitations was asked in the NHIS) were not significantly different. Hence the controversial declines in the relative employment rate of people with disabilities captured in Figure 12.2 using the work-activity limitation question in the CPS-ASEC are not significantly different from the declines found by using the impairment question in the NHIS; therefore, they can be used by researchers trying to explain trends in the employment of working-age people with disabilities.

Despite this evidence in support of the value of the work-activity limitation question and, in 2006, the warning of the then president of the American Statistical Society that "research on technical and methodological adjustments to a work-activities question continue until such a question could be added to the American Community Survey to improve its measure of work disability" (Keller-McNulty 2006), the work-activity limitation question was dropped from the set of six questions in the ACS in 2008. In addition, as described in the data section above, beginning in June 2008, this same six-question sequence without a work-activity limitation question was also included in the CPS-BMS.

In the next section we revisit Figures 12.1 and 12.2 and compare the prevalence of disability in the ICF-inspired six-question sequence in the ACS data in 2005–07, when it included a work-activity limitation question, with the CPS-ASEC trends reported in those years. We then do the same with the more recent ACS and CPS using the new six-question sequence that no longer includes a work-activity limitation question. We then focus on the possible reasons for these results.

COMPARING CPS- AND ACS-BASED DISABILITY
PREVALENCE AND EMPLOYMENT TRENDS

Between 2005 and 2007 the ACS six-question sequence included a work-activity limitation question. Not surprisingly, based on our concentric circle concept (and by definition since it is only one of the six questions), the prevalence rates of disability in the ACS using this six-question sequence for these three years are substantially greater (just over 12 percent) than when using only the work-activity limitation question (around 8 percent)—i.e., there are respondents in the ACS who report impairments or other activity limitations but do not report work limitations (Figure 12.1). So as Burkhauser et al. (2002) showed with NHIS data, using a work-activity limitation question alone to capture the broader working-age population with impairments or other activity limitations will understate the size of that population.

It is important to note, however (and not consistent with the aspirations of capturing the full population with disabilities) that not all persons who report a work-activity limitation in the 2005–07 ACS are also captured by the other five questions because the prevalence rate found using the five-question sequence (around 11 percent) is below that of the six-question sequence. Much more important, in 2008 and 2009 when the sensory question in the ACS was broken into separate vision and hearing impairments (but the work-activity limitation question was dropped) what should have resulted in an increase in the prevalence rate relative to the five-question sequence in 2005–07 that also did not include the work-activity limitation question, instead resulted in a substantial blip downward (to around 10 percent) in prevalence rates and an even bigger blip downward from the original six-question sequence, which included the work-activity limitation question.[3]

Figure 12.1 thus shows that from 2005 to 2007, excluding the work-activity limitation question from the old six-question sequence in the ACS substantially understates measured prevalence of disability among the working-age population in the United States. It is likely that the new six-question sequence that excludes the work-activity limitation question has missed an even larger number of those who would have reported work-activity limitations if asked. (See Burkhauser, Houtenville, and Tennant, 2012, for a more complete discussion.) To the degree that these respondents "truly" have health condition-based work limitations, the new six-question sequence in the ACS will undercount the true ICF-based conceptualization of the population with disabilities.

Once again, and not surprisingly, based on our concentric circle concept (and by definition since it is only one of the six questions), in 2005 the employment rate of working-age persons with disabilities relative to those without disabilities is substantially greater (about 50 percent) using the six-question sequence in the ACS than using only the work-activity limitation question (around 24 percent) in the ACS (Figure 12.2). Consistent with Burkhauser et al. (2002), this finding shows that using a work-activity limitation question alone to capture the broader working-age population with impairments or other activity limitations will understate the employment rate of that population. However, the relative trends in the employment rate in both the five- and six-question sequence-based disability populations and in the work-activity limitation-based disability population between 2005 and 2007 are all downward sloping during this three-year time period when such information was available in the ACS, suggesting that while the work-activity limitation-based disability population and these other two broader measures of the working-age population with disabilities generate substantially different levels of relative employment, they all capture similar downward trends (Burkhauser et al. 2002).

Nevertheless, in 2008, when the work-activity limitation question was dropped from the old six-question sequence, what should have resulted in another year of decline in the relative employment rate of people with disabilities, as the economy headed into recession, instead resulted in an uptick in their relative employment rate compared to both the five- and six-question-sequence populations used in the previous year. To the degree that this uptick is the result of excluding respondents who would have reported a work-activity limitation and would have been more likely not to be employed, this new six-question sequence will overstate the relative employment rates of the true ICF-based conceptualization of the population with disabilities. (Burkhauser et al. 2002)

DISABILITY PREVALENCE AND EMPLOYMENT IN 2010 USING THE COMBINED CPS

In this section we focus on the 2010 CPS-ASEC population because, as discussed in the data section, all respondents in this supplement were asked the work-activity limitation question in March and the six-question sequence (not including a work-activity limitation question) either in March or in their first or fifth month in the CPS-BMS sample. This allows us to compare how using these alternative definitions of disability, or a combination of the two, changes the prevalence of disability in 2010 as well as the social success outcomes of employment, program participation, and economic well-being within them.

Table 12.1 reports the number of working-age people ages twenty-five to sixty-one using the single work-activity limitation question in the CPS-ASEC (column 1), the six-question sequence in the CPS-BMS (column 2), and the seven-question sequence that pulls the work-activity limitation question from one part of the CPS and the six-question sequence from another part (column 3). Using our concentric circles model of the disability population, we see that when we add the six questions that capture impairments and other activity limitations to our work-activity limitation question, the combined CPS-ASEC population expands from 12.5 million (a prevalence rate of 8.3 percent) to 17.5 million (a prevalence rate of 11.6 percent) people. This is a dramatic increase that suggests that using the work-activity limitation question alone will undercount this broader ICF-based population. But the same is the case if we only use the new ACS six-question sequences in the CPS-BMS to capture the broader population with disabilities. Only 11.9 million working-age people with disabilities (a prevalence rate of 7.9 percent) are captured by these six questions versus the 17.5 million (11.6 percent prevalence rate) using all seven questions.

More important, the characteristics of those missed by using either the six-question sequence or the work-activity limitation question are quite different. The six-question-sequence-based population is much more likely to be employed across all of our measures of employment. The employment rate in 2010 using the six-question population is almost twice that of the work-activity limitation-based population—30.8 to 16.6 percent. The relative employment rate in 2010 is also much higher for the six-question-sequence-based population. Because of the higher employment rates, the six-question-sequence-based population, not surprisingly, has greater average income and a lower risk of poverty than the work-activity limitation-based population. The six-question-sequence-based population is also much less likely to receive any of the major disability-related program benefits than the work-activity limitation-based population (41.8 versus 53.1 percent, respectively).

As can be seen in Figure 12.1, while a comparison of the prevalence of disability using the six-question sequence in the CPS-BMS is

TABLE 12.1

Population size, prevalence rate, demographics, socioeconomic outcomes, and program participation of noninstitutionalized civilians ages 25–61, by disability measure

	WORK-ACTIVITY LIMITATION	SIX-QUESTION SEQUENCE	EITHER SIX-QUESTION SEQUENCE OR WORK-ACTIVITY LIMITATION	WORK-ACTIVITY LIMITATION SUBSET	SIX-QUESTION SUBSET
	B + C	A + B	A + B + C	C	A
Population size[a]	12,531,314	11,934,894	17,538,186	5,006,872	5,603,293
Prevalence rate[a] (%)	8.3	7.9	11.6	3.7	3.3
Male[a] (%)	48.7	48.6	48.8	49.3	49.0
25 to 29 years[a] (%)	6.9	6.6	7.1	8.1	7.5
White non-Hispanic[a] (%)	65.2	68.2	66.4	62.7	69.5
High school or equivalent[a] (%)	37.7	36.3	36.7	37.6	34.1
Percentage employed[a]	16.6	30.8	28.2	22.8	57.3
Relative employment rate[a]	0.213	0.402	0.358	0.304	0.779
Percentage in the labor force[a]	20.6	36.5	33.7	27.9	66.5
Percentage working at least 52 hours in the prior calendar year[b]	23.4	37.9	35.5	30.5	65.9
Percentage working full-time, full-year in the prior calendar year[b]	7.5	20.4	17.4	11.0	42.3
Median wages and salaries of full-time, full-year workers[b] (dollars)	32,120	35,152	35,000	33,100	36,500
Poverty rate[b] (%)	30.1	25.6	26.5	28.5	17.5
Median household size-adjusted income[b] (dollars)	19,486	22,066	21,779	21,245	30,235
Social Security Disability Insurance (SSDI)[b] (%)	32.3	25.5	25.0	23.9	6.6
Supplemental Security Income–disabled adults (SSI)[b] (%)	20.8	16.8	16.5	15.9	5.9
SSDI and/or SSI–disabled adults narrow definition[b] (%)	49.2	38.9	38.5	37.6	11.6

SSDI and/or SSI–disabled adults gross definition[b] (%)	52.4	41.8	41.7	41.4	14.8
Workers' compensation[b] (%)	1.7	1.1	1.4	2.1	0.8
Veterans disability[b] (%)	3.8	3.1	3.2	3.5	1.7
Any of the above programs[b] (%)	53.1	41.8	41.9	42.2	13.8

SOURCE: Authors' calculations using March 2010 Current Population Survey.

NOTE: Sample weights are used to obtain representative estimates.

[a]2010

[b]2009

approximately the same as the prevalence of disability using the single work-activity limitation question in the CPS-ASEC, this is a coincidence that is a result of each missing an approximately equal amount of respondents who report either a work-activity limitation or a six-question-sequence limitation but not both. Hence neither does a good job of capturing a broader ICF-based conceptualization of disability, which would include those who those report impairments, a work-activity limitation, or the other activity limitations operationally captured in these seven questions. The prevalence rate of disability using this broader seven-question-population definition is much closer to the old six-question-sequence-based population in the 2005–07 ACS that it resembles. That is, there is less of a difference in disability prevalence rates between data sets (ACS and CPS) using similar definitions of the disability population than there is across definitions using the same data set.

The differences in the relative employment rates of these three populations with disabilities found in Table 12.1 and reported in Figure 12.2 are similar to those found by using these same three population definitions with the old six-question sequence in the ACS 2005–07. The employment rates in the work-activity limitation-based population in the CPS are substantially below those in the new six-question disability sequence-based population or the seven-question sequence-based population in the CPS but close to those in the work-activity limitation-based population in the ACS.

Results from Table 12.1, Figure 12.1, and Figure 12.2 show that while the overall prevalence of disability using the six-question sequence is approximately the same as the prevalence of disability using a single work-activity limitation question, as are the broad demographic characteristics (age, race, gender, and education) of these populations, there are large differences in the employment, program participation, and economic well-being of these populations.

The reason for these differences in the employment, program participation, and economic well-being of these two populations is made clearer in Figure 12.3. The total population found using the broader seven-question sequence, which is closest to the old six-question sequence in the ACS, is denoted by (A + B + C) in the diagram. Only 40 percent of the people in this broader disability category are the same people—that is, they report having both one of the impairments or other activity limi-

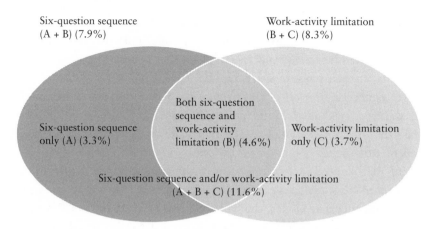

Figure 12.3 Prevalence rate of noninstitutionalized civilians ages 25–61, by disability type

SOURCE: Authors' calculations using the 2010 March Current Population Survey.
NOTE: Sample weights are used to obtain representative estimates.

tations in the six-question sequence in the CPS-BMS and a work-activity limitation in the CPS-ASEC, represented by (B) in the diagram. The rest of the population consists of the 30 percent of the population who only reported having one or more of the six-question sequence, (A) in the diagram, or the 30 percent who only report a work-activity limitation, (C) in the diagram. These two subpopulations have very different employment rates, incomes, poverty rates, and public program use. This can be seen in columns 4 and 5 of Table 12.1.

While the work-activity limitation question, (B + C) in the diagram, is operationally a subcircle of the broader seven-question sequence (A + B + C), this is not the case when the six-question-sequence, which does not include the work-activity limitation question, is considered to be the operational set of questions to capture the "true" ICF-based conceptualization of disability. In this case, the entire area (C) is missed by the six-question-sequence (A + B) and vice versa. That is, unlike the model of concentric circles we outlined above, the new six-question sequence-based population fails to capture (C), just as the work-activity limitation-based question fails to capture (A). This leads to an undercounting of the broader disability population represented by (A + B + C) when using these two alternative disability populations but more importantly, neither measure captures a random sample of that population.

This implicitly assumes that (A + B + C) best represents the true ICF-based conceptualization of the population of working-age people with disabilities. Burkhauser, Houtenville, and Tennant (2012) provide a pragmatic test of this proposition, based on the fact that the Census 2000 documentation spelled out a goal for the set of questions that should be used in the ACS to capture the population with disabilities—*generating data relevant to the Social Security disability programs.* They argue, using the model of concentric circles, that the subcircle of SSDI and SSI-Disabled Adult beneficiaries who have been determined by the Social Security Administration to have a work-activity limitation that is severe enough for them not to be able to perform any substantial gainful employment, should be a subcircle of the work-activity-limitation population (B + C), which in turn is a subcircle of a broader conceptualization that includes those with impairments or other activities limitations (A + B + C).

Then, using the population receiving SSDI or SSI benefits in the 2010 CPS-ASEC data sample, they find that 55.4 percent of this SSDI/SSI population report both a work-activity limitation and one of the six-question impairments or other activity limitations (B). The marginal increase in the share of this SSDI/SSI population captured by adding the work-activity limitation-only population (C) is 28.7 percent and the marginal increase by adding the six-question-sequence-only population (A) is 7.9 percent. Altogether, 92.0 percent of the SSDI/SSI population is captured by the seven-question (A + B + C) population. Thus the work-activity-limitation-based population does a far better job (84.1 percent) of capturing the SSDI/SSI population than does the six-question-sequence-based population (63.3 percent). Using the six-question-sequence-based population will miss over 2.1 million SSDI-SSI beneficiaries found in the seven-question sequence-based working-age population with disabilities (Table 12.1, subset C, fourth row from the bottom).

CONCLUSION

In this chapter, we show that not only is disability hard to conceptualize, but it is even harder to use operationally in two national data sets that are widely used by researchers and policymakers interested in providing the evidence for policymaking for vulnerable populations. Our analysis finds that while there are well-known problems with the work-activity limitation question used in the CPS-ASEC since 1981, it is far from clear that the decision to discard the work-activity limitation question from the new six-question disability sequence beginning in 2008 in the ACS and in June 2008 in the CPS-BMS resulted in a superior operational use of an ICF-based conceptualization of the working-age population with disabilities. This is unlikely to be the case because a significant portion of those who report a work-activity limitation in the CPS-ASEC are not captured by this new ACS-inspired and official BLS measure of the population with disabilities in the CPS-BMS. To the degree that respondents who reported a work-activity limitation in the CPS-ASEC should be included in the true working-age population with disabilities, the population of working-age people captured by the ACS-inspired six-question sequence in the CPS-BMS will undercount the true population with disabilities, overstate its relative employment rates and income, and understate the public program use it was specifically developed to capture.

CPS-ASEC, 1981–ONWARD

Work limitation: Does anyone in this household have a health problem or disability which prevents them from working or which limits the kind or amount of work they can do?

ACS, 2005–2007

Sensory: Does this person have any of the following long-lasting conditions: Blindness, deafness, or a severe vision or hearing impairment?

Physical: Does this person have any of the following long-lasting conditions: A condition that substantially limits one or more basic physical activities such as walking, climbing stairs, reaching, lifting or carrying?

Cognitive: Because of a physical, mental, or emotional condition lasting 6 months or more, does this person have any difficulty in doing any of the following activities: Learning, remembering, or concentrating?

Activities of Daily Living: Because of a physical, mental, or emotional condition lasting 6 months or more, does this person have any difficulty in doing any of the following activities: Dressing, bathing, or getting around inside the home?

Instrumental Activities of Daily Living: Because of a physical, mental, or emotional condition lasting 6 months or more, does this person have any difficulty in doing any of the following activities: Going outside the home alone to shop or visit a doctor's office?

Work Limitation: Because of a physical, mental, or emotional condition lasting 6 months or more, does this person have any difficulty in doing any of the following activities: Working at a job or business?

CPS-BMS, 2008–ONWARD; ACS 2008–ONWARD

Hearing: Is anyone deaf or does anyone have serious difficulty hearing?

Vision: Is anyone blind or does anyone have serious difficulty seeing even when wearing glasses?

Physical: Does anyone have serious difficulty walking or climbing stairs?

Cognitive: Because of a physical, mental, or emotional condition, does anyone have serious difficulty concentrating, remembering or making decisions?

Activities of Daily Living: Does anyone have difficulty dressing or bathing?

Instrumental Activities of Daily Living: Because of a physical, mental or emotional condition, does anyone have difficulty doing errands alone such as visiting a doctor's office or shopping?

NOTES

1. Each housing unit is followed for a 16-month period—four months in-sample, eight months out-of-sample, and then four months in-sample. That is, a respondent in a selected housing unit is interviewed with respect to all persons living in that housing unit for four consecutive months. After eight consecutive months out-of-sample, a respondent in that housing unit is interviewed for another four consecutive months, after which the housing unit is retired from the CPS sample. In any sample month, one-eighth of the sample is being interviewed for the first time (month-in-sample, or MIS = 1), one-eighth is being interviewed for the second time (MIS = 2), and so on (CPS, 2006, 3–13).

2. In all of our figures and charts we focus on working-age (twenty-five to sixty-one) civilians not living in group quarters. We use age twenty-five as the lower bound to minimize the influence of schooling on the employment differentials between people with and without disabilities. Similarly, we use age sixty-one as the upper bound to minimize the influence of retirement. The employment variable is "employed in the reference period—either at the time the question was asked or in the previous year." In all cases when referring to CPS-ASEC income, the question is asked in March but the reference is to the previous year's income, and the program participation rate is based on those receiving SSDI and/or SSI benefits as part of the previous year's income.

3. Burkhauser, Houtenville, and Tennant (2012) argue that because the work-activity limitation question directly followed the five impairment and other activity limitation questions in the 2005–07 ACS, it was more likely that enumerators would revisit the five-question sequence if a respondent reported a work-activity limitation but not one of the impairments or other activity limitations or vice versa and check the responses for consistency (consistent with the view that work-activity limitations are a subset of general impairment and activity-limitation questions). The fact that the prevalence of work-activity limitations in the CPS-ASEC during these three years is consistently above the prevalence of work-activity limitations in the ACS, together with the fact that the 2008–09 six-question sequence (which drops the work-activity limitation question) yields disability prevalence rates that are below the disability prevalence rates for both the five- and six-question sequences found in 2005–07 ACS is consistent with this view.

REFERENCES

Acemoglu, D., and J. Angrist. 2001. "Consequences of Employment Protection? The Case of the Americans with Disabilities Act." *Journal of Political Economy* 109(5): 915–57.

Bound, J., and R. V. Burkhauser. 1999. "Economic Analysis of Transfer Programs Targeted on People with Disabilities." In Orley C. Ashenfelter and David Card (eds.), *Handbook of Labor Economics*. Volume 3C. Amsterdam: Elsevier Science, 3417–528.

Brault, M., S. Stern, and D. Raglin. 2007. *2006 ACS Content Test Evaluation Report Covering Disability*, U.S. Census Bureau, Washington, DC.

Burkhauser, R. V., and M. C. Daly. 2011. *The Declining Work and Welfare of People with Disabilities: What Went Wrong and a Strategy for Change.* Washington, DC: American Enterprise Press.

Burkhauser, R., M. Daly, A. Houtenville, and N. Nargis. 2002. "Self-Reported Work Limitation Data: What They Can and Cannot Tell Us." *Demography* 39(3): 541–55.

Burkhauser, R., and A. Houtenville. 2010. "Employment Among Working-Age People with Disabilities: What the Latest Data Can Tell Us." In E. M. Szymanski and R. M. Parker (eds.), *Work and Disability: Contexts, Issues, and Strategies for Enhancing Employment Outcomes for People with Disabilities.* Austin, TX: Pro-Ed, 49–86.

Burkhauser, R., A. Houtenville, and J. Tennant. 2012. "Capturing the Elusive Working-Age Population with Disabilities: Reconciling Conflicting Social Success Estimates from the Current Population Survey and American Community Survey." *Journal of Disability Policy Studies.*

Current Population Survey. 2006. Design and Methodology, Technical Paper 66. Available at: http://www.census.gov/prod/2006pubs/tp-66.pdf.

Current Population Survey. 2009a. Annual Social and Economic (ASEC) Supplement Technical Documentation. Available at: http://www.census.gov/apsd/techdoc/cps/cpsmar09.pdf.

Current Population Survey. 2009b. "Frequently Asked Questions about Disability Data." Available at: http://www.bls.gov/cps/cpsdisability_faq.htm.

Hale, T. 2001. "The Lack of a Disability Measure in Today's Current Population Survey." *Monthly Labor Review* (June): 38–41.

Hotchkiss, J. 2004. "A Closer Look at the Employment Impact of the Americans with Disabilities Act." *Journal of Human Resources* 39:887–911.

Houtenville, A. J., D. C. Stapleton, R. R. Weathers II, and R. V. Burkhauser (eds.). 2009. *Counting Working-Age People with Disabilities: What Current Data Tell Us and Options for Improvement.* Kalamazoo, MI: W. E. Upjohn Institute for Employment Research.

Keller-McNulty, S. 2006. Reference: American Community Survey and Disability (Letter to Dr. Lewis Kincannon, Director, U.S. Census Bureau). Reproduced in *AmStat News*, June 2006, 4.

Kirchner, C. 1996. "Looking Under the Street Lamp: Inappropriate Uses of Measures Just Because They Are There." *Journal of Disability Policy Studies* 7(1): 77–90.

Miller, K., and T. DeMaio. 2006. *Report of Cognitive Research on Proposed American Community Survey Disability Questions*, U.S. Bureau of the Census, Washington, DC.

Nagi, S. 1965. "Some Conceptual Issues in Disability and Rehabilitation." In M. B. Sussman (ed.), *Sociology and Rehabilitation*. Washington, DC: American Sociological Association, 100–113.

Nagi, S. 1969. *Disability and Rehabilitation: Legal, Clinical and Self-Concepts of Measurement*. Columbus: Ohio State University Press.

Nagi, S. 1991. "Disability Concepts Revisited: Implications to Prevention." In A. M. Pope and A. R. Tarlove (eds.), *Disability in America: Toward a National Agenda for Prevention*. Washington, DC: National Academy Press, 307–27.

Stapleton, D. C., and R. V. Burkhauser (eds.). 2003. *The Decline in Employment of People with Disabilities: A Policy Puzzle*. Kalamazoo, MI: W. E. Upjohn Institute for Employment Research.

Swanson, G., L. Carrothers, and K. Mulhorn. 2003. "Comparing Disability Survey Questions in Five Countries: A Study Using ICF to Guide Comparisons." *Disability and Rehabilitation: An International Multidisciplinary Journal* 25:665–75.

U.S. Bureau of the Census. 2000. Census 2000 Needs Requirements, March 23, 2000. Retrieved November 18, 2004, from http://www.census.gov/dmd/www/pdf/09h_di.pdf.

Weathers, R. 2009. "The Disability Data Landscape." In Houtenville, A., D. Stapleton, R. Weathers, and R. Burkhauser (eds.), *Counting Working-Age People with Disabilities: What Current Data Tell Us and Options for Improvement*. Kalamazoo, MI: W. E. Upjohn Institute for Employment Research.

World Health Organization. 2001. *International Classification of Disability, Health, and Functioning*. Geneva: World Health Organization.

CHAPTER THIRTEEN

The Economic Consequences of Disability
Evidence from the PSID

Bruce D. Meyer and Wallace K. C. Mok

INTRODUCTION

Disability is one of the main risks individuals face in their lifetimes, and it has become a significant concern among policymakers in many countries. The U.S. Social Security Administration (SSA) estimates that a twenty-year-old worker has nearly a 30 percent chance of becoming disabled before reaching age sixty-five.[1,2] Census of Population data for 2000 indicate that 20.9 million families (28.9 percent of all American families) have at least one disabled member, and 12.8 percent of these families live in poverty; the corresponding poverty rate for families without disabled members is only 7.7 percent.[3] This chapter examines the consequences of disability on a wide range of household economic outcomes.

Public insurance spending on the disabled has increased significantly. In 2009, Social Security Disability Insurance (SSDI) payments amounted to $118 billion, and Supplementary Security Income (SSI) for the blind and the disabled reached $41 billion.[4] Private spending on the disabled was also substantial, with $57.6 billion spent on workers' compensation in 2008.[5] These expenditures are high even compared to such social insurance or welfare programs as unemployment insurance ($80 billion in 2009) and food stamps ($50 billion in fiscal year 2009).[6] Autor and Duggan (2006) predict that the SSDI receipt rate will rise 71 percent before reaching a steady state rate of approximately 7 percent of nonelderly adults. Despite the high disability rates and program costs, few studies examine the long-term economic circumstances of the disabled.[7]

This chapter contributes to the literature by studying the impact of disability on personal earnings, family income, receipt of public benefits, and poverty using data collected over a thirty-eight-year period from the Panel Study of Income Dynamics (PSID). The longitudinal structure of these data allows us to examine changes in the variables of interest before and after individuals become disabled. To analyze these outcomes, we must rely on a self-reported measure of disability. We argue that self-reports are the only feasible option, given that a large proportion of disabilities, even those compensated by SSDI, cannot be determined by an explicit physical marker (because they are psychological or involve pain).[8] In addition, program-based definitions miss nonrecipients and nonreporting recipients. Several studies also indicate that self-reported disability has many desirable features (Stern 1989; Benitez-Silva et al. 2004), although this view is not universally held. Although we follow the methodology of Meyer and Mok (2012), the present study differs in its focus on changes in income, in particular public-benefit receipt. We show that the onset of disability is associated with a significant reduction in an individual's earnings and income and a significant increase in poverty. That is coupled with the receipt of public transfers for a large group of individuals, many of whom have insufficient assets to cushion the shock. We find that these effects vary substantially depending on the extent of an individual's disability.

The remainder of this chapter proceeds as follows. The next section describes our data set and sample, how we define and categorize the disabled, and the empirical strategy used. The following section examines changes in earnings, income, poverty, and receipt of public transfers following disability onset.

DATA AND METHOD

Data

Our data are from the 1968–2005 waves of the PSID.[9] We focus on male household heads twenty-two to sixty-one years of age in the survey year; those under age twenty-two are unlikely to be household heads.[10,11] The PSID defines the household head in a married-couple family to be the male, except when the household head is so severely disabled that he is unable to respond to the survey, which is rare. To insure sufficient information on the variables of interest, we selected male household heads who were interviewed for at least six years and who were between twenty-two and sixty-one years old for at least four interviews, three of which were consecutive. To identify the disabled, we use the response to the disability question in the PSID: *Do you have any physical or nervous condition that limits the type or amount of work you can do?* This question is asked of household heads consistently throughout the life of the survey.[12] We divide our sample of male household heads into disabled and nondisabled individuals. The nondisabled sample consists of those who never reported that they had a physical or nervous limitation during the survey years. Members of the disabled sample must have reported a limitation in at least one year. Given we are mostly interested in the effects of working age disability, we also delete those who became disabled after the age of 56.

We replace missing demographic information (age, marital status, years of education, number of family members, number of children, and state of residence) by the nonmissing value in the nearest wave.[13] We exclude, however, individuals who are missing key demographic variables (education, age, and marital status).[14] The application of these restrictions results in a primary sample of 6,301 male household heads, 1,819 (29 percent) of whom are classified as ever disabled.

Disability Questions, Limitations, and Severity

We are interested in how the degree of disability affects economic outcomes, and we therefore follow the disaggregation strategy adopted by Meyer and Mok (2012), by grouping the disabled along persistence and severity dimensions. The three persistence groups are: *One-Time Disabled*—those who report a disability once, but do not report a disability again during the next ten years; the *Temporarily Disabled*—those who have one or two positive limitation reports within the ten years following disability onset; and the *Chronically Disabled*—those who have three or more positive limitation reports over the ten years following disability onset. To reduce the dependence of definitions on the number of years a household head participates in the survey, we use all the survey waves and require that a disabled individual be in the survey for at least three years within the ten years following onset.[15]

After establishing the presence of a work-limiting condition, a severity question addresses the extent to which this condition limits the work capability of the household head. We group responses to this question into two categories: *Severely Disabled* and *Not Severely Disabled*. We define *Not Severely Disabled in Year t* as individuals who respond "Just a little," "Somewhat," "Not limiting," or "Not at all" to the severity question in the year t survey. *Severely Disabled in Year t* are those who respond "Can do nothing," "Completely," "A lot," or "Severely." We define the *severity ratio* as the proportion of time the individual reports being severely disabled in the year of onset and the ten years following onset.[16] We define the *Severely Disabled* as individuals whose severity ratio is greater than 0.5. That is, starting from year of onset to the tenth year following onset, more than 50 percent of the observed severity reports consist of the following responses: "Can do nothing," "Completely," "A lot," or "Severely." The *Not Severely Disabled* are those individuals whose severity ratio is less than 0.5. When exactly half the responses indicate severe disability (that is, a severity ratio of 0.5), we classify the disabled individual based on the first observed severity report.[17]

We combine the two disability dimensions in our main analysis by splitting the Chronically Disabled into two groups. The *Chronic-Not Severe* are chronically but not severely disabled under the severity classification. The *Chronic-Severe* are chronically and severely disabled. Hence, this classification yields four groups of interest: *One-time, Temporary, Chronic-Not Severe*, and *Chronic-Severe*—collectively, the *Extent of Disability* groups.[18]

The use of these self-reported disability responses is controversial, but past researchers have also pointed out the merits of self-reported disability measures. Benitez-Silva et al. (2004) suggest that self-reported disability responses are an unbiased indicator of SSDI eligibility decisions. Stern (1989) finds that a self-reported disability question is close to exogenous. To the extent that self-reported disability is endogenous, the relationship is opposite to what is hypothesized in the literature (i.e., health tends to deteriorate when working rather than disability being used to justify not working). In their comparison of the Current Population Survey (CPS) and the National Health Interview Survey (NHIS),

Burkhauser et al. (2002) argue that the self-reported work-limitation-based definition of disability may even underestimate disability rates. Given that alternative definitions have their own endogeneity problems or are often too narrow, we believe that self-reported disability status responses, while not perfect, offer the best available method of measurement.[19]

Our sample consists of 6,301 individuals,1,819 of whom have had a disability. Of these disabled individuals, 418 (23 percent) are One-Time Disabled; 555 (31 percent) are Temporary Disabled, 531 (29 percent) are Chronic-Not Severe; and 315 (17 percent) are Chronic-Severe. Meyer and Mok (2012) provide a more comprehensive overview of the characteristics of the sample. The average age at disability onset is highest for the Chronic-Severe group (41.6 years), followed in descending order by the Chronic-Not Severe group (36.7 years); the Temporary group (35.2 years); and the One-Time group (35 years). The Chronic-Severe group is also the least-educated group—only 18 percent have ever attended college; by comparison, 46 percent of the One-Time group have attended college.[20]

Members of the Chronic-Severe group have more persistent disabilities on average than the Chronic-Not Severe group. The Chronic-Severe group reports a mean of 6.3 positive limitation reports within ten years after disability onset, while the Chronic-Not Severe group reports a mean of 5.4. The average severity ratio of the Chronic-Severe group at 0.84 is more than six times that of the Chronic-Not Severe group rate of 0.12. Meyer and Mok (2012) report that by the time a male household head reaches age fifty, there is an 11 percent chance that he has begun a Chronic-Severe disability. Thus, we emphasize that the Chronic-Severe group represents a substantial share of working-age household heads.

Estimation Technique

To measure the change in economic outcomes before and after the onset of disability, we estimate the following fixed-effect linear regression model for person i in year t:

$$(1) \qquad y_{it} = \alpha_i + \gamma_t + X_{it}\beta + \sum_g \sum_k \delta_k^g S_{kit}^g + \varepsilon_{it},$$

where y_{it} is the outcome of interest (such as labor earnings) for person i in year t, α_i is an indicator variable for individual i and γ_t is an indicator variable for year t. X_{it} is a set of time-varying explanatory variables including marital status, state of residence, age and age-squared, education, and number of children. Additional controls are included, depending on the dependent variable.[21] S_{kit}^g is an indicator variable that equals one if in year t, individual i belongs to disability group g and is in time period k (defined below), and ε_{it} is a potentially serially correlated error term. Four different time periods (k = {1,2,3,4}) are of interest:

Before onset (k = 1): $-5 \leq j \leq -2$

Around onset (k = 2): $-1 \leq j \leq 1$

Short run (k = 3): $2 \leq j \leq 5$

Long run (k = 4): $6 \leq j \leq 10$,

where j is year from disability onset, with j = 0 being the year of onset.

Our sample consists of the nondisabled and the disabled during all years prior to disability onset through the ten years following onset. Given the inclusion of individual fixed effects, δ_k^g measures the change in the dependent variable for individuals in disability group g in time period k, relative to the value of their dependent variable more than five years prior to disability. Because we include control variables such as age, age-squared, and year, the coefficients can also be taken to measure the change in the outcome relative to what would have happened if not for the disability. The nondisabled are included to improve the precision of the estimated effects of age, education, and the other control variables. This way of modeling the time pattern of economic outcomes is similar to the approach of Jacobson, LaLonde, and Sullivan (1993); Stephens (2001); and Charles (2003).[22]

CHANGES IN EARNINGS, AFTER-TAX INCOME, AND PUBLIC TRANSFERS, BEFORE AND AFTER DISABILITY ONSET

Earnings of Head

Section A of Table 13.1 shows the changes in earnings from estimating Equation (1) when we first treat the disabled sample as a single group and, second, when the disabled are disaggregated. For each group, we report the estimated dollar change, followed by its standard error and the implied percentage change beneath. The denominators of the percentage

TABLE 13.1

Changes in earnings and after-tax income including noncash benefits
before and after disability onset

	All disabled	EXTENT OF DISABILITY GROUPS			
		One-time	Temporary	Chronic-not severe	Chronic-severe
A. EARNINGS (DOLLARS)					
Before onset	−2,888	−2,500	−1,552	−4,336	−5,325
	(871)**	(1,168)*	(1,434)	(1,656)**	(1,393)**
	−7.39%	−5.92%	−4.13%	−10.53%	−15.36%
Around onset	−6,363	−4,613	−3,679	−7,318	−14,248
	(1,175)**	(1,478)**	(2,157)	(1,886)**	(1,748)**
	−7.29%	−10.70%	−9.67%	−17.73%	−39.46%
Short run	−8,944	−5,406	−3,084	−10,188	−24,673
	(1,527)**	(1,996)**	(2,985)	(2,069)**	(1,927)**
	−21.81%	−11.50%	−7.83%	−23.78%	−68.11%
Long run	−9,878	−5,477	−2,370	−11,934	−28,952
	(1,863)**	(2,244)*	(3,472)	(2,542)**	(2,151)**
	−23.04%	−10.80%	−5.62%	−26.79%	−78.45%
B. AFTER-TAX INCOME INCLUDING NONCASH BENEFITS (DOLLARS)					
Before onset	−1,996	−1,592	−530	−1,796	−6,190
	(815)*	(1,148)	(1,390)	(1,523)	(1,527)**
	−4.03%	−3.04%	−1.09%	−3.63%	−13.11%
Around onset	−3,656	−4,368	−1,527	−2,573	−8,894
	(1,092)**	(1,582)**	(1,874)	(1,840)	(1,798)**
	−7.17%	−7.89%	−3.05%	−5.13%	−18.37%
Short run	−5,094	−4,420	−2,565	−3,733	−13,782
	(1,385)**	(1,834)*	(2,425)	(2,243)	(2,081)**
	−9.51%	−7.30%	−4.92%	−7.01%	−28.06%
Long run	−6,162	−4,203	−2,305	−5,696	−17,871
	(1,761)**	(2,616)	(2,919)	(2,657)*	(2,318)**
	−10.62%	−6.14%	−4.02%	−10.07%	−34.79%

NOTES: The estimates reported are the coefficient estimates on the time from onset indicator variables interacted with the extent of disability groups in a fixed-effect regression (see equation (1) in text). The omitted period is more than five years before disability onset. Standard errors clustered by person are in parentheses with implied percentage changes reported beneath. The statistical significance of each estimate is indicated as follows: *Significant at 5 percent level, **Significant at 1 percent level; dollars are CPI-U adjusted 2005 dollars.

changes are obtained from the average of the predicted earnings of members of the disabled groups as if disability had not occurred (setting all the time from onset indicators to zero). Earnings are estimated to decline by 7 percent in the before-onset period, as well as in the period around onset. In the short run following disability onset, we expect the disabled to suffer from a 22 percent decline in earnings. In the long run, earnings drop by 23 percent. Our results are similar to those of Stephens (2001), and show little evidence of a recovery in earnings among the average disabled over the course of a disability.

When the disabled are disaggregated, the results show pronounced heterogeneity in the earnings changes across the disability groups. For the One-Time group, earnings are expected to drop by 10.7 percent around the onset period. Earnings further drop by 11.5 percent in the short run after disability, but this drop stabilizes and remains at 10.8 percent in the long run. For the Temporary group, the drop in earnings around onset is about 9.7 percent, but earnings do recover over time, as suggested by the smaller and statistically insignificant estimates for both the short run and the long run. However, the drop in earnings is large for the Chronic-Not Severe and the Chronic-Severe groups. For the Chronic-Not Severe, earnings are estimated to drop by 17.7 percent around onset, by 23.8 percent in the short run, and by 26.8 percent in the long run. For the Chronic-Severe, the drop in earnings is even larger, amounting to 39.5 percent around onset, 68 percent in the short run, and 78.5 percent in the long run. These declines for the most disabled are often more than twice as large as those of the Chronic-Not Severe group, and they are about three times as large as those of the average disabled. Meyer and Mok (2012) show that the pronounced drop for the Chronic-Severe disabled is due to the high proportion who work zero hours following disability—by the tenth year after disability onset, about 65 percent of the Chronic-Severe group have zero hours of work.

After-Tax Family Income

The large drop in earnings observed above, especially for the Chronic-Severe group, may not translate into a large reduction in family economic well-being because of the presence of nonlabor income, intrafamily risk sharing through earnings of a spouse or children, interfamily transfers such as support from friends and relatives, and reductions in taxes or increases in tax credits from programs such as the Earned Income Tax Credit that supplement income for the working poor.

Using the summary family income variable provided by the PSID, which is the sum of labor, assets, and transfer income, may be unsatisfactory even after accounting for federal income tax liabilities.[23] First, this measure does not include in-kind transfers such as food stamps and subsidized housing. Second, public transfer income is generally under-reported in household surveys, and transfers to the disabled in the PSID are no exception.[24] We follow Meyer and Mok (2012) and obtain income figures by summing up after-tax family income, food stamps, and any housing subsidy received.[25] In addition, we account for underreporting in the main public benefit programs by scaling the benefits received using the program-specific reporting rates as reported in Meyer, Mok, and Sullivan (2009). These reporting rates are calculated by comparing the weighted sum of the benefits received by the entire PSID sample with those reported to have been paid out by government agencies. By scaling up benefits in this way, we implicitly assume that nonreporting recipients share the same characteristics as reporting recipients.

Section B of Table 13.1 shows the estimated changes in after-tax income for the average disabled and each of the disability groups. The denominators used for the percentage changes again are calculated as the average of the predicted income of the disability groups with the time from onset dummies set to zero. These percentage changes are reported below the standard errors, which are in turn below the coefficient estimates. For the average disabled, the long-run drop in after-tax income is approximately 10.6 percent. However, disaggregating reveals a very different picture. For the One-Time and Temporary disability groups, the estimated drop in after-tax income in the long run is small (6.1 percent and 4.0 percent, respectively) and imprecisely measured. For the Chronic-Severe group, however, the decline is large, amounting to almost 18.4 percent around onset, increasing to 28.1 percent in the short run, and 34.5 percent in the long run. This large drop in the long run is much smaller than the large drop in earnings observed earlier.

Public Transfers

We next investigate the role of public transfers in alleviating the decline in material well-being of the disabled head and family. Section A of Table 13.2 shows the change in public transfers to the family across disability groups. The Chronic-Severe group receives by far the largest public transfers; total benefits increase by $5,700 around onset and are estimated to double in the long run. Given the large drop in earnings we observe above, the smaller reduction in income than earnings is largely due to the receipt of public transfers.

TABLE 13.2
Public transfers receipt before and after disability onset

	All disabled	EXTENT OF DISABILITY GROUPS			
		One-time	Temporary	Chronic-not severe	Chronic-severe
A. ALL PUBLIC TRANSFERS (DOLLARS)					
Before onset	209	391	220	235	589
	(156)	(281)	(225)	(286)	(456)
Around onset	2,167	919	1,710	2,185	5,733
	(232)**	(291)**	(320)**	(420)**	(876)**
Short run	2,869	503	1,310	2,775	10,057
	(265)**	(279)	(343)**	(510)**	(932)**
Long run	2,757	450	1,046	2,338	11,362
	(284)**	(406)	(310)**	(445)**	(1,065)**
B. SOCIAL SECURITY RETIREMENT AND DISABILITY					
Before onset	0.029	0.029	0.025	0.026	0.044
Around onset	0.051	0.026	0.041	0.045	0.122
Short run	0.104	0.035	0.049	0.063	0.361
Long run	0.138	0.034	0.053	0.104	0.482
C. SSI					
Before onset	0.007	0.002	0.011	0.009	0.008
Around onset	0.015	0.005	0.014	0.010	0.038
Short run	0.023	0.006	0.015	0.014	0.073
Long run	0.025	0.009	0.014	0.015	0.086
D. FOOD STAMPS					
Before onset	0.078	0.070	0.080	0.078	0.089
Around onset	0.119	0.088	0.120	0.116	0.170
Short run	0.124	0.061	0.120	0.117	0.224
Long run	0.111	0.051	0.088	0.108	0.238
E. OTHER PUBLIC BENEFITS					
Before onset	0.146	0.144	0.153	0.131	0.163
Around onset	0.190	0.163	0.188	0.208	0.206
Short run	0.160	0.133	0.160	0.170	0.183
Long run	0.131	0.096	0.131	0.151	0.126
F. POVERTY RATE BEFORE PUBLIC TRANSFERS					
Before onset	0.124	0.091	0.114	0.120	0.205
Around onset	0.180	0.113	0.166	0.165	0.332
Short run	0.215	0.083	0.180	0.178	0.496
Long run	0.204	0.088	0.109	0.168	0.587
G. POVERTY RATE AFTER PUBLIC TRANSFERS					
Before onset	0.090	0.056	0.081	0.092	0.161
Around onset	0.116	0.073	0.121	0.100	0.200
Short run	0.128	0.055	0.131	0.109	0.243
Long run	0.116	0.067	0.076	0.123	0.231

NOTES: In Panel A the estimates reported are the coefficient estimates on the time from onset indicator variables interacted with the extent of disability groups in a fixed effect regression (see equation (1) in text) with the total amount of public transfers received as the dependent variable. The omitted period is more than five years before onset. Standard errors clustered by person are in parentheses. The statistical significance of each estimate is indicated as follows: *Significant at 5 percent level, **Significant at 1 percent level. Panels B through E report the fraction of families receiving a given benefit. Dollars are CPI-U adjusted 2005 dollars. For Panels F and G, the numbers reported are the fraction living below poverty before and after the inclusion of public transfers (underreporting adjusted).

The remainder of Table 13.2 shows the receipt of various public benefits by the different disability groups. We first focus on Social Security retirement and disability benefits. While on average 13.8 percent of the disabled receive Social Security benefits in the long run after disability onset, this is mostly due to the Chronic-Severe group, with about 48 percent of its members receiving such benefits. For SSI, again the Chronic-Severe group has a long-run receipt rate more than three times that of the average disabled. For food stamps, a program mostly targeting the poor, we also see the Chronic-Severe group has a much higher receipt rate than the average disabled in the long run. This result is consistent with the higher poverty rate among the Chronic-Severe group as we shall see below. For other public benefits—unemployment insurance (UI), workers' compensation (WC) and public housing—the receipt rate is similar across the disability groups. This finding is expected, as UI targets the unemployed but actively searching for work, WC benefits are mostly temporary, and public housing is not a program specifically targeting the disabled. We should emphasize that these receipt rates are likely lower than the actual receipt rates given the frequency of underreporting receipt. However, the bottom-line message is clear: The probability of benefit receipt varies substantially across the extent of disability groups, so that an analysis based on the average disabled is misleading.

Poverty

The goal of any public social insurance program is to alleviate material deprivation that might result from an unexpected bad event. With the high benefit-receipt rates we observe above, a natural question to ask is to what extent these public benefits alleviate poverty. To answer this question, we study the poverty rates of families in the various disability groups across time with and without these public benefits included in their incomes. These estimates are reported in Panels F and G in Table 13.2. For the average disabled before disability onset, the poverty rate is about 12 percent before accounting for public transfers, a number close to the national average. In the long run after disability onset, that number rises to about 20 percent, but is almost halved after public transfers are included. The importance of public transfers is more evident for the Chronic-Severe group. In the long run after disability, almost 60 percent of such families would fall into poverty in the absence of public transfers.

However, the poverty rate falls to 23.1 percent when these public transfers are included. This finding suggests that there may be too few alternative private income sources for the Chronic-Severe disabled given their relatively high poverty rate in the absence of public transfers. However, we should also suspect that the availability of these public transfer programs may "crowd out" other income sources, such as spousal earnings.

Changes Before and After 1980

Given the length of the PSID panel, it is also of interest to see how the recent disabled fare relative to their earlier counterparts. We split the disabled roughly in half, based on the period of disability onset. Estimates are reported in Table 13.3.[26] Panel A shows the long-run changes in earnings, after-tax income, public transfers and receipt of OASDI/SSI for those who started their first observed disability spell on or before 1980. Panel B reports these estimates for those who became disabled after 1980. Although the change in earnings for the average disabled is similar in these two periods, the percentage change differs. The more recent disabled experience a lower percentage decline in earnings in the long run than their older counterparts. In terms of after-tax income (including noncash benefits), the more recent disabled sample also have a lower loss, at about 9 percent compared with about 12 percent of their earlier counterparts. Such findings may lead us to conclude that the economic situation for the disabled has improved over time, but a closer examination of the changes in earnings and income across the disability groups gives us a somewhat different picture. Looking at the most disabled Chronic-Severe group in the most recent period, earnings drop by 82 percent in the long run, which is much greater than the 73 percent drop suffered by their earlier counterparts. The drop in after-tax income is also greater for the more recent Chronic-Severe disabled, while the drop in after-tax income for the Temporary and the Chronic-Not Severe groups is smaller (and not statistically significant at 5 percent). Note that we use the entire time period to classify disabilities, so those with onset in the later period have fewer years after onset, on average, to be classified as chronic, leading to a lower Chronic-Severe prevalence. Another point to note is that the more recent Chronic-Severe disabled receive relatively more public transfers (and more of them receive OASDI/SSI), which partly mitigates the very large drop in earnings. Overall, it is

TABLE 13.3

Long-run changes in earnings, after-tax income, and public transfers,
by year of onset

	All disabled	One-time	Temporary	Chronic-not severe	Chronic-severe
				EXTENT OF DISABILITY GROUPS	
A. DISABILITY ONSET ON OR BEFORE 1980					
Earnings ($)	−10,870	−2,283	−2,732	−9,264	−26,608
	(1,687)**	(2,579)	(2,688)	(2,139)**	(2,445)**
	−28.57%	−5.30%	−6.96%	−22.12%	−72.93%
After-tax income ($)	−5,852	1,248	−4,378	−5,184	−13,166
	(1,727)**	(4,824)	(2,438)	(1,955)**	(2,892)**
	−11.83%	2.27%	−8.82%	−10.31%	−26.90%
Public transfers ($)	3,967	350	1,404	1,885	11,501
	(608)**	(507)	(528)**	(678)**	(1,598)**
Receipt of OASDI or SSI	0.177	0.101	0.062	0.106	0.491
Number of disabled	832	77	256	291	208
B. DISABILITY ONSET AFTER 1980					
Earnings ($)	−9,163	−5,999	−1,318	−11,911	−31,254
	(2,307)**	(2,566)*	(4,506)	(3,575)**	(3,019)**
	−18.63%	−11.23%	−2.84%	−24.29%	−82.03%
After-tax income ($)	−6,255	−5,421	−1,488	−6,086	−20,652
	(2,243)**	(2,951)	(3,860)	(3,916)	(3,219)**
	−8.97%	−7.38%	−2.16%	−8.93%	−35.02%
Public transfers ($)	2,213	357	539	2,101	12,323
	(341)**	(486)	(337)	(563)**	(1,547)**
Receipt of OASDI or SSI	0.122	0.022	0.066	0.121	0.604
Number of disabled	987	341	299	240	107

NOTES: The first three sets of rows in both panels report the coefficient estimates on the long-run time from onset indicator variable interacted with the extent of disability groups (see equation (1) in text) in a fixed-effect regression. The omitted period is more than five years before onset. Standard errors clustered by person are in parentheses with implied percentage changes reported beneath. The statistical significance of each estimate is indicated as follows: *Significant at 5 percent level, **Significant at 1 percent level. The final row of each panel reports the share of those in each disability group who are OASDI/SSI recipients. Dollars are CPI-U adjusted 2005 dollars.

important to note that the predicament of the most disabled has not been alleviated in more recent years.

Pre-Onset Net Wealth and Changes in After-Tax income

It is possible that those disabled with a large fall in income have assets upon which they can draw to prevent a drop in living standards. Thus, we next investigate how the income changes differ between high- and low-wealth disabled. Data on wealth come from the 1984, 1989, 1994, 1999, 2001, 2003, and 2005 waves of the PSID. Because many years are missing asset information, we focus only on those disabled who became disabled in 1984 or later.[27] We sort each disabled head into one of two subgroups—those with pre-onset net wealth above and below twice their average annual pre-onset after-tax income (high and low pre-onset net wealth). Table 13.4 reports the changes in after-tax income for these two net wealth groups. We should first note that about half of all disabled and 60 percent of the Chronic-Severe disabled have assets of less than two years' income prior to onset. Among the average disabled with high pre-onset net wealth, the results suggest that the long-run decline in after-tax income is small, as the estimate is statistically insignificant (the point estimate is positive).[28] In contrast, those with low pre-onset net wealth suffer from a very large 19 percent decline in after-tax income. Turning to the Chronic-Severe group, the long-run drop in after-tax income is very large—36 percent for the high pre-onset net wealth group. For their low-wealth pre-onset counterparts, the drop is nearly as large, at 32 percent. In most cases, these low net wealth groups suffer from much greater losses in after-tax income than their wealthier counterparts. With less than two years' after-tax income in the form of net wealth, these households seem unlikely to be able to shield themselves from a substantial fall in their living standards by drawing down assets, as these assets would quickly be exhausted. Given the small subsample of disabled heads with wealth information, these results are only suggestive.[29] A more definitive examination of the living standards of the disabled will require examining consumption patterns (Meyer and Mok 2012) or material hardship indicators.

DISCUSSION

This chapter investigates how a wide range of economic outcomes change following the onset of disability. Data from the PSID suggest that treating the disabled as a single group in economic analyses may give a distorted picture of changes in well-being. Earnings and income drop significantly over the course of disability, but the drop is felt most profoundly by the most disabled group, which sees its income fall by more than 30 percent and has a poverty rate of more than 23 percent in

TABLE 13.4

*Changes in after-tax income including noncash benefits before and after
disability onset, by high and low pre-onset net wealth*

	All disabled	EXTENT OF DISABILITY GROUPS			
		One-time	Temporary	Chronic-not severe	Chronic-severe
A. HIGH PRE-ONSET NET WEALTH (MORE THAN TWO YEARS' INCOME)					
Before onset	2,850	2,048	4,078	4,167	–1,730
	(1,757)	(2,203)	(2,946)	(4,759)	(3,315)
	4.57%	3.22%	6.44%	6.71%	–3.44%
Around onset	1,949	–2,060	6,959	5,112	–7,787
	(2,427)	(3,184)	(4,038)	(6,196)	(4,104)
	2.98%	–3.05%	10.73%	7.79%	–15.48%
Short run	1,548	–3,819	6,453	11,134	–16,453
	(3,108)	(3,327)	(5,712)	(8,104)	(4,715)**
	2.19%	–5.26%	9.46%	14.64%	–29.82%
Long run	3,279	1,029	9,737	6,002	–21,315
	(4,453)	(5,663)	(7,627)	(11,162)	(5,468)**
	4.11%	1.23%	12.67%	7.53%	–35.56%
Number of disabled	354	133	126	67	28
B. LOW PRE-ONSET NET WEALTH (LESS THAN TWO YEARS' INCOME)					
Before onset	–5,422	–3,791	–5,626	–4,666	–10,359
	(921)**	(1,450)**	(1,528)**	(1,724)**	(2,531)**
	–11.57%	–8.04%	–12.31%	–10.04%	–21.52%
Around onset	–8,150	–7,683	–7,989	–7,233	–10,905
	(1,196)**	(1,963)**	(2,072)**	(1,771)**	(3,280)**
	–15.37%	–13.96%	–15.50%	–13.93%	–20.79%
Short run	–10,139	–8,393	–9,348	–10,857	–14,435
	(1,660)**	(2,144)**	(3,213)**	(2,454)**	(4,816)**
	–17.03%	–13.49%	–16.10%	–18.34%	–26.33%
Long run	–12,418	–10,352	–8,613	–13,997	–20,005
	(2,128)**	(3,122)**	(4,302)*	(2,563)**	(4,936)**
	–18.77%	–14.81%	–13.30%	–21.85%	–31.27%
Number of disabled	341	119	95	85	42

NOTES: The estimates reported are the coefficient estimates on the time from onset indicator variables interacted with the extent of disability groups in a fixed effect regression (see equation (1) in text) with income as the dependent variable. The omitted period is more than five years before disability onset. Standard errors clustered by person are in parentheses with implied percentage changes reported beneath. The statistical significance of each estimate is indicated as follows: *Significant at 5 percent level, **Significant at 1 percent level. Dollars are CPI-U adjusted 2005 dollars.

the long run. We also show that the most disabled group receives much more in public benefits. Despite the receipt of benefits, the situation for this chronic and severely disabled group is dire. As discussed in detail in Meyer and Mok (2012), this most disabled group is large, so its situation should not be overlooked. When we split our time period in two, the fall in earnings and in after-tax and transfer income is even greater in the most recent years for the chronic and severely disabled. To make matters worse, the fall in household income is even greater for those with little in the way of assets to draw upon. These results call for further examination of the living standard of the disabled, including an analysis of their consumption. The results in this chapter also raise the stakes in the discussion of disability policy, which has tended to focus on the rise in benefit receipt and its disincentive effects. Our results suggest that there is substantial deprivation that existing benefits do not prevent.

NOTES

1. See Baldwin and Chu (2006), who estimate that the probability of receiving Social Security Disability Insurance by age sixty-seven is 38 percent for men and 31 percent for women.

2. A recent report by the Institute of Medicine (2007) concludes that the number of people in the U.S. with disabilities currently exceeds 40 million. This conclusion is based on reviewing a selection of survey results, including results from the National Health Interview Survey, Survey of Income Program Participation, Census of Population, and American Community Survey.

3. See Wang (2005).

4. Specifically, the federal government spent $38 billion on SSI for the blind and the disabled (age 0–64), while another $3 billion was spent in federally administered state supplementation (U.S. Social Security Administration 2010).

5. See Sengupta et al. (2010). The reported amount includes payments for medical treatment and cash benefits.

6. For unemployment insurance, see Department of Labor (2011). For food stamps, see U.S. Department of Agriculture, Food and Nutrition Service Program Data (2011).

7. Important work on this topic includes Haveman and Wolfe (1990), who study the difference between the incomes and earnings of the disabled and nondisabled using the Current Population Survey. Bound and Burkhauser (1999) compare earnings of the disabled and the nondisabled. Charles (2003) examines earnings, hours, and wages after disability. Stephens (2001) analyzes several of these outcomes along with food consumption.

8. Autor and Duggan (2006) report that more than half of SSDI awards in 2003 were for either mental disorders or musculoskeletal disorders (e.g., back pain).

9. The PSID is a longitudinal data set started in 1968 with an initial sample of approximately 4,800 U.S. households comprising approximately

18,000 individuals. See Meyer and Mok (2012) for more background information about the survey.

10. We retain data on disability for people outside this age range because they may prove useful in determining the persistence or severity of an individual's disabling condition. As we explain later, the degree of persistence is determined based on the frequency of positive limitation reports after disability onset. Thus, ignoring information after age sixty-one may lead to an individual being misclassified, especially if his or her age of disability onset is close to sixty-one. Similarly, the age of onset cannot be correctly determined if we exclude all data outside the age range. For example, a person whose disability began at age eighteen could have his or her onset age mistakenly set to twenty-two if we disregard the responses to the disability question outside the age range.

11. The focus on male household heads is necessary because the PSID does not ask disability questions of spouses prior to 1981 (see Burkhauser et al. 2006).

12. See also Meyer and Mok (2012) for how the year of disability onset is determined for the disabled.

13. Approximately 400 individuals have missing data substituted in this way.

14. We exclude seventy-five individuals (1.2 percent of the sample) because key demographic information is unavailable.

15. If we require more than three (four to six) postonset positive limitation reports to be in the chronic group, the results are quite similar. Our disability persistence classification differs from that of Charles (2003), who defines the most chronically disabled group as individuals who report a positive limitation in every year after onset (as long as they are in the survey). Thus, in this author's classification system, whether an individual is chronic partly depends on the number of years an individual is in the survey; the use of a shorter panel (1968–1993) increases this dependence. Thus, a disabled person is more likely to be in the most chronic group the closer the year of onset is to 1993.

16. Twenty-five individuals in the main analysis who never respond to the severity question in this eleven-year period (year of onset and the subsequent ten years) are dropped.

17. Of the 1,819 disabled, 100 have a severity ratio of 0.5. Of the 846 chronically disabled individuals, only 43 have a severity ratio of 0.5.

18. In principle, these four groups are not fully ordered. We cannot say, a priori, that the Chronic-Not Severe group is "more disabled" than the Temporary group. In practice, though, the Chronic-Not Severe group fares much worse than the nonchronic groups, as shown in our analysis.

19. See Bound et al. (2007) and Kreider (1999) for discussions of the limitations of self-reported disability.

20. Members of each of the four disabled groups participate in the survey on average for at least 17.3 years in total and 10.0 years following disability onset. This long participation in the survey, particularly after onset, should reduce any concerns that the One-Time group members are categorized as such because they have exited the survey soon after disability onset. However, when we split the sample into shorter subperiods in Table 13.4, we will see that the classification is affected by the length of observation.

21. The number of family members is included in the income regressions. For earnings and income, we include interactions of education with age, age-squared, and time since 1968. For more details, see appendix 3 of Meyer and Mok (2012).

22. The analysis of Charles (2003) includes individual-specific time trends, which is one of the approaches in the Jacobson, LaLonde, and Sullivan (1993) analysis of earnings of the displaced. We suspect that disabling conditions have effects prior to disability onset, however, and we find that the results tend to be sensitive to the period over which such trends are estimated.

23. We use TAXSIM to generate tax liability estimates. See appendix 3 in Meyer and Mok (2012) for details.

24. See Meyer, Mok, and Sullivan (2009) for evidence of underreporting of public transfers in several data sets including the PSID.

25. See appendix 3 of Meyer and Mok (2012) for the method of estimating the value of housing subsidies used here.

26. The denominators of the percentage changes are obtained from the average of the predicted outcomes for the disability groups based on coefficients estimated using the entire sample.

27. For those surveyed in a year without wealth information, we use data from the most recent previous year with such information.

28. See note 27.

29. As noted above, the Chronic-Severe group is less numerous in these data because it only includes those with onset after 1984 when there are fewer years left on average to be classified as chronic. Higher attrition and every-other-year interviewing add to this tendency.

REFERENCES

Autor, David H., and Mark G. Duggan. "The Growth in the Social Security Disability Rolls: A Fiscal Crisis Unfolding." *Journal of Economic Perspectives* 20, no. 3 (2006): 71–96.

Baldwin, Robert, and Sharon Chu. "A Death and Disability Life Table for Insured Workers Born in 1985." In *Actuarial Note*. Baltimore MD: Office of the Chief Actuary, Social Security Administration, 2006.

Benitez-Silva, Hugo, Moshe Buchinsky, Hiu Man Chan, John Rust, and Sofia Sheidvasser. "An Empirical Analysis of the Social Security Disability

Application, Appeal, and Award Process." *Labour Economics*, no. 6 (1999): 147–78.

Bound, John, and Richard V. Burkhauser. "Economic Analysis of Transfer Programs Targeted on People with Disabilities." In *Handbook of Labor Economics*, edited by Orley Ashenfelter and David Card. Amsterdam: Elsevier Science North-Holland, 1999, 3417–528.

Bound, John, Todd R. Stinebrickner, and Timothy Waidmann. "Health, Economic Resources and the Work Decisions of Older Men." NBER Working Paper 13657, 2007.

Burkhauser, Richard V., Mary C. Daly, Andrew J. Houtenville, and Nigar Nargis. "Self-Reported Work-Limitation Data: What They Can and Cannot Tell Us." *Demography* 39, no. 3 (2002): 541–55.

Burkhauser, Richard V., Robert R. Weathers II, and Mathis Schroeder. "A Guide to Disability Statistics from the Panel Study of Income Dynamics." Ithaca, NY: Rehabilitation Research and Training Center on Disability Demographics and Statistics, Cornell University, 2006.

Charles, Kerwin Kofi. "The Longitudinal Structure of Earnings Losses among Work-Limited Disabled Workers." *Journal of Human Resources* 38, no. 3 (2003): 618–46.

Haveman, Robert H., and Barbara L. Wolfe. "The Economic Well-Being of the Disabled: 1962–84." *Journal of Human Resources* 25, no. 1 (1990): 32–54.

Institute of Medicine. *The Future of Disability in America*. Edited by Committee on Disability in America. Prepublication Copy, Board on Health Sciences Policy. Washington, DC: The National Academy Press, 2007.

Jacobson, Louis S., Robert J. LaLonde, and Daniel G. Sullivan. "Earnings Losses of Displaced Workers." *American Economic Review* 83, no. 4 (1993): 685–709.

Kreider, Brent. "Latent Work Disability and Reporting Bias." *Journal of Human Resources* 34, no. 4 (1999): 734–69.

Meyer, Bruce D., and Wallace K. C. Mok. "Disability, Earnings, Income and Consumption." Working Paper, University of Chicago, 2012.

Meyer, Bruce D., Wallace K. C. Mok, and James X. Sullivan. "The Under-Reporting of Transfers in Household Surveys: Its Nature and Consequences." NBER Working Paper 15181, 2009.

Sengupta, Ishita, Virginia Reno, and John F. Burton Jr. "Workers' Compensation: Benefits, Coverage, and Costs, 2008." Washington, DC: National Academy of Social Insurance, 2010.

Stephens, Melvin, Jr. "The Long-Run Consumption Effects of Earnings Shocks." *Review of Economics and Statistics* 83, no. 1 (2001): 28–36.

Stern, Steven. "Measuring the Effect of Disability on Labor Force Participation." *Journal of Human Resources* 24, no. 3 (1989): 361–95.

U.S. Department of Agriculture, Food and Nutrition Service Program Data. "U.S. Department of Agriculture." Food and Nutrition Service Program Data, Food and Nutrition Service, U.S. Department of Agriculture. Accessed April 2011. http://www.fns.usda.gov/fsp.

U.S. Department of Labor. "Unemployment Insurance Financial Data Handbook." Employment and Training Administration, ET Handbook No. 394. Accessed April 2011. http://workforcesecurity.doleta.gov/unemploy/hb394.asp.

U.S. Social Security Administration. "Annual Statistical Supplements to the Social Security Bulletin." Washington, DC: Social Security Administration, 2010.

Wang, Qi. "Disability and American Families: 2000." In *Census 2000 Special Reports*. Washington, DC: U.S. Department of Commerce, U.S. Census Bureau, 2005.

CHAPTER FOURTEEN

Health and Wealth in Early Retirement

Geoffrey L. Wallace, Robert Haveman, Karen Holden, and Barbara Wolfe

INTRODUCTION

Retirement years are a precarious time for many older Americans. Even if they are successful in accumulating resources expected to be sufficient to maintain their preretirement standard of living, many retirees face unexpected adverse health shocks after retirement. Because of the uncertainty of shocks to physical and cognitive health, there is potential for significant deterioration in resource adequacy both at the time of retirement and into the retirement years.

In this study, we select a sample of new retirees constructed from the Health and Retirement Study (HRS) data and follow them during the first decade of their retirement. Using these data, we identify the nature of shocks to physical and cognitive health for which individuals are at risk during their retirement years, and estimate both the absolute and

The research reported herein was performed pursuant to a grant from the U.S. Social Security Administration (SSA) funded as part of the Financial Literacy Research Consortium. The opinions and conclusions expressed are solely those of the authors and do not represent the opinions or policy of SSA, any agency of the federal government, or the Center for Financial Security at the University of Wisconsin—Madison. The authors are grateful for feedback from discussants and participants at the summer CFS FLRC workshop in Madison, WI. In addition, we would like to thank William Nicholson and Jacob Schindler for their valuable research assistance.

relative risk of these shocks. We then estimate the impact of the occurrence of these shocks on wealth-based measures of retirement adequacy.

We begin by discussing the existing literature on this topic and indicating how our study adds to the existing body of knowledge regarding economic status during retirement years. We then describe the data and measures used, including the basic sample selection criteria and the criteria for being selected into any of the event-specific samples. Third, we present evidence on the rate at which retirees experience these shocks and describe their impact on annuitized net wealth (ANW) and an ANW-based retirement adequacy indicator. The final section concludes with a description of policy implications.

PREVIOUS LITERATURE

Much recent economic literature on older Americans examines the question of whether Americans save enough to maintain preretirement living standards. Far less attention has been given to the question of the evolution of wealth and wealth-based retirement adequacy during retirement; few studies relate the incidence of adverse health shocks to changes in resources over retirement years. Resources that may have been more than adequate early in retirement may be strained after retirees confront health problems.

Several studies provide evidence on how wealth and its components evolve during retirement, in particular the preservation of IRAs and 401(k) pensions and housing wealth as forms of self-insurance (Holden and Schrass 2009; Poterba et al. 2008; Coile and Milligan 2009; Megbolugbe et al. 1997, 1999; Venti and Wise 2002, 2004). Coile and Milligan (2009) provide evidence that the drawdown in home equity increases with the time from the occurrence of adverse shocks, and that at least some of the drawdown in housing assets is offset by increases in more liquid assets. Poterba, Venti, and Wise (2010) examine how nonpension wealth is affected by family status and health changes and report on the evolution of nonpension assets into retirement. They find strong evidence that the response of couples to adverse shocks to both individual and household health status leads to temporal decreases in the stock of available wealth. In addition, they find that individuals facing adverse family-structure and health shocks have lower asset trajectories in the years following the shock than similar individuals who did not face such shocks.

Our research is in the spirit of Coile and Milligan (2009) and Poterba, Venti, and Wise (2010), and uses the analytic framework of Haveman, Holden, Wolfe, and Romanov (2007a, 2007b).[1] We advance this prior work by using a more comprehensive wealth measure, omitting only what we label *unsmooth* pensions, never-dispersed pensions, and the value of nonprimary residences from our wealth measure, and by studying for the first time a broad array of health related shocks, including both self-reported and survey-administered assessments of cognitive decline.

Two other chapters in this volume also contribute to this early literature on the implications of experiencing an adverse shock. Chapter 15 by Daly and Gardiner uses the HRS data used in our study; the authors measure the effects of becoming disabled on both subjective well-being and mental health, but not on the economic impact of this event. Chapter 13 by Meyer and Mok uses working-age men in the Panel Study of Income Dynamics (PSID) to study the effect of becoming disabled on a range of economic outcomes, including lifecycle earnings, income, public transfers, and consumption.

DATA AND MEASURES

The data used in this study were drawn from the initial cohort of the HRS, which consists of individuals born between 1931 and 1941 and their spouses. Initial HRS cohort households were first interviewed in 1992, when they were between fifty-one and sixty-one years old, and subsequently reinterviewed every two years.[2] At each two-year wave interview respondents are asked about their living arrangements (family structure), health status, health insurance, health care utilization, and cognition, including a brief assessment. Moreover, at each wave interview one of the two (potential) individuals in an HRS household is selected to be the financial respondent and answer questions about the household's income and wealth. Those include the value of primary residences, the outstanding value of mortgages on the primary residence, the net value of other real estate and businesses, the value of checking and savings deposits, stocks, bonds, money market accounts, and IRAs, as well as flows of income from Social Security benefits, pensions, annuities, and veteran's benefits.[3]

Postretirement Shocks

The primary goal of this analysis is to provide information on the propensity of retired individuals to experience adverse physical and cognitive health shocks after retirement, and then to estimate the impact of these changes on ANW and on the adequacy of retirement resources. The HRS contains a great deal of information on health, such as the onset of disease, medical-care utilization, self-assessments of physical and cognitive health, self-assessment of various functional limitations, and interviewer-administered assessments of cognitive functioning. From this we select three measures of physical and cognitive health decline. The health decline measures chosen were parsed down from an expanded list of measures used in our prior work on this topic (Wallace et al. 2009). They were selected because of their simplicity, availability, and consistency across waves and because they were found to have an impact on wealth among some groups. Declines in physical health are based on 1) decreases in self-reported health to "poor", 2) having trouble with three or more (out of five) gross motor skills (GMS), and 3) having trouble with three or more (out of five) activities of daily living (ADLs). Declines in cognitive health are based on 1) self-reported decreases in memory to "poor", 2) falling below a threshold of 8 (out of 10) on an interviewer administered Telephone Interview for Cognitive Status and 3) falling below a threshold of 4 in an interviewer administered ten-noun recall test.

In defining postretirement shocks we track respondents as they enter retirement, and record both their risk for and exposure to various shocks. We then follow the respondents who are eligible for a particular shock until they experienced the shock, or they are no longer eligible to experience the shock (we also stop following them if information concerning their eligibility or exposure to the shock is no longer available). Being eligible for a shock requires that an individual has not already experienced the shock. Thus, the baseline for the analysis of the timing of events is always the first wave of retirement, and the samples used to estimate the rate of events will only include respondents who are eligible for such events in the first wave they were observed retired.[4]

Wealth Measures

For each wave in which any respondent in the analysis sample is observed, we compute household total wealth and annuitized net wealth (ANW). ANW is defined as the amount of income that would equal the total wealth in present value, if received annually over a person's expected remaining years of life (including that of the surviving spouse, if married). Total wealth is divided into five components: Nonhousing wealth; the net value of the primary residence; Social Security wealth; smooth pension wealth; smooth veteran's benefit wealth, and smooth annuity wealth.[5]

Means of sample characteristics for the first period postretirement by couple household and sex are shown in Table 14.1. Sample sizes are large for women and men in couple households, but smaller for single women and, especially, for single men.[6] Mean retirement age is similar across groups, but the means mask significant differences in the distribution. Married men are considerably more likely to retire (i.e., receive retirement benefits) at ages sixty- five to sixty-seven or later, relative to other groups; married women are much more likely to retire at earlier ages. "Received SSDI first (=1)" is a binary variable that indicates whether we code a respondent as retired because they were observed between the ages of sixty-two and sixty-four receiving Social Security Disability Insurance (SSDI) versus receiving (age-reduced) Social Security retirement or survivor benefits. The sample is predominately non-Hispanic white. Whites make up about 80 percent of the sample of couple respondents and around 64 percent of the sample of single respondents.

Overall, both respondents report good physical health, with only 7 and 8 percent of married respondents, and between 11 and 12 percent of single respondents, reporting poor health. In addition to reporting low rates of poor health, respondents generally reported low rates of functional limitations associated with GMS and ADL, and poor memory. The cognitive assessments administered by interview, particularly the TICS, indicate higher rates of memory cognitive problems with nearly over a quarter of respondents with nonmissing data registering TICS scores below 8.[7]

Mean values of wealth and ANW in the first wave of retirement are shown in Table 14.1. All dollar-denominated figures are inflation

TABLE 14.1
Means of sample characteristics

	Coupled men	Coupled women	Single men	Single women
Sample size	2,979	2,462	511	1,384
Retirement age	64.4	63.7	64.0	63.8
62–64	0.575	0.745	0.673	0.688
65–67	0.350	0.223	0.272	0.270
68–70	0.075	0.032	0.055	0.042
Received SSDI first (=1)	0.077	0.058	0.125	0.105
RACE				
White	0.804	0.809	0.689	0.626
Black	0.103	0.090	0.204	0.271
Hispanic	0.075	0.086	0.090	0.085
Other	0.018	0.015	0.018	0.019
EDUCATION LEVEL				
Less than HS	0.251	0.218	0.288	0.324
HS	0.355	0.446	0.358	0.365
Some college	0.183	0.210	0.182	0.184
4+ college	0.210	0.126	0.172	0.126
SELF-REPORTED HEALTH				
Very good or excellent	0.418	0.451	0.376	0.339
Good	0.319	0.320	0.295	0.294
Fair	0.190	0.158	0.217	0.252
Poor	0.074	0.071	0.112	0.115
GROSS MOTOR SKILLS (GMS) INDEX				
Trouble with 0 GMS	0.847	0.805	0.800	0.680
Trouble with 1–2 GMS	0.118	0.145	0.142	0.219
Trouble with 3+ GMS	0.035	0.050	0.057	0.101
ADL INDEX				
Trouble with 0 ADL	0.902	0.880	0.843	0.810
Trouble with 1–2 ADL	0.076	0.091	0.143	0.130
Trouble with 3+ ADL	0.021	0.050	0.035	0.061
SELF-REPORTED MEMORY				
Very good or excellent	0.223	0.259	0.258	0.249
Good	0.333	0.447	0.341	0.359
Fair	0.177	0.200	0.229	0.262
Poor	0.037	0.030	0.074	0.056
Missing	0.227	0.064	0.098	0.074
TICS SCORE				
TICS score 8 or higher	0.334	0.335	0.368	0.383
TICS score less than 8	0.114	0.170	0.174	0.176
TICS score missing	0.551	0.495	0.458	0.441
NOUN RECALL SCORE				
Noun recall score 4 or higher	0.604	0.837	0.722	0.837
Noun recall score less than 4	0.063	0.042	0.133	0.058
Noun recall score missing	0.333	0.121	0.145	0.105
Total wealth (thousands of dollars)[a]	905.4	877.6	503.84	399.3
Annuitized net wealth (ANW) (thousands of dollars)	0.349	0.364	0.389	0.258
ANW less than 1.5 times FPT (=1)	0.260	0.220	0.399	0.493

[a] 2008 dollars

adjusted to 2008 using the CPI-U. There are also large differences in wealth across couple-household and gender categories, but differences in ANW are much smaller. ANW are adjusted via an equivalency scale to single-person equivalents. Some of the most striking figures in Table 14.1 are very high near asset inadequacy rates, calculated by comparing ANW to 1.5 times the official poverty threshold for singles. Although not shown, there are large differences in wealth, ANW, and asset in-adequacy between whites and nonwhites and between more educated respondents and those with less than a high school diploma.

OUR FINDINGS

In this section, we present evidence on the incidence of negative unex-pected shocks that are likely to adversely affect the level of available resources. We do this by estimating the rate at which shocks to physical and cognitive health occur. We explore which shocks are most likely to occur in the early retirement years as well as the characteristics of individuals who are at increased risk for these events. Having identified these shock patterns among various household types, we then estimate the effect of these events on the evolution of economic resources during the course of retirement. We identify those groups that are vulnerable to having their economic resources so eroded that they fall into poverty or near-poverty because of these events.

Patterns of Shocks Overall, and by Demographic Group

In Figure 14.1, we present the patterns of these shocks over the first eleven years of retirement for those households that are at risk of expe-riencing these shocks. The average of the occurrence over relevant two-year periods is presented.[8] Many of the cognitive and health events occur with a relatively high frequency, particularly the change in health to 'Fair/Poor' and self-reported declines in memory.

While the average rate at which these shocks occur is an important indicator of the relative frequency of a particular event, it does not tell us how these rates vary over individuals with various background char-acteristics. To reveal these group-specific patterns, we estimated models that reveal the probability that an individual will experience a specific shock, depending on his or her characteristics. The characteristics that

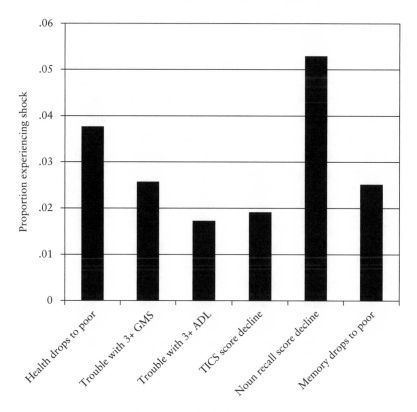

Figure 14.1　Average two-year risk for shock in early retirement
SOURCE: Authors' calculations from the 1992–2008 HRS.

we have identified are gender, household type (couples or singles), race/
ethnicity, education level, whether retired after age 65, and retiring after
receiving SSDI.[9]

From this multivariate analysis of the impact of background variables
on the probability of transition to poor physical health we determine that
men and women tend to have similar rates of physical health decline.
Being a member of a couple indicates a lower likelihood of shocks to
physical health than for singles. There is also a strong relationship between the likelihood of physical health decline and race, with black and
Hispanic men and women being substantially more likely to experience
a physical health decline. More-educated men and women are less likely
to experience these negative physical health shocks relative to individuals

with less education. Finally, individuals whom we code as retired upon the receipt of SSDI at ages sixty-two to sixty-four are at an increased likelihood of events signaling physical health decline.[10] The results for the cognitive health events mirror those for the events signaling physical decline. Singles, nonwhites, those with less than a high school education, and those we code as retiring receiving SSDI are at a substantially, and in most cases statistically significant, increased risk of self-reported memory declines to poor and dropping below threshold levels of the TICS and ten-noun recall test scores.

The Impact of Physical and Cognitive Health Decline on ANW

To examine the impact of shocks/events on ANW, we estimate a fixed-effects regression with ln(ANW) as the dependent variable, and the specific event plus a set of time-varying control variables as independent variables. More formally we estimate

$$\ln(ANW_{it}) = \alpha_i + \gamma_t + \eta_y + X_{it}\beta + \delta(PoorHealth_{it}) + \varepsilon_{it},$$

where α_i is an individual level fixed effect, γ_t is a postretirement wave effect (t=1,2,3,4,5,6,7+), η_y is a year effect (y = 1996, 1998, 2000, 2002, 2004, 2006, and 2008), $PoorHealth_{it}$ is an indicator of transition to poor health using the measures described above, and X_{it} is a vector of time-varying covariates. The above specification is estimated separately for single males and females, and separately for males and females in couple households. In all specifications for coupled individuals, X_{it} includes the spouse's self-reported health on a four-point scale (poor, fair, good, or excellent). In addition, in the specifications aimed at estimating the wealth response to shocks to cognitive health, X_{it} includes indicators for the respondent's self-reported physical health status.

Prior research has established a positive association between wealth and health (Smith 2007). This positive association can arise because wealth or other resource measures have a protective effect on health, or because poor health erodes wealth or wealth accumulation.[11] Our interest is in the latter mechanism. In the case of retirees, contemporaneous health status, the risk of transition to poor health, and the level of retirement resources may all be affected by resource levels prior to retirement. We deal with this potential for reverse causality by including fixed effects in the specification above and by selecting individuals into the sample who were not in poor health during the first period of retirement. Because the specifications contain an individual fixed effect, the impact of each health shock on ln(ANW) is identified within (rather than between) individual variation in shock status. In effect, we are estimating relationships between transition to poor health during retirement and variation of ln(ANW) away from *individual* conditional mean levels. Excluding the individual fixed effect from the above specification dramatically inflates the size of the estimated impact because individuals who are observed experiencing health shocks have lower average levels of retirement wealth.

Estimates of the effect of shocks indicating physical and cognitive health decline on ln(ANW) are shown in Figure 14.2.[12] Nearly all event coefficients are negative, indicating that physical health decline is associated with a decrease in ANW. One of the more interesting findings shown in Figure 14.2 concerns the relative vulnerability of women in couple households to ANW declines associated with health decline. The impact of each health decline indicator is nearly twice as large for women in couple households as for men, with estimates ranging from −4 percent of ANW (health decline to fair or poor) to 6 percent of ANW (for those with troubles in three or more ADLs). In addition, all of the health status decline indicators are statistically significant for women whether single or in couple households. All of the indicators of health status decline have a statistically significant and negative effect on ANW among single women, but only trouble with three or more ADLs is statistically significant among single men.[13]

In contrast to the coefficients on the physical health decline indicators, a majority of the impacts of indicators of cognitive decline on ln(ANW) shown Figure 14.2 are not statistically significant, although most have the expected sign. ('Sign' here refers to positive or negative, indicating direction of effect.) Only a drop in the ten-noun recall score below four has an effect on ANW that is statistically different from zero for men in couple households, single men, and single women. In addition, for men in couples, having a TICS score that drops below eight is associated with an estimated 8 percent decline in ANW that is statistically different from zero at the 5 percent level.

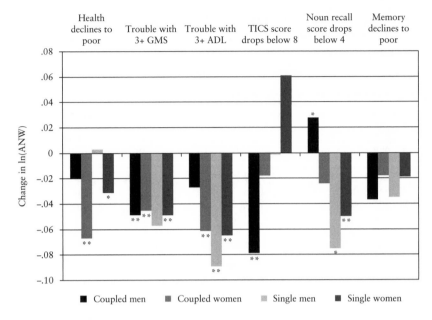

Figure 14.2   The impact of physical and cognitive health decline on ln(ANW) by couple status and sex

*Statistically significant at the 10 percent level
**Statistically significant at the 5 percent level

The Impact of Cognitive and Health Declines on the Probability of Becoming Poor/Near-Poor

The measure of the inadequacy of retirement resources employed in this analysis is a simple indicator as to whether ANW is below 1.5 times the federal poverty threshold for a single person under age sixty-five. There is no analog to the fixed-effect model in the case where the outcome is a binary variable. Estimating a fixed-effect version of a model where the outcome variable is binary results in any observations in which the individual identifier perfectly predicts the outcome being dropped. Practically speaking, this means that any individual who was never observed to have experienced a particular event postretirement would be dropped from the estimation pertaining to this event.

Rather than present results from a traditional estimation, which would be flawed for reasons discussed above, we take a different approach. Assuming that we know the actual data-generating process, an individual would fall below an adequacy standard of 1.5 times the poverty threshold in any period if and only if the value of the random component (error) of ln(ANW) in that period were sufficiently small relative to the expected level of ln(ANW). For example, if an individual had expected ln(ANW) 0.04 greater than the natural log of 1.5 times the poverty threshold, he or she would need a negative error of at least −0.04 to be pushed into asset poverty. Suppose an individual experienced a health shock that resulted in the expected value of ln(ANW) being reduced by 0.06. In this case the same individual would be asset-poor if he or she experienced an error of smaller than positive 0.02. For this individual the impact of the shock on the probability of being poor can be calculated as $F(0.02)$ less $F(-0.04)$ where $F(\ )$ is the cumulative distribution function of the error distribution.

The above approach to calculating the impact of a shock to health or cognition relies on knowledge of the expected ANW as well as knowledge of the error distribution, both of which are unknown. In the absence of knowledge of the true value of expected ANW and the error distribution, we utilize estimates of expected ln(ANW) from the fixed-effects estimation in the prior subsection. Estimates of the expected ln(ANW) are obtained conditioning on a shock having occurred and conditioning on a shock not having occurred. For each level of estimated expected ln(ANW), we calculate the value of the error needed to push the individual into asset poverty. Then, using kernel density estimates of the error distribution, we compute the probability of drawing an error that is sufficiently small to push the individual into asset poverty conditional on having realized a shock, and conditional on not having realized a shock. Finally, the impact of a shock to health or cognition on the probability of being asset-poor is then calculated as the difference in the probability of drawing an error sufficiently small to lead to asset poverty conditional on a shock and conditional on not having a shock.

The impact of transitioning to three or more ADLs on falling below 1.5 times the Federal Poverty Threshold (FPT) among single men is shown in Figure 14.3. Among the results reported in Figure 14.2, transitioning to difficulty with three or more ADLs among single men is the combination of health event and demographic group with the largest negative impact, at −8.7 percent. The results in Figure 14.3 represent an upper bound on the impact of health events on the likelihood of

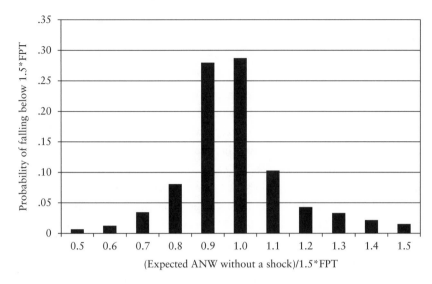

Figure 14.3 Impact of trouble with 3+ ADL on the probability of inadequate ANW among single men (coefficient = −0.089)

being asset-poor in retirement. The most striking result from Figure 14.3 is the large effect that transitioning to three or more ADLs has on the likelihood of falling below adequacy levels, but these effects are only large for individuals who would, in the absence of the event, have ANW levels very near the threshold value of 1.5 times the FPT. For example, the impact of transitioning to three or more ADLs on the probability of insufficient retirement assets among single men approaches 0.30 at the adequacy threshold, but is less than 0.05 at 1.2 times the adequacy threshold.[14]

Vulnerable Populations

Within the population we study there are subgroups that have a high average vulnerability to cognitive or health decline or both resulting in a decrease of their ANW below 1.5 times the FPT adequacy standard. These groups can be thought of as vulnerable with respect to a set of events because they fit three specific criteria. First, they have characteristics that are associated with an increased likelihood of experiencing the set of events for which they are vulnerable. Second, the event to which the group is deemed to be vulnerable must have a modest-to-large effect on their ANW, where modest and large are effects in the range of 5 and 10 percentage points, respectively, and there is some evidence of statistical significance. Lastly, a sizable fraction of the group has inadequate or near inadequate levels of ANW. For our purposes, inadequate or near inadequate levels of ANW are defined as no more than 20 percent higher than 1.5 times the FPT adequacy standard.

In Table 14.2, we place a box around group-event category combinations that meet these three criteria. We consider a group to be at risk for multiple events if they meet the three stated criteria both for events indicating cognitive decline and those indicating health decline. These groups are noted in the table in bold. In all we identify fourteen overlapping groups that are vulnerable to having their ANW fall below or further below 1.5 times the FPT adequacy standard due to cognitive decline or health decline, and three groups that are vulnerable to both types of risk. Because the groups are overlapping it is possible for individuals to face more than one elevated risk category. Some individuals are particularly vulnerable because they have multiple characteristics associated with elevated risk of declines in physical and cognitive health. For example, single nonwhite males with less than a high school degree are particularly vulnerable to physical and cognitive health decline because they have multiple characteristics associated with elevated risk for such declines.

The groups that we identify as being vulnerable to adverse events postretirement are traditionally viewed as disadvantaged; males in couple households with disadvantaged characteristics, females in couple households with disadvantaged characteristics, and singles with disadvantaged characteristics. For example, single males comprise 6.97 percent of the sample, and they face a high risk of experiencing a cognitive decline. However, they face a modest risk of falling below the adequacy threshold should they experience such a decline, as less than 40 percent of them have ANWs within 20 percent of the threshold.

CONCLUSIONS

We have used a sample of recent retirees from the HRS original cohort to examine the role of cognitive and health shocks that occur after retirement on the evolution of wealth. Our results indicate that a number of

TABLE 14.2
Assessing vulnerable groups

| | | PHYSICAL HEALTH DECLINE | | | | COGNITIVE HEALTH DECLINE | | | |
| | | Coupled male | Coupled male | Single male | Single female | Coupled male | Coupled female | Single male | Single female |
Individual attribute	Effect of event	Small	Modest	Modest	Modest	Modest	Small	Modest	Small
Single	% of sample	na	na	6.97	18.87	na	na	6.97	18.87
	Relative risk	low	low	high	high	low	low	high	high
	% near poor	26.0	22.0	39.9	49.3	26.0	22.0	39.9	49.3
Nonwhite	% of sample	7.9	6.4	2.2	7.1	7.9	6.4	2.2	7.1
	Relative risk	high	high	high	high	high	high	high	high
	% near poor	54.4	49.8	62.2	67.6	54.4	49.8	62.2	67.6
Low education	% of sample	10.2	7.3	2.0	6.1	10.2	7.3	2.0	6.1
	Relative risk	high	high	high	high	high	high	high	high
	% near poor	52.9	48.6	60.5	77.2	52.9	48.6	60.5	77.2
Retired with SSDI	% of sample	3.1	2.0	0.1	2.0	3.1	2.0	0.1	2.0
	Relative risk	high	high	high	high	high	high	high	high
	% near poor	49.6	43.8	64.1	73.9	49.6	43.8	64.1	73.9
Retired at age 62–65	% of sample	17.2	8.6	2.3	5.9	17.2	8.6	2.3	5.9
	Relative risk	no effect	no effect	no effect	no effect	no effect	no effect	no effect	no effect
	% near poor	30.7	22.7	43.0	53.5	30.7	22.7	43.0	53.5

negative cognitive and health events are among the most frequent occurrences for the retired population. For instance, the probability among those with initial better memory of experiencing a memory decline to fair or poor over any two-year period during early retirement is 0.11 on average.

The analysis of the probability of shock occurrence also revealed large differences in the incidence by background characteristics, with nonwhites, those who retire with SSDI, and those with less education being more likely to experience events indicating cognitive and health decline. These risks of exposure between individuals with traditionally advantaged versus disadvantaged background characteristics implies a relatively large risk for the disadvantaged.

We found evidence of some differences in the risk of cognitive decline between men and women, with men being at greater risk of such events, but the risk rates for other shocks appear to be similar across sex. Our analysis of the impact of events on ANW and ANW-based inadequacy indicates that cognitive and health decline events have effects ranging from small and not statistically different from zero to as large as a 9 percent loss in ANW depending on the event and subgroup. In general, events indicating cognitive decline had smaller effects than events indicating health decline. There is also evidence that the effects on ANW of shocks indicating health decline are larger for women, whether single or in couples.

In examining the impact of events indicating cognitive and health decline on the likelihood of having ANW fall below 1.5 times the FPT, we find that the effects are potentially very large only for individuals who, in the absence of the event, would be expected to have ANW levels close to the adequacy standard. Thus, the average impact of these events on the probability of adequacy in a population depends in large part on what fraction of the population has ANW levels near the threshold. If a population is clustered below and around the adequacy standard, then it may be very vulnerable to having its resources eroded to below the threshold level by adverse health and cognitive events.

An important and interesting question concerns the process by which declines in health and cognitive status seem to lead to resource declines. One possibility is that health insurance may be able to play a more protective role for the vulnerable populations. As Social Security recipients, these retired individuals are eligible for Medicare, though it is not known if they have supplemental medigap insurance coverage. If not, the spending down of resources necessary to cover the costs of medical care is a real possibility. Moreover, many of the costs of care associated with health and cognitive declines may involve nonmedical caregivers, home modifications, and other expenses that are difficult to insure. Loss of resources may also occur if spouse adjustments to work and earnings are related to a partner's loss of health or cognitive status.

NOTES

1. These authors estimate the adequacy of economic resources of individuals at the time of retirement using data from both the Social Security New Beneficiary Survey and the Health and Retirement study. Their work is preceded by several other studies of the adequacy of resources available to older workers upon retirement, including Moore and Mitchell (2000); Engen, Gale, and Uccello (1999); Wolff (2002); and Scholz, Seshadri, and Khitatrakun (2006). These studies arrive at quite disparate conclusions regarding overall levels of retirement resource adequacy, caused in part by basic differences in data, assumptions, estimation procedures, and the definition of adequacy used. Engen, Gale, and Uccello (1999), in assessing differences among these studies, suggest that when a variety of adjustments are made for differences in assumptions and estimating procedures, there may be less disagreement regarding the overall adequacy of retirement savings than is generally recognized. Haveman et al. (2007a) examine changes in retirement resource adequacy (defined as the level of annuitized net wealth, or ANW, relative to the poverty line and twice the poverty line). Haveman et al. (2007b) compare resource adequacy for the group that retired in the early 1980s with a cohort that retired in the 1990s; they find similar levels of adequacy between the two cohorts of retirees.

2. The initial HRS was constructed by selecting households in which at least one person born between 1931 and 1941 resided, and then collecting information from these persons and their spouses. Thus, the HRS includes spouses who may be younger or older than the respondents themselves. While these spouses never enter our sample as newly retired, their income and assets and characteristics are included when describing adequacy of the couple's resources.

3. To construct our analysis sample, we used the RAND HRS Data, Version J (2010). Data on cognition and assets and income come from the HRS core data, which are publically available every two years between 1992 and 2008. The RAND HRS Data file is an easy-to-use longitudinal data set based on the HRS data. It was developed at RAND with funding from the National

Institute on Aging and the Social Security Administration. We track individual respondents from the wave in which they are first observed as "retired" (defined by first receipt of Social Security benefits, including spousal benefits, or Social Security disability insurance (SSDI) benefits at age sixty-two or older), until they die, attrite from the sample, or until the information available from the panel expires; the last available year is 2008. This age criterion eliminates individuals who were disability insurance recipients earlier in life and were automatically converted to retired-worker status, per program rules. While some may receive benefits without having ceased work just prior to receipt, receipt signals a dependence for support on retirement income rather than work.

4. The chapters by Daly and Gardiner and Meyer and Mok in this volume also use this "transition into" framework in identifying shocks.

5. Total wealth is divided into five components: nonhousing wealth; the net value of the primary residence; Social Security wealth; smooth pension wealth; smooth veteran's benefit wealth; and smooth annuity wealth.

6. Men and women in the first two columns are not necessarily in the same households. Households in which the first receipt of Social Security is not observed for one spouse will have only one spouse in our sample. Among reasons why only one spouse may be observed is if the other spouse's initial receipt is prior to 1992, the spouse is too young for eligibility prior to 2008, or he or she works in noncovered employment.

7. A substantial number of female respondents are missing cognitive health measures during the first period postretirement. In the case of the TICS and noun-recall-based measures, the high amount of missing data is at least partially attributable to the fact that the data on these measures was not collected until 1996. In the case of self-reported memory, there was a high fraction of respondents with missing data in 1994.

8. For example, the rate shown for a marriage event is approximately 0.02, indicating that over a two-year period an average of 2 percent of the people who were single and not married two years earlier will marry.

9. In particular, we estimated logistics models for the probability that an individual experiences an event by sex as a function of whether individuals were in a couple household, their race/ethnicity and education level, whether they retired at sixty-five or later, and whether they were coded as retiring while receiving SSDI.

10. We emphasize that these are declines that occur *after* SSDI receipt. Thus, the observed decline may be related to the health condition on which their SSDI determination is based but is not that same health condition.

11. Research designed to establish the tie between resources and health has attempted to link resources (or resource changes) to various health states (or changes in health status). For example, large observed increases in wealth (Smith 2007) and the growth in American Indian casino gambling (and the income/wealth associated with it) have been related to the health status of

those experiencing the change. Earlier research has been more descriptive and has linked the level of assets and credit card debt to health status (Robert and House 1996; Drentea and Lavrakas 2000) and the level of wealth to changes in health (Smith 2007).

12. A complete set of estimates is available upon request.

13. The absence of statistically significant effects for single men may be a result of the very limited number of single men in our sample.

14. This observation concerning the impact of events on adequacy at various points in the distribution of the ratio of ANW to the adequacy standard suggests that overall vulnerability in terms of ANW-based retirement adequacy in a population of Social Security beneficiaries to events indicating cognitive and health decline depends on the extent to which the population is clustered around the adequacy standard. If few in the population were clustered around the adequacy standard, adverse events would still result in a loss of ANW, and while this might be tragic on its own, the average impact of such a loss of ANW on threshold-based, ANW-based adequacy would not be large. Similarly, if a large proportion of the retired population had ANW levels within 10 percent of the adequacy standard (1.5 times the FPT), events that result in a loss of ANW are expected to have a large average effect on adequacy in the population.

REFERENCES

Coile, Courtney, and Kevin Milligan (2009). "How Household Portfolios Evolve After Retirement: The Effect of Aging and Health Shocks." *Review of Income and Wealth* 55 (2): 226–48.

Drentea, Patricia, and Paul J. Lavrakas (2000). "Over the Limit: The Association Among Health Status, Race and Debt." *Social Science & Medicine* 50:517–29.

Engen, Eric M., William G. Gale, and Cori E. Uccello (1999). "The Adequacy of Household Saving." *Brookings Papers on Economic Activity* 2:65–187.

Haveman, Robert, Karen Holden, Barbara Wolfe, and Andrei Romanov (2007a). "Assessing the Savings Sufficiency over the First Decade of Retirement." *International Tax and Public Finance* 14(4): 481–502.

Haveman, Robert, Karen Holden, Barbara Wolfe, and Andrei Romanov (2007b). "The Sufficiency of Retirement Savings: Comparing Cohorts at the Time of Retirement." In Brigette Madrain, Olivia S. Mitchell, and Beth J. Soldo (eds.), *Redefining Retirement: How Will Boomers Fare?* New York: Oxford University Press, 36–69.

Holden, Sarah, and Daniel Schrass (2009). *The Role of IRAs in U.S. Households' Saving for Retirement, 2008*. Research Fundamentals. Washington, DC: Investment Company Institute.

Megbolugbe, Issac, Jarjisu Sa-Aadu, and James Shilling (1997). "Oh Yes, the Elderly Will Reduce Housing Equity Under the Right Circumstances." *Journal of Housing Research* 8(1): 53–74.

Megbolugbe, Issac, Jarjisu Sa-Aadu, and James Shilling (1999). "Elderly Female-Headed Households and the Decision to Trade Down." *Journal of Housing Economics* 8(4): 285–300.

Moore, James, and Olivia S. Mitchell (2000). "Projected Retirement Wealth and Saving Adequacy." In O. S. Mitchell, B. Hammond, and A. Rappaport (eds.), *Forecasting Retirement Needs and Retirement Wealth*. Pension Research Council. Philadelphia: University of Pennsylvania Press: 68–94.

Poterba, James M., Steven F. Venti, and David A. Wise (2008). *Tapping Assets in Retirement: Which Assets, How, and When?*, ed. Retirement Research Center, NBER Working Paper No. NB08-06 Sep-08. Cambridge, MA: National Bureau of Economic Research.

Poterba, James M., Steven F. Venti, and David A. Wise (2010). *Family Status Transitions, Latent Health, and the Post-Retirement Evolution of Assets*. NBER Working Paper No. 15789. Cambridge, MA: National Bureau of Economic Research.

RAND Corporation (2010). "Health and Retirement Study: Data Version J." *Center for the Study of Aging*; with funding from National Institute on Aging and the Social Security Administration. Santa Monica, CA.

Robert, Stephanie A., and James S. House (1996). "SES Differentials in Health by Age and Alternative Indicators of SES." *Journal of Aging and Health*, 8(3): 359–88.

Scholz, John Karl, Ananth Sheshadri, and Surachai Khitatrakun (2006). "Are Americans Saving Optimally for Retirement?" *Journal of Political Economy*, 114(4): 607–43.

Smith, James. P. (2007). "The Impact of Socioeconomic Status on Health over the Life Course." *Journal of Human Resources*, 42(4): 739–64.

Social Security Administration (2009). *Annual Statistical Supplement to the Social Security Bulletin*, SSA Publication No. 13-11700. Washington, DC: Office of Research, Evaluation, and Statistics.

Venti, Steven F., and David A. Wise (2002). "Aging and Housing Equity." In Olivia S. Mitchell et al. (eds.), *Innovations in Retirement Financing*. Philadelphia: University of Pennsylvania Press, 251–81.

Venti, Steven F., and David A. Wise (2004). "Aging and Housing Equity: Another Look." In David A. Wise (ed.), *Perspectives in the Economics of Aging*. National Bureau of Economic Research. Chicago: University of Chicago Press, 127–80.

Wolff, Edward N. (2002). *Retirement Insecurity: The Income Shortfalls Awaiting the Soon-to-Retire*. Washington, DC: Economic Policy Institute.

CHAPTER FIFTEEN

Disability and Subjective Well-Being

Mary C. Daly and Colin S. Gardiner

INTRODUCTION

A considerable literature, including Chapters 13 and 14 of this volume, finds that the onset of a disability can have a large and persistent impact on the income and wealth of individuals and families.[1] These economic impacts have been recognized by policymakers in the United States and other industrialized nations and are the rationale for public cash assistance programs targeted at those with disabilities.[2] Increasingly, however, policymakers, especially in European nations, are calling for researchers to broaden their scope of analysis of the impact of disability to include the noneconomic side of well-being.[3] This interest has been spurred, in part, by a growing academic literature on the importance of subjective well-being in determining the health and welfare of societies (Diener 2000; Kahneman and Krueger 2006; Layard 2006; Stiglitz, Sen, and Fitoussi 2009). And, as discussed in Chapter 5, in some nations, promoting and protecting subjective well-being has become an important social goal in its own right.

In this chapter, we consider the relationship between disability and subjective well-being in the United States. The goal of the analysis is

The views in this essay are solely the responsibility of the authors and should not be interpreted as reflecting the views of the Federal Reserve Bank of San Francisco or the Board of Governors of the Federal Reserve System. The authors thank Robert Haveman for comments and Leila Bengali for excellent research assistance.

to increase understanding of the noneconomic toll that disability might take on individuals. Such understanding is important for evaluating the total costs of disability and for considering potential service additions to existing public disability programs. Our analysis is based on data from the Health and Retirement Survey (HRS), a nationally representative survey. Our chapter contributes to the existing literature in several ways. First, we provide estimates of the impact of disability on subjective well-being using nationally representative data for the United States— something that, to our knowledge, has not been done before. Second, we show that people with disabilities report substantially lower levels of subjective well-being than people without disabilities. This negative relationship holds across gender, age, race, educational attainment, and income, and in both cross-sectional and longitudinal analysis. Although all people with disabilities have some reduction in subjective well-being, the declines are largest for those with more-severe disabilities. Finally, we provide some initial evidence regarding the permanence of the decline in subjective well-being associated with disability. Based on pooled cross-sectional surveys, we find that the differences in subjective well-being between those with and without disabilities are decreasing in the duration of disability, suggesting that over time the impact of disability on subjective well-being may attenuate.

This chapter proceeds with a brief review of previous research examining the links between subjective well-being and disability. Next, we describe our data source, the HRS, and define the variables used in our analysis. With the data in place, we provide a descriptive overview of the relationship between disability and subjective well-being. We then turn to more formal regression analysis and lay out our methods and results. We end with a summary of our findings and a discussion of their implications.

BACKGROUND AND MOTIVATION

A small literature, largely in psychology and epidemiology, has examined the impact of disability on noneconomic aspects of well-being including happiness, social connectedness, and mental health. For the most part these studies have been cross-sectional and limited to small populations of individuals with particular disabilities, such as spinal cord injuries or burns (Brickman, Coates, and Janoff-Bulman 1978; Schulz and Decker 1985; Tyc 1992; Patterson et al. 1993; Frederick and Loewenstein 1999).[4] Data from these studies find that although there is an initial drop in happiness following the disabling event, people with relatively debilitating conditions, over time, are able to maintain positive attitudes and nonpathological levels of subjective well-being. This finding has led to speculation that people habituate to their disability and return to their predisability state of self-reported subjective well-being.

More recently, researchers have turned to large, nationally representative surveys to investigate the linkages between disability and subjective well-being. In the first of this type of study, Lucas (2007), using data from the German Socio-Economic Panel (GSOEP) and the British Household Panel Survey (BHPS), finds a strong and statistically significant negative relationship between subjective well-being and disability. He finds little evidence that these effects moderate over time, suggesting that individuals may not adapt to their disability and return to the level of well-being they had before the event.

Conversely, Oswald and Powdthavee (2008) using the BHPS and a broader measure of disability, find that following an initial drop in subjective well-being, individuals with disabilities return to their predisability levels of subjective well-being within two years. Restricting the sample to those with a severe disability limits measured adaptation; within the smaller, more severely disabled sample, there is no return to predisability levels of subjective well-being. Powdthavee (2009), again using the BHPS, finds very similar results. A final longitudinal study by Pagan-Rodriguez (2010), using the GSOEP, finds that working-age males with a disability achieve complete adaptation on global measures of well-being. However, this habituation does not occur across all domains of well-being.

To summarize, all of these studies point to a significant decline in subjective well-being following the onset of a disability. However, there is considerable disagreement about how long the negative impact lasts, whether it varies with different measures of subjective well-being, and whether it is different for less- and more-severe disabilities. Additional work is required to refine our knowledge of the impact that disability has on noneconomic well-being and the extent to which this impact moderates over time. Moreover, given documented cross-country differences in definitions of and reactions to disability, research using U.S. data would be useful.[5] In this chapter, we work to fill these gaps.[6]

DATA AND KEY VARIABLES

The Health and Retirement Survey

The HRS is a nationally representative longitudinal survey of individuals who were at least fifty-one years of age in 1992—the first year the survey was conducted.[7] The HRS is funded by the National Institute on Aging and managed by the University of Michigan. The survey is conducted biennially and currently contains nine waves of data from 1992 through 2008. Data from the HRS are also used in the chapters by Kalil and DeLeire and by Stevens and Moulton in this volume.

The main purpose of the HRS is to provide insight into health and work transitions of older Americans. As such, each of the HRS surveys includes a core set of questions related to demographics, income, wealth, employment status, health, and disability. Periodically, the HRS also includes add-on questions intended to measure specific aspects of late-life transitions in greater detail. These special surveys, or "modules," provide the data for our research.

Specifically, we rely on data from the Leave-Behind Participant Life-style Questionnaire, also known as the Leave Behind Survey. The Leave Behind Survey collected information about a variety of psychosocial issues including subjective well-being. As the name denotes, this part of the questionnaire was "left behind" for respondents to complete on their own and return by mail.[8]

The Leave Behind Survey was piloted in 2004. The pilot questionnaire was administered to a random subsample of about 7,600 HRS respondents. About half of those (3,273) were given the psychosocial questionnaire, which we rely on for our analysis. Following the pilot, the questionnaire was revised and administered to the full sample of HRS respondents over the next two survey years: one-half in 2006 and the remaining half in 2008. Only those who completed face-to-face interviews received the Leave Behind Survey.

Our analysis makes use of two samples: a cross-sectional sample and a panel sample. Our cross-sectional sample pools responses from the 2004 pilot with responses from the 2006 and 2008 waves. After adjusting this pooled sample for missing or unusable subjective well-being and disability data, we have a total cross-sectional sample of 12,261 individuals. The panel sample is composed of individuals who were part of the psychosocial pilot survey in 2004 and who were reinterviewed in 2006 or 2008. To be included in our sample, respondents must have completed the survey in both years. Our panel sample contains 1,359 individuals.

As noted earlier, we make several adjustments to the data to arrive at our final samples. First, we eliminate all records containing proxy respondents. We then exclude anyone who failed to answer the subjective well-being questions used in our analysis. Like Kalil and DeLeire (Chapter 5), we drop category 4 responses to the subjective well-being question in 2004 and 2008 (we describe the rationale for this step in detail in the variable description section). Finally, we delete records with incomplete or missing information on disability.

Key Variables

Our two key variables for analysis are disability and subjective well-being. We describe the definitions of each in detail below. We also briefly review our key control variables.

Disability. As Burkhauser, Houtenville, and Tennant describe in Chapter 12 of this volume, disability is a difficult concept to define and measure. The Americans with Disabilities Act defines disability as a physical or mental impairment that substantially limits one or more life activities of an individual. Although we cannot follow that definition precisely in the HRS, we do have information on whether individuals consider themselves to have a work limitation. Burkhauser and Daly (1996, 2012), Burkhauser et al. (2002), and Burkhauser, Houtenville, and Tennant (Chapter 12) find that, while not perfect, self-reported work limitation measures of disability capture a population of individuals that is highly correlated with objective measures of physical limitation and health.[9]

Specifically, the HRS asks, "Now I want to ask how your health affects paid work activities. Do you have any impairment or health problem that limits the kind or amount of paid work you can do?" The respondent has the following response options: *Yes, No,* or *Too old to work.* We define disability as a Yes in response. For those individuals who say they have a work disability, the HRS goes on to inquire about the year of onset. These onset questions ask when the disability appeared and when it began to limit paid work. The onset questions are important for understanding whether individuals habituate to their disability.

Using these questions, we construct several disability variables. The first is a dummy variable equaling 1 if the respondent reports having a work limitation. We also create a disability transition variable that we use in the panel analysis. The transitions represent state changes (from no disability to disability and vice versa) between 2004 and 2006 and between 2004 and 2008. In addition, for our panel analysis, we create a dummy indicating whether an individual ever had a disability, and if so, a duration variable indicating how long ago the disability occurred.

Subjective Well-Being. In Chapter 5, Kalil and DeLeire consider two types of noneconomic well-being: hedonic and eudaimonic. In our study, we focus only on the hedonic because it is the measure most typically evaluated in the economics and disability literatures. Like Kalil and DeLeire, we measure hedonic or subjective well-being using the "satisfaction with life scale" available in the HRS Leave Behind Survey (Diener and Pavot 1993; Diener et al. 1985).[10] This measure captures an individual's perceived distance from long-term goals or aspirations rather than his or her emotional satisfaction with current circumstances (Keyes, Shmotkin, and Ryff 2002). The satisfaction with life scale contains five statements, and respondents are asked to rate how much they agree or disagree with each of them. The statements are as follows: "In most ways my life is close to ideal"; "The conditions of my life are excellent"; "I am satisfied with my life"; "So far, I have gotten the important things I want in life"; and "If I could live my life again, I would change almost nothing." The average of the scores from the five questions creates the "satisfaction with life scale."

Although this five-question measure is available in all years (2004–08), the scaling and the coding differ from year to year, requiring us to adjust the data. The most important of these adjustments is related to scaling. In all years respondents are asked to respond to the above statements by choosing along a spectrum of responses that range from strongly agree to strongly disagree. In 2004 and 2008, respondents had a seven-point scale that includes an option to neither agree nor disagree

(4 on the numeric scale). Respondents in 2006 had no such option and thus have a six-point scale. We adjust for this difference in scaling by excluding individuals who report Neither agree nor disagree in 2004 or 2008. We then rescale the 2004 and 2008 data to a six-point scale. As Kalil and DeLeire report in Chapter 5, our results are not drastically changed by excluding these individuals and then rescaling, which suggests that the neither agree nor disagree response only adds noise to our results.

We make two other minor adjustments to the data. First, we reverse the order of the 2004 scaling to account for the fact that in the questionnaire the scale went from strongly disagree to strongly agree while in subsequent years the scale went from strongly agree to strongly disagree. Second, following Diener et al. (1985) we mark as missing those respondents who fail to answer three or more of the five life satisfaction questions.

Activities of Daily Life. To account for the severity of a disability, we use two measures designed to assess the ability of individuals to perform everyday activities and tasks. The first assesses general difficulty with daily life tasks, including bathing, eating, dressing, walking across a room, and getting in or out of bed. The second assesses difficulties with instrumental activities of daily life, including using the telephone, managing money, taking medications, shopping for groceries, and preparing hot meals. For each measure we construct a disability severity indicator that is the sum of the number of tasks with which the respondent reports having difficulty; for example, an individual who has difficulty with all of the activities of daily living would be assigned a five.

Self-Reported Health. To separately account for the role that health rather than disability might have on subjective well-being, we include a measure of self-reported health. The self-reported health variable is categorical and the respondent is asked, "Would you say your health is excellent, very good, good, fair, or poor?" We consider a respondent reporting fair or poor to have low self-reported health.

Family Income and Wealth. To account for the fact that income and wealth are frequently lower for those with disabilities, we include family income and wealth gradients in most of our regression models. For family income, we create dummies for income levels from $0–$24,999; $25,000–$49,999; $50,000–$74,999; $75,000–$99,999; and $100,000 plus. Likewise, for family wealth the dummy groupings are $0; $1–$49,999; $50,000–$99,999; $100,000–$149,999, and $150,000 plus. All family income and wealth values are reported in 2007 dollars.

Other Controls. We include controls for educational attainment defined as: less than high school, less than a BA, a BA, or a graduate degree, and for labor force status defined as: employed, unemployed, retired, and not in the labor force. In addition, we control for age (continuous) and have dummy variables for marital status, gender, Hispanic, race, and whether the respondent was interviewed in multiple years.

DISABILITY AND SUBJECTIVE WELL-BEING
IN THE HRS

We begin by reporting on the prevalence of disability in the HRS and its correlation with other demographic, economic, and health variables in the HRS. Table 15.1 shows the characteristics of those with and without disabilities in our HRS sample. The numbers in Table 15.1 are based on pooled data from the 2004, 2006, and 2008 surveys. All data are weighted with the Leave Behind Survey person-weight so they can be interpreted as population values (see Clarke et al. 2007 for details).

As Table 15.1 shows, in the cross-section there are notable differences in the populations with and without disabilities. On average, individuals with self-reported work limitations have lower levels of education, lower attachment to the labor force, and lower family income and family wealth across the income distribution. Those with work disabilities also are far more likely to report that they are in fair or poor health than those without disabilities. Only a small fraction of those with a disability participate in the labor market, while most are retired or out of the labor force. In contrast, about 50 percent of the population without disabilities report being employed and only 42 percent report being retired. Of course, some of this is due to the difference in age across the two groups. Although not large in year terms, the difference in average age in the two populations crosses the important age sixty-five threshold, meaning that

TABLE 15.1
Disability status by demographic characteristics

	Disabled	Not disabled
AGE AND GENDER		
Age	66	63
Female	55.2%	49.9%
EDUCATION (%)		
Less than high school	22.1	11.4
Less than BA	62.0	57.4
BA	9.2	16.9
Graduate degree	6.6	14.3
LABOR STATUS (%)		
Employed	14.0	50.7
Unemployed	1.0	1.5
Retired	70.3	41.7
Not in the labor force	14.8	6.0
INCOME (DOLLARS)		
Family income	49,004.95	97,023.70
Family wealth	359,729.10	705,735.90
Family income (median)	30,122.44	$1,585.20
Family wealth (median)	116,799.50	313,235.10
HEALTH AND WELL-BEING		
Subjective well-being	3.83	4.61
Self-reported low health (%)	54.0	11.2
Self-reported low mental health[a] (%)	14.9	3.3

SOURCES: Health and Retirement Survey and authors' calculations.
[a]Mental health score is less than or equal to two.

some of the difference in labor market attachment could be associated with normal retirement behavior rather than health.

For mean and median family income and wealth, the differences across the two populations are even more evident. The median person reporting a work disability has about one-half of the family income and one-third of the wealth of the median person without a work limitation. The mean disparities are somewhat smaller but still point to a considerable difference in the economic well-being between those with and those without disabilities. These findings are consistent with Bound and Burkhauser (1999); Burkhauser and Daly (1996, 1998, and 2012); Burkhauser and Stapleton (2003); Haveman and Wolfe (1990); and Meyer and Mok (2009).

Turning to our measures of nonfinancial well-being—subjective well-being—we also find sizeable differences between those with and those without disabilities. People with disabilities have lower subjective well-being and self-reported mental health. This result is consistent with those reported in other cross-sectional and longitudinal studies—Dijkers (1997, 1999); Livneh and Martz (2003); Lucas (2007); Oswald and Powdthavee (2008); Schulz and Decker (1985); and Tyc (1992).

The data in Table 15.1 show that in addition to lower employment, income, and wealth, people with disabilities also have lower subjective well-being. But previous research has shown that education, income, and wealth are important correlates of subjective well-being, so it is difficult from the evidence in Table 15.1 to conclude that disability has an independent effect on subjective well-being.[11]

Table 15.2 provides more suggestive evidence that having a disability is independently associated with lower subjective well-being. The table reports weighted mean subjective well-being scores for those with and those without disabilities. The results show that subjective well-being gaps between those with and those without disabilities persist across a wide variety of characteristics including gender, overall health, mental health, severity, education, labor status, income, and wealth. The gaps are slightly larger for women than for men, for those with lower education, income, and wealth, and for those who are out of the labor force but not retired. These descriptive statistics suggest that having a disability may independently contribute to subjective well-being.

FORMAL ANALYSIS

Analytic Approach

To better identify the linkages between subjective well-being and disability we perform two types of regression analysis: cross-sectional and panel. Finally, using the retrospective nature of the disability questions in the HRS, we take an initial step toward understanding whether people adapt to their disabilities over time.

Our cross-sectional model is a simple multivariate regression that allows us to refine the descriptive results highlighted in Tables 15.1 and 15.2. This model examines whether individuals with disabilities report

TABLE 15.2

Subjective well-being by disability status and demographic characteristics

	Disabled	Not disabled
GENDER		
Male	3.87	4.59
Female	3.81	4.62
HEALTH		
Self-reported low health	3.48	3.98
Self-reported low mental health[a]	2.66	3.09
Some difficulties with activities of daily living[b]	3.28	4.15
Some difficulties with instrumental activities of daily living[b]	3.26	3.77
EDUCATION		
Less than high school	3.75	4.52
Less than BA	3.78	4.52
BA	4.12	4.76
Graduate degree	4.21	4.85
LABOR STATUS		
Employed	3.81	4.46
Unemployed	3.33	3.93
Retired	3.90	4.81
Not in the labor force	3.55	4.65
FAMILY INCOME		
Percentiles: 0–25	3.50	4.35
Percentiles: 25–50	3.91	4.52
Percentiles: 50–75	4.14	4.57
Percentiles: 75–100	4.28	4.82
FAMILY WEALTH		
Percentiles: 0–25	3.39	4.15
Percentiles: 25–50	3.89	4.49
Percentiles: 50–75	4.18	4.67
Percentiles: 75–100	4.41	4.92
Overall sample	3.83	4.61

SOURCES: Health and Retirement Survey and authors' calculations.

[a]Mental health score is less than or equal to two.

[b]Index score of two or greater indicating difficulty with two or more activities of daily living.

lower levels of subjective well-being controlling for other observable variables. Our basic cross-sectional model takes the form

(1) $SWB_i = \alpha_i + \beta_1 Disability_i + x_i \beta_2 + \varepsilon_i,$

where SWB_i is subjective well-being measured by the Diener life satisfaction scale. $Disability_i$ is a binary variable equaling 1 if the individual reports having a work limitation. X_i is a set of control variables including age, gender, marital status, race/ethnicity, education, labor force status, whether the individual was interviewed in more than one year, interview year, and, depending on the model, self-reported health, difficulties with activities of daily life, income, and wealth. The cross-sectional regressions are estimated on pooled data from the 2004, 2006, and 2008 surveys and are weighted by the Leave Behind Survey person-weight. Standard errors are robust and clustered by individual.

The cross-sectional models provide a useful reference point and link our work to previous cross-sectional studies, but they do not allow us to distinguish declines in subjective well-being associated with the onset of a disability from low subjective well-being related to an unobserved factor that is correlated with becoming disabled. For this we turn to the panel data aspect of the HRS. Using the panel, we are able to control for unobserved time-invariant characteristics of individuals that might affect subjective well-being.

Like several other authors in this volume including Kalil and De-Leire, we estimate a standard first-difference panel model of the following form:

$$(2) \quad \Delta SWB_{i,\,04-06,\,04-08} = \alpha_i + \beta_1 Disability\ Transitions_{i,\,04-06,\,04-08} \\ + \beta_2 \Delta x_{i,\,04-06,\,04-08} + \varepsilon_i.$$

The dependent variable in the regression is the change in subjective well-being from 2004–06 or 2004–08. *Disability Transitions*$_{i,\,04-06,\,04-08}$ is measured as the change in work-limitation status between 2004–06 or 2004–08. It is divided into four transition variables: *no disability to disability, disability to no disability, disability to disability,* and *no disability to no disability* (omitted category). The panel models are clearly superior to the simple cross-sectional analysis, but they do come with the cost of smaller sample sizes, which limits the precision of our estimates.

We end our analysis with a preliminary examination of the extent to which individuals with disabilities might adapt to them over time and return to their predisability levels of subjective well-being. We address this question of habituation by estimating a regression that includes a variable indicating whether or not a person has a disability and, for those who do have a disability, how long in years the disability has been present. Specifically, we estimate the following model:

$$(3) \quad SWB_i = \alpha_i + \beta_1 Disability_i + Tenure_i \beta_2 + Disability_i * Tenure_i \beta_3 \\ + x_i \beta_4 + \varepsilon_i,$$

where *Disability$_i$* is a dummy variable equaling 1 if the individual ever reports having a work limitation. *Tenure$_i$* is a measure of the length of a work limitation. *Disability$_i$*Tenure$_i$* is an interaction term of the binary disability variable and the continuous work limitation tenure variable.; X_i is a set of controls, as defined in equation 1.

Results

Table 15.3 reports the results of the cross-sectional and panel regressions of the effect of disability on subjective well-being as well as the results from the cross-sectional models testing for adaptation to disability. All cross-sectional regressions include the demographic controls as well as year dummies and a variable indicating whether an individual responded in multiple years. Within Table 15.3, columns 1–3 report results for the simple binary measure of disability, columns 4–6 report results for the change in disability status, and columns 7–9 report results for the adaptation/habituation models.

As Table 15.3 shows, disability is associated with statistically significant lower levels of subjective well-being (column 1). The measured negative association between disability and subjective well-being is reduced by half (from −0.712 to −0.369) when measures of self-reported low health and functional limitations are included; that said, the effect remains statistically significant (column 2). The inclusion of income and wealth variables reduces the effect further, although the magnitude of the reduction is far smaller than the one associated with the inclusion of the low health and functional limitation variables—to −0.324 from −0.369 (column 3). To put the magnitude of the coefficient on disability in context, relative to the standard deviation of life satisfaction (1.22), the association with disability reported in column 3, which controls for self-reported low health, severity, income, and wealth, is about 27 percent.

Columns 4–6 show results for the simple first-difference model. Recall that the model is based on partitioning the sample into transition states defined by disability status. The panel results show that relative to having no disability at any point, a transition to a period of disability from no disability has a statistically significant negative effect on subjective well-being. The other transition states also have negative effects on subjective well-being but they are not statistically significant, although

TABLE 15·3
Cross-sectional and panel models of disability and subjective well-being (SWB)

Dependent variable	Model 1 SWB	Model 2 SWB	Model 3 SWB	Model 4 SWB	Model 5 SWB	Model 6 SWB	Model 7 SWB	Model 8 SWB	Model 9 SWB
Disability	-0.712*** (0.0354)	-0.369*** (0.0380)	-0.324*** (0.0375)						
Self-reported low health		-0.562*** (0.0429)	-0.505*** (0.0427)					-0.549*** (0.0418)	-0.496*** (0.0416)
Difficulties with activities of daily living		-0.109*** (0.0274)	-0.0998*** (0.0274)					-0.107*** (0.0273)	-0.0993*** (0.0272)
Difficulties with instrumental activities of daily living		-0.122*** (0.0298)	-0.108*** (0.0299)					-0.121*** (0.0298)	-0.107*** (0.0299)
Transition: disability to no disability				-0.194 (0.147)	-0.194 (0.147)	-0.195 (0.147)			
Transition: no disability to disability				-0.247* (0.130)	-0.220* (0.121)	-0.224* (0.123)			
Transition: disability to disability				-0.251 (0.162)	-0.236 (0.167)	-0.235 (0.167)			
Transition: no low health to low health					-0.132 (0.167)	-0.131 (0.167)			
Ever reported a disability							-0.765*** (0.0415)	-0.430*** (0.0427)	-0.374*** (0.0421)
Tenure of disability							-0.0244 (0.0163)	-0.0215* (0.0130)	-0.0229* (0.0134)
Interaction term: ever reported and tenure of disability							0.0329** (0.0164)	0.0272** (0.0131)	0.0277** (0.0135)
Income controls	No	No	Yes	No	No	Yes	No	No	Yes
N	11,359	11,359	11,359	1,118	1,118	1,118	11,359	11,359	11,359
R-squared	0.165	0.208	0.225	0.010	0.011	0.011	0.169	0.212	0.227
P-value: F-test of coefficient equality				0.949	0.980	0.980			

sources: Health and Retirement Survey and authors' calculations.

notes: Control variables include age, gender, marital status, race/ethnicity, education, year, whether interviewed in multiple years, labor force status, and whether had disability for less than a year. All income variables are reported in 2007 dollars. Income controls are either levels or changes of continuous family income and wealth. Clustered and robust (panel) standard errors are reported in parentheses. Clustering is on individual identifier due to observations in multiple years. P-values of the F-test are calculated across all four of the disability tenure dummy variables.

*p < 0.1, **p < 0.05, ***p < 0.01.

the sample size is so small for these states that it is hard to draw any firm conclusions. That said, we cannot reject the hypothesis that the coefficients on the disability state transitions variables are equal.

Similar to the cross-sectional results, the coefficient on the no disability to disability transition variable is robust to the inclusion of changes in health, income, and wealth. This is consistent with the onset of a disability having an independent negative effect on subjective well-being that is not simply a reflection of the postdisability loss of income and wealth that the previous chapters highlighted. Relative to the standard deviation of life satisfaction in our panel sample (1.12), the association of subjective well-being with moving from no disability to disability is 20 percent. The results from our panel analysis generally confirm the findings in the cross-sectional regressions. Disability has an impact on subjective well-being that is not mediated by income or wealth.

The final set of results, shown in columns 7–9, utilizes the retrospective questions about disability in the HRS to consider whether the decline in subjective well-being associated with disability is permanent or transitory. These results shed some light on whether individuals with disabilities eventually adapt to their new health state and return to their predisability level of subjective well-being. The regressions are based on a cross-sectional model that in addition to the standard controls includes three key variables: (1) whether the respondent ever reported a disability during our sample frame, (2) the duration in years of the reported work-limitation, and (3) the interaction of these two variables. This empirical structure separates the effect of having a work limitation from the duration of the work limitation. In this framework, if adaptation occurs, we would expect a significant and positive coefficient on the interaction term implying that the overall effect of ever reporting a disability decreases in the duration of disability. Of course, because we are estimating a cross-sectional model of individuals with different disability durations, we cannot rule out that those who were not able to adapt attrited from the sample or that those with higher life satisfaction live longer and thus have longer disability durations. Those are issues for future research.

The results in column 7 show that before controlling for health, severity, income, or wealth, the interaction term on ever reported a disability and disability duration is positive and statistically significant. Controlling for health and severity (column 8) and for income and wealth (column 9), we find similar results that are again statistically significant. To put the habituation results in context, we can consider what the results imply about the time it would take to make up the initial drop in subjective well-being associated with the onset of a disability. For example, compare the coefficient on the interaction term (0.0277; column 9) with the drop in subjective well-being associated with a transition from no disability to disability (−0.244; column 6). Numerically, the coefficient on the interaction term is about one-eighth the size of the transition coefficient, implying it takes on average about eight years for subjective well-being to recover from the initial decline associated with the onset of disability.

While much more work is needed to fully understand the long-term impacts of disability on subjective well-being, these results are consistent with prior research that finds individuals adapt to their disabilities over time. That said, like previous studies investigating the issue of adaptation or habituation to disability, our study's results are suggestive but not definitive. Future research on this issue is required.

CONCLUSION

Policymakers in industrialized nations are increasingly asking researchers to broaden their scope of analysis of population outcomes to include noneconomic as well as economic metrics of well-being. Although a large literature exists documenting the effects of disability on income and wealth, there are relatively few studies examining the impact of disability noneconomic measures. The analysis in this chapter adds to this research by examining the effect of work-limiting disability on subjective well-being. Our findings suggest that much like economic measures, subjective well-being declines at the onset of disability. The negative association between disability and subjective well-being is robust to the inclusion of a variety of controls including health, functional ability, education, income, wealth, and employment status. The general finding holds in pooled cross-sectional analysis and in more appropriate panel data regressions, which allow us to take account of unobserved individual characteristics that may affect both the onset of disability and the level of reported subjective well-being. We also find evidence, although it is preliminary, that the impact of disability on subjective well-being may not be permanent. Regression analysis using data about individuals with disabilities of different durations suggests that the impact of disability on subjective well-being declines with duration. Although interesting and consistent with previous research on the ability of people with disabilities to adapt to their new health status, our results on this topic require additional validation.

Why are these findings important? For researchers these outcomes point to the potential value of exploring noneconomic metrics when evaluating the costs of lifecycle shocks. Increasingly, nationally representative panel data sources include such metrics, and future research can begin to examine whether the associations described in this chapter are causal and if so what mechanisms might drive the observed reactions. For policymakers, these findings suggest that lifecycle shocks have larger costs than most current public programs address. Programs that include psychosocial as well as economic consequences may reduce the overall impact of lifecycle shocks on individuals and families. The findings in this chapter and in Chapter 5 of this volume suggest that such programs may be worth considering.

NOTES

1. In addition to the chapters in this volume, examples are Bound and Burkhauser (1999); Bjelland et al. (2009); Burkhauser, Daly, and Houtenville (2001); Burkhauser and Stapleton (2003); Burkhauser and Daly (1996 and 2012); McNeil (2000); Meyer and Mok (2009); and Stern (1989).

2. In the United States there are two main public cash transfer programs for people with disabilities: Social Security Disability Insurance and Supplemental Security Income.

3. This interest is especially clear in European nations. In France, President Nicolas Sarkozy formed the Commission on the Measurement of Economic Performance and Social Progress, which issued a report supporting calls for a statistical indicator of economic well-being that includes social progress. A similar project is also underway in the U.K. (Office of National Statistics 2010).

4. Lucas (2007) provides a thorough survey of the literature.

5. Smith et al. (2005) consider the buffering effect wealth has on well-being following the onset of a disability using cross-sectional data from the HRS, but they do not use the panel nature of the data to track onsets of disability.

6. One reason for the research gap on this topic in the United States is a lack of available data. In this chapter, we take advantage of the psychosocial

module included in the Health and Retirement Study beginning in 2004 with data through 2008. These data are the first in the United States that will allow us to replicate the work of Lucas (2007) for the United States.

7. The HRS began as two distinct but closely related surveys: the HRS and the AHEAD. The surveys were merged in 1998.

8. The questionnaire was the product of collaborative efforts of an expert panel of individuals in psychology, epidemiology, demography, and economics. (See HRS Documentation Report 2008 for more detailed information on the Psychosocial Survey design and the survey work group.)

9. These measures are not without critics. For an example of this criticism, see Hale (2001), Kirchner (1996), and McNeil (2000). Nonetheless, we find that our self-reported work limitation measure of disability is highly correlated with low self-reported health and those who report having difficulties with multiple activities of daily life.

10. For a more detailed account of the Diener's satisfaction with life index in the HRS consult Clarke et al. (2007).

11. For reviews of the correlates of subjective well-being in the literature, see Dolan et al. (2008) and Kahneman and Krueger (2006).

REFERENCES

Bjelland, Melissa J., Richard V. Burkhauser, Sarah von Schrader, and Andrew J. Houtenville. *2009 Progress Report on the Economic Well-Being of Working-Age People with Disabilities.* Policy Brief, Ithaca, NY: Rehabilitation Research and Training Center on Employment Policy for Persons with Disabilities, Cornell University, 2009.

Bound, John, and Richard V. Burkhauser. "Economic Analysis of Transfer Programs Targeted on People with Disabilities." In *Handbook of Labor Economics*, by Orley C. Ashenfelter and David Card, 3417–528. Amsterdam: Elsevier, 1999.

Brickman, Philip, Dan Coates, and Ronnie Janoff-Bulman. "Lottery Winners and Accident Victims: Is Happiness Relative?" *Journal of Personality and Social Psychology* 36, no. 8 (1978): 917–27.

Burkhauser, Richard V., and Mary C. Daly. *The Declining Work and Welfare of People with Disabilities: What Went Wrong and a Strategy for Change.* Washington DC: AEI Press, 2012.

Burkhauser, Richard V., and Mary C. Daly. "Disability and Work: The Experiences of American and German Men." *Economic Review*, Federal Reserve Bank of San Francisco no. 2 (1998): 17–29.

Burkhauser, Richard V., and Mary C. Daly. "Employment and Economic Well-Being Following the Onset of a Disability." In *Disability, Work, and Cash Benefits*, edited by Jerry L. Mashaw, Virginia Reno, Richard V. Burkhauser, and Monroe Berkowitz, 59–102. Kalamazoo, MI: W. E. Upjohn Institute for Employment Research, 1996.

Burkhauser, Richard V., Mary C. Daly, and Andrew J. Houtenville. "How Working-Age People with Disabilities Fared over the 1990s Business Cycle." In *Ensuring Health and Income Security for an Aging Workforce*, edited by P. Budetti, R. V. Burkhauser, J. Gregory, and H. A. Hunt. Kalamazoo MI: W. E. Upjohn Institute for Employment Research, 2001.

Burkhauser, Richard V., Mary C. Daly, Andrew J. Houtenville, and Nigar Nargis. "Self-Reported Work-Limitation Data: What They Can and Cannot Tell Us." *Demography* 39, no. 3 (August 2002): 541–55.

Burkhauser, Richard V., and David C. Stapleton. "Introduction." In *The Decline in Employment of People with Disabilities*, edited by Richard V. Burkhauser and David C. Stapleton, 1–20. Kalamazoo, MI: W. E. Upjohn Institute for Employment Research, 2003.

Clarke, Philippa, Gwenith Fisher, Jim House, Jacqui Smith, and David Weir. *Guide to Content of the HRS Psychosocial Leave-Behind Participant Lifestyle Questionnaires: 2004 & 2006*. Survey Research Center, University of Michigan, 2007. Available at http://hrsonline.isr.umich.edu/sitedocs/userg/HRS2006LBQscale.pdf.

Diener, Edward. "Subjective Well-Being: The Science of Happiness and a Proposal for a National Index." *American Psychologist* 55, no. 1 (January 2000): 34–43.

Diener, E., R. A. Emmons, S. Griffin, and R. J. Larsen. "The Satisfaction with Life Scale." *Journal of Personality Assessment* 49, no. 1 (1985): 71–75.

Diener, E., and W. Pavot. "Review of the Satisfaction with Life Scale." *Psychological Assessment* 5, no. 2 (1993): 164–72.

Dijkers, M. "Correlates of Life Satisfaction Among Persons with Spinal Cord Injury." *Archives of Physical Medicine and Rehabilitation* 80, no. 8 (1999): 867–76.

Dijkers, M. "Quality of Life After Spinal Cord Injury: A Meta-Analysis of the Effects of Disablement Components." *Spinal Cord* 35 (1997): 829–40.

Dolan, Paul, Tessa Peasgood, and Matthew White. "Do We Really Know What Makes Us Happy? A Review of the Economic Literature on the Factors Associated with Subjective Well-Being." *Journal of Economic Psychology* 29 (2008): 94–122.

Frederick, Shane, and George Loewenstein. "Hedonic Adaptation." In *Well-Being: The Foundations of Hedonic Psychology*, edited by Daniel Kahneman, E. Diener, and N. Schwartz, 302–29. New York: Russell Sage Foundation, 1999.

Hale, Thomas W. "The Lack of a Disability Measure in Today's Current Population Survey." *Monthly Labor Review*, June 2001: 38–41.

Haveman, Robert H., and Barbara L. Wolfe. "The Economic Well-Being of the Disabled: 1962–84." *Journal of Human Resources* 25, no. 1 (1990): 32–54.

Kahneman, Daniel, and Alan Krueger. "Developments in the Measurement of Subjective Well-Being." *The Journal of Economic Perspectives* (American Economic Association) 20, no. 1 (2006): 3–24.

Keyes, Corey L. M., Dov Shmotkin, and Carol D. Ryff. "Optimizing Well-Being: The Empirical Encounter of Two Traditions." *Journal of Personality and Social Psychology* 82, no. 6 (2002): 1007–22.

Kirchner, Corinne. "Looking Under the Street Lamp: Inappropriate Uses of Measures Just Because They Are There." *Journal of Disability Policy Studies* 7 (1996): 77–90.

Layard, Richard. "Happiness and Public Policy: A Challenge to the Profession." *The Economic Journal* 116 (March 2006): 24–33.

Livneh, H., and E. Martz. "Psychosocial Adaptation to Spinal Cord Injury as a Function of Time Since Injury." *International Journal of Rehabilitation Research* 26 (2003): 191–200.

Lucas, Richard. "Long-Term Disability Is Associated with Lasting Changes in Subjective Well-Being: Evidence from Two Nationally Representative Longitudinal Studies." *Journal of Personality and Social Psychology* 92, no. 4 (2007): 717–30.

McNeil, John. "Employment, Earnings, and Disability." *75th Annual Conference of the Western Economic Association,* 2000.

Meyer, Bruce D., and Wallace C. Mok. "Disability, Earnings, and Consumption." *Harris School of Public Policy Studies Working Paper #06.10,* 2009.

Office of National Statistics. *More Information About Measuring National Well-Being.* November 25, 2010. http://www.ons.gov.uk/ons/about-ons/consultations/closed-consultations/measuring-national-well-being/index.html.

Oswald, Andrew J., and Nattavudh Powdthavee. "Does Happiness Adapt? A Longitudinal Study of Disability with Implications for Economists and Judges." *Journal of Public Economics* 92, no. 5–6 (June 2008): 1061–77.

Pagan-Rodriguez, Ricardo. "Longitudinal Analysis of the Domains of Satisfaction Before and After Disability: Evidence from the German Socio-Economic Panel." *German Institute for Economic Research.* 2010. Available at http://www.diw.de/documents/dokumentenarchiv/17/diw_01.c.357849.de/soep2010_paper_pagan.pdf (Accessed 2011).

Patterson, David. R., John J. Everett, Charles H. Bombardier, Kent A. Questad, Victoria K. Lee, and Janet A. Marvin. "Psychological Effects of Severe Burn Injuries." *Psychological Bulletin* 113 (1993): 362–78.

Powdthavee, Nattavudh. "What Happens to People Before and After Disability? Focusing Effects, Lead Effects, and Adaptation in Different Areas of Life." *Social Science & Medicine* 69 (2009): 1834–44.

Ryff, Carol D., Burton H. Singer, and Gayle Dienberg Love. "Positive Health: Connecting Well-Being with Biology." *The Royal Society: Biological Sciences* 359 (2004): 1383–94.

Schulz, R., and S. Decker. "Long-Term Adjustment to Physical Disability: The Role of Social Support, Perceived Control, and Self-Blame." *Journal of Personality and Social Psychology* 48 (1985): 1162–72.

Smith, Dylan M., Kenneth M. Langa, Mohammed U. Kabeto, and Peter A. Ubel. "Health, Wealth, and Happiness: Financial Resources Buffer Subjective Well-Being After the Onset of a Disability." *Psychological Science*, 2005: 663–66.

Stern, Steven. "Measuring the Effect of Disability on Labor Force Participation." *The Journal of Human Resources* 24, no. 3 (1989): 361–95.

Stiglitz, Joseph E., Amartya Sen, and Jean-Paul Fitoussi. *Report by the Commission on the Measurement of Economic Performance and Social Progress.* Commission on the Measurement of Economic Performance and Social Progress, 2009.

Tyc, V. L. "Psychosocial Adaptation of Children and Adolescents with Limb Deficiencies: A Review." *Clinical Psychology Review* 2 (1992): 275–91.

CHAPTER SIXTEEN

Health Shocks

A Discussion

Robert Haveman

Within this volume, four of the chapters deal with a variety of issues related to the impact of unexpected health related events (shocks) on various aspects of the well-being of the American population at different points in the lifecycle. Two of them—the Wallace et al. and the Daly and Gardiner Chapters 14 and 15—focus on the older population, while Meyer and Mok, in Chapter 13, study the short- and long-term effects of shocks experienced by middle-aged people. All of these chapters focus on one or another negative health event, including the onset of disability. The focus on health and disability shocks suggests the importance of the question asked by Burkhauser, Houtenville, and Tennant in Chapter 12: "How should we measure the prevalence of Americans with disabilities; how best to establish whether or not a surveyed person is disabled?"

In this discussion, I will first deal with the three chapters that estimate the effects of a variety of health-related shocks on the well-being of Americans. While each of the chapters makes a significant contribution either to what we know about the prevalence of health problems or their onset, I will raise a number of issues regarding the results of the studies and the methods used, focusing the discussion on providing suggestions for further research on these topics.

OVERALL FINDINGS OF THE STUDIES ON THE EFFECTS OF HEALTH-RELATED SHOCKS

As noted above, three of the chapters focus on the impact of the onset of some adverse health or disability problem on a measure of well-being.

While the chapters vary widely in several dimensions, it is nonetheless possible to summarize the general effects of the health related events studied. Some of the dimensions in which the studies vary, a topic I will return to below, are contained in Table 16.1 along with a summary of impacts, which are contained in the final column. Clearly, all of the adverse shocks summarized in the table have negative effects on the lives and well-being of those who experience them. For those studies that measure these shocks by the "transition" from a robust state to a vulnerable state (e.g., the onset of disability), the magnitude of the impact is substantial. For example, Meyer and Mok show that at the time that working-age people become chronically and severely disabled, earnings fall by about one-third and income falls by one-fifth. In the long run, that disabling event results in a one-third decline in wealth (from a median of $39,000, to $23,000), a one-fifth decline on food and housing consumption, and a doubling in the average amount of public transfers received.

When the event is a change (e.g., a decline) in some health indicator (rather than the onset of a disabling condition), the estimated negative effects are quantitatively smaller. For example, Wallace et al. measure the effect of moving from some prior level of self-reported health (such as good or fair health) to a deteriorated level of health (say, poor health), and find negative impacts on annuitized net wealth of about 2 percent up to 9 percent for the health and cognitive shocks that they study. Daly and Gardiner estimate that overall subjective well-being declines by about 20 percent of a standard deviation of life satisfaction at the onset of a limitation of the ability to work.

In addition to these overall findings, the studies also revealed a number of other important patterns. Here are some of these:

Attenuation of Negative Shock

In the Daly and Gardiner chapter, the large negative effect of the onset of work limitations (disability) on subjective well-being (a decrease of about 20 percent of a standard deviation of life satisfaction) was found to persist for several periods after the onset. While there appears to be some diminution of the negative effect on well-being of the initial disability shock with the passage of time, the recovery is very slow; they calculate that on average it would take eight years to make up this initial drop in

TABLE 16.1

The health/disability studies and their characteristics

Study	Population studied	Health-related shock	Indicators of well-being	Non-health-related variables statistically controlled	Estimated impact
Meyer-Mok	Male household heads 22–61 years of age (observed 1968–2004)	Self-reported measure of work limitations (classified into one-time, temporary, chronic not severe and chronic severe)	Life cycle patterns of earnings, income, public transfers, and consumption	Marital status, state of residence, age and age-squared, education, year, number of children, *fixed effect*	For chronic severe, earnings/income decline 33/20 percent at onset increasing to 67/35 percent in the long run. From onset to long run, public transfers double, median net wealth falls from \$35k to \$23k, food/housing consumption falls 20 percent
Daly-Gardiner	People older than 51 years (observed 2004–2008)	Onset, presence, and duration of self-reported work limitations	Subjective well-being and mental health	Health, economic resources, education, labor force status, age, gender, race, marital status, poor health = 1, prior well-being, and mental health	20 percent decrease in subjective well-being due to onset, with little evidence of attenuation with time after onset
Wallace et al.	New retirees among 51–61 year-olds (observed 1992–2008)	Declines in self-reported health and cognitive capabilities	Level of asset-based re-source adequacy and the probability of near-poverty resources	Marital status, health, education, spouse health/education, period, year, *fixed effect*	Cognitive/health declines reduce ANW by up to 9 percent; vulner-able groups (single, nonwhite, low education) are more likely to experience shocks and have a larger probability of having inad-equate resources because of them

subjective well-being. Recovering the predisability level of well-being appears to be impossible for many older persons.

The Meyer and Mok chapter also studied this attenuation effect. For example, they find that the short-run effect of the onset of a disability is to decrease earnings by varying amounts depending on the severity of the disabling condition (e.g., by more than one-half for the chronic-severe condition group), and that for none of the groups does the decline tend to reverse itself with the passage of time after onset. Notably, the authors find that even though receipt of public transfers offsets some of the earnings loss (so that the fall in family income is not so severe), experiencing a severe disability leads to both long- and short-run decreases in food/housing consumption (material well-being).

Incidence and Effect of Shocks on Population Subgroups

All of the chapters reveal the effects of health-related shocks on the entire population group that they are studying—prime-age male household heads (Meyer-Mok), people older than fifty-one years (Daly-Gardiner), and new retirees ages fifty-one to sixty-one from 1992–2008 (Wallace et al.). However, only Chapter 14, by Wallace et al., reveals both the incidence of shocks and their impact on subpopulations within these groups. In the chapter, several subgroups are distinguished—single men and women and married men and women, and within these groups, racial groups, age groups, those retiring with SSDI benefits, and education groups. Their estimates show that singles, but especially men, have a higher relative risk of experiencing a shock than do married men and women. They also indicate that the groups that are the most vulnerable to adverse events postretirement are those traditionally viewed as disadvantaged; males in couple households with disadvantaged characteristics (e.g., nonwhites and those with low education), disadvantaged females in couple households, and disadvantaged singles.

Cross-Study Interpretations of Health Impacts

These chapters are emblematic of a difficulty commonly encountered when making cross-study comparisons. While the variety of topics examined is interesting and the findings are important, the field will move forward as measures become more standardized in disparate areas of inquiry so that results become more comparable.

Consider the variation across the three chapters that examine health shocks that is shown in Table 16.1. In addition to the different ages of the population groups studied, the measures used by the authors to characterize a health related shock vary substantially across the studies, as do the outcomes measured. Further, in doing statistical analyses of the *ceteris paribus* effects of these health related events, the studies vary in the phenomena for which they statistically control in obtaining their estimates.

For example, Meyer and Mok (Chapter 13) identify the effects of various measures of disability onset—one-time, temporary, chronic-not severe and chronic-severe—while Daly and Gardiner (Chapter 15) study the effects of the onset, the presence, and the duration of self-reported work limitations. Wallace et al. (Chapter 14) analyze the effects of declines in a variety of self-reported health and cognitive capabilities. In terms of the outcomes studied, Meyer and Mok focus on life-cycle patterns of earnings, income, public transfers, and consumption of working-age men; Daly and Gardiner on subjective well-being; and Wallace et al. study the effects on the level of asset-based resource adequacy and the probability of near-poverty resources.

The use of such disparate populations studied, measures of health related shocks, well-being indicators monitored, and varying statistical controls make it difficult to compare the quantitative effects that are revealed in the studies. While I draw this point in the context of the studies in this volume, the same point might be made of any such collection examining the different set of outcomes these chapters consider. Nonetheless, this points toward the value of researchers in this field beginning to think about how to standardize as many of these features across studies as possible to assist in cross-study comparisons.

Also, as researchers, we should move further toward explanations of which types of unexpected events tend to have the largest negative effect on well-being. This will assist policymakers in understanding which types of events should be the focus of efforts to buffer people from their negative consequences. Conceptually, inquiries regarding the impact of health shocks should move to understanding; if actions to avoid an unexpected shock are possible, on which sort of shocks should people concentrate their avoidance efforts?

For example, from the Wallace study (of which I am a coauthor), it appears that declines in physical health have a larger negative effect on resource adequacy than do declines in mental health. However, the measures of the magnitude or severity of the shock are not necessarily the same across the types of shock. For example, a drop in the ten-noun recall score to below four may be a larger (or smaller) event than transitioning to difficulty with three or more ADLs. Given this, it is not clear that physical health shocks tend to have the larger effect on well-being.

A similar issue that arises in assessing results across disparate studies of health events is understanding which of the measures of impact have the greatest salience. Does a 10 percent decline in after-tax income attributed to a shock (as measured in the Meyer-Mok study) represent a smaller or larger real effect on well-being than a 10 percent decline in expected annuitized net wealth (as measured in Chapter 14)? Clarifying this point would require further research that systematically explores the impact of different types of shocks on a standardized outcome variable.

LESSONS TO GUIDE THE NEXT GENERATION OF RESEARCH

While attempting to coordinate the data and methods of researchers studying a phenomenon is difficult and probably unproductive, a review of Chapters 13–15 of this section does suggest some guidance for future research.

First, it is clear that the shocks that are studied have differential effects on various population groups. While sample sizes may limit the extent of more detailed analyses, breaking out such subgroup impacts would seem to be of high priority for the next generation of research on the effect of shocks.

Second, future research on the effect of unexpected shocks should attend to both the short-run and the long-run effects of the shock. Evidence presented in these studies suggests that the negative impact of an adverse shock on more concrete economic measures, such as earnings and income, actually increase with the passage of time (Meyer-Mok), while the level of self-reported well-being tends to slowly recover the longer an individual experiences a disabling condition (Daly-Gardiner). Future research should strive to clarify the relationship of both monetary and nonmonetary (subjective) impacts associated with adjustment to a disabling condition or a work limitation.

Third, future studies should strive to report the effects of shocks that are of similar magnitude so as to enable more reliable interpretation of estimated impacts. Studies should also seek to report impacts of negative shocks on comparable outcome variables, perhaps, indicating percentage changes from some baseline level (as in Meyer-Mok) or probabilities of failure to meet some known standard (as in Wallace et al.).

Finally, the wide range of estimation models and specifications has hindered the reliable comparison of findings among the studies. Perhaps future research could proceed by reporting results that move from the estimation of impacts using straightforward regression models to more advanced and complex estimation strategies. Similarly, comparison among studies would be aided if researchers would systematically move from including few controls for other potentially intervening variables to as much control as the available data support.

THE DEFINITION OF DISABILITY—A BASIC ISSUE

Chapter 12 in the health section is by Burkhauser, Houtenville, and Tennant. This chapter looks at a basic issue of disability measurement and its consequences; the other chapters work with disability and work limitation information available in the data sets that they use. As Burkhauser et al. emphasize, disability is a devilishly difficult concept to define and measure. The Americans with Disabilities Act defines disability as a physical or mental impairment that substantially limits one or more life activities of an individual. A quite different standard is set by the nation's primary disability support program—the Social Security Disability Income program (SSDI). That program requires that benefit recipients have demonstrated that they are totally and permanently unable to do the work that they did prior to onset, that they cannot adjust to other work because of their medical condition(s), and that the condition has lasted or is expected to last for at least one year or to result in death. Clearly, to understand the dynamics leading to SSDI receipt, trends in the take-up and employment trends among the impaired, and other important policy issues, the empirical definition of disability needs to be resolved. As noted in the table above, the studies reported here adopt a variety of definitions of health related negative shocks. They range from self-reported measures of disability onset, self-reported indicators of work limitations, and changes in self-reported health and cognitive capabilities.

Chapter 12 addresses the question of how best to measure disability status of working-age people. As the varying standards used by public programs and legislation suggest, this is not an easy task. Indeed, the prominent data sets—American Community Survey (ACS), the Current Population Study Basic Monthly Survey (CPS-BMS), and the Current Population Survey Annual Social and Economic Supplement (CPS-ASEC)—adopt quite different approaches for measuring the disabled working-age population. These approaches range from a six-question sequence on specific limitations (in the CPS-BMS and ACS), to a work-limitation question (in the CPS-ASEC), to a combination of the two measures. Interestingly, the questions on the CPS-ASEC survey are controlled by the Bureau of the Census, while those on the CPS-BMS survey are controlled by the Department of Labor.

By exploiting the fact that for some respondents to the CPS both the six-question sequence and the single work-limitation question are asked, the authors are able to test the ability of various combinations of these measures to identify the population of SSDI and SSI-D beneficiaries. The authors recognize that this test is less than ideal, but justified when "true disability" cannot be observed. They find that the single work limitation question of the CPS-ASEC does a better job than the six-question impairment approach of the CPS-BMS and ACS in passing this test, while an approach that includes both information on impairments and report of a work limitation does an even better job. Using this last approach, Burkhauser et al. capture about 92 percent of the program beneficiaries. They find that differences in the prevalence of disability differ substantially across the measures, but trends in the employment of the disabled (and the take-up of SSDI and SSI-D benefits) are roughly similar.

The most important conclusion of the chapter is that the single work-limitation question performs better than relying only on responses to the presence of specific limitations, as reflected in the six-question impairment approach, which conclusion is cited by Daly and Gardiner to justify the measure of disability that they employ. Burkhauser et al. argue that the single work-limitation question "can be used by researchers trying to explain trends in the employment of working-age people with disabilities." They urge the federal statistical agencies to maintain use of this question to enable researchers to best capture the population with disabilities, and especially to reliably measure the trend in disability over time.

The effort to develop a sensible and coordinated approach to empirically measuring disability and disability shocks is of high priority, and the Burkhauser et al. study is an important start in this effort. However, the test of which various survey-based reports of impairments/work limitations should be used to identify SSDI and SSI-D participants needs more defense. The dynamics leading to SSDI receipt are complicated and involve discretion in both the interpretation of program rules (by program administrators and administrative law judges) and in the evidence provided regarding the degree of disablement (by the potential beneficiary); indeed, many errors of both exclusion and inclusion are made. Many applicants become recipients who do not in fact meet the standard, as some who claim a work disability are not truly disabled; becoming a recipient of publicly provided benefits appears to be, in part, a matter of self-selection. Other people do not apply or are rejected even though they meet the standard because they are working or have been erroneously rejected.

If, in fact, people respond to questions regarding impairments or work limitations in order to ratify their efforts to secure (or their actual receipt of) public disability income support, it is unclear what we learn from the test applied by Burkhauser et al. Given this, a relevant question is whether the measure of disability used in Chapters 13 and 15 is an "unexpected shock" or a self-reported statement of health status meant to achieve some personal objective.

On this matter of the so-called moral hazard problem in self-reports of disability and the process of securing public disability benefits, there is substantial evidence that moving onto public disability benefit rolls (entering what Burkhauser et al. consider disability status) is a planned decision.[1] Among those who apply for and obtain disability benefits, some have experienced a shock leading to true loss of earning capacity, while others have rationally decided that securing SSDI benefits is their most attractive economic option. Clearly, further research to attempt to distinguish the role of "shock" from the rational response to incentives in determining a reliable measure of disability is of high priority.

NOTE

1. See Richard Burkhauser and Mary Daly, *The Declining Work and Welfare of People with Disabilities: What Went Wrong and a Strategy for Change* (Washington, DC: American Enterprise Institute Press, 2011) and David Autor and Mark Duggan, "The Rise in the Disability Rolls and the Decline in Unemployment," *Quarterly Journal of Economics*, Feb. 2003, 157–205.

Italic page numbers indicate material in tables or figures.